Friedrich Heckmann,
Dominique Schnapper

The Integration of Immigrants
in European Societies

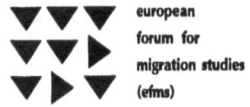

european
forum for
migration studies
(efms)

Forum Migration 7
The Integration of Immigrants in European Societies
National Differences and Trends of Convergence

The Integration of Immigrants in European Societies
National Differences and Trends of Convergence

Friedrich Heckmann, Dominique Schnapper (eds.)

In Memory of Hans Mahnig

 Lucius & Lucius · Stuttgart · 2003

Bibliografische Information der Deutschen Bibliothek
Die Deutsche Bibliothek verzeichnet diese Publikation in der Deutschen
Nationalbibliografie; detaillierte bibliografische Daten sind im Internet über
http://dnb.ddb.de abrufbar

europäisches forum für migrationsstudien (efms)

Institut an der Universität Bamberg

Katharinenstraße 1

D-96052 Bamberg

www.efms.de

© Lucius & Lucius Verlagsgesellschaft mbH Stuttgart 2003

Gerokstraße 51, D-70184 Stuttgart
www.luciusverlag.com

Design: Barbara Meyer, D-90542 Eckental

Satz: efms, D-96052 Bamberg

Druck und Einband: Rosch-Buch, Scheßlitz

Printed in Germany

ISSN 0949-1960

ISBN 3-8282-0181-4

Preface

This book is one product of the EFFNATIS project (1998-2000) studying integration policy and its effects in eight European countries. Researchers from Finland, France, Germany, Great Britain, Spain, Sweden, Switzerland and the Netherlands took part in the project which was coordinated by the *european forum for migration studies* at the University of Bamberg (efms). Authors' institutional affiliations are shown at the end of the volume.

We thank the European Union for financing the EFFNATIS project within the TSER programme. The EFFNATIS project was not only a study on the integration of immigrants in European countries, but a truly European and Europeanizing experience in itself. Susanne Worbs of the efms did a tremendous job in coordinating this large international project and relating it to the European Commission. She also had a most valuable part in the editorial work for this volume. Special thanks for their contribution go to Harald Lederer, Edda Currle, Wolfgang Bosswick, Maria Matreux and Gerald Kubik (all of efms).

This book is dedicated to the memory of Hans Mahnig, who died suddenly in 2001 at the age of only 35. His tragic death was a shock to the whole project team, in which he had been our Swiss partner and colleague. Hans was bright, amiable, dedicated and had a very fine sense of humour. His article in this book in joint authorship with Andreas Wimmer is a fine document of his intellectual standing. Hans cared for people and was particularly sensitive to the needs of underprivileged people. We won't forget him.

Friedrich Heckmann   Dominique Schnapper

Bamberg   Paris

Contents

Friedrich Heckmann / Dominique Schnapper

Introduction

European societies have experienced large scale immigration since the end of World War II. The illusion of temporary immigration has disappeared and confronts the new immigration countries with the necessity of integrating the new groups. The integration of migrants is a challenge to the established patterns of nation building and to welfare state policies. European societies are struggling with the problem of how to include the immigrants in their social structures.

In this situation a search for "models" has occurred and different national patterns of integration are being discussed as to their relative merits or problems. A prevailing discourse in Europe compares images of different national patterns: for instance, a French republican, culturally unifying, universal model is confronted with British or Dutch "multiculturalism", and with a German social policy orientation towards migrants. According to this "national difference paradigm" there is an "Intégration à la Française" linked to the tradition of nation building since the foundation of the Republic and aiming at a culturally homogenous nation. British or Dutch "multiculturalism", according to these images, seem to be willing to retain cultural differences and ethnic identities of migrants. And Germany, due to its "Volk" centered ethnic nation concept, supposedly, has problems of accepting immigrants as citizens, but nevertheless includes them in almost all social policy institutions. The texts that follow will compare these images with past and present integration policies on an empirical basis.

The countries represented in this volume are – in alphabetical order – France, Germany, Great Britain, Sweden, Switzerland and The Netherlands as countries with a relevant history of immigration and integration since World War II. Finland and Spain which follow have only recently turned into countries with a net immigration gain.

The articles originate from the EU funded EFFNATIS project which was primarily interested in the question whether there are different national patterns of integration, and if so, what they are like and what effect they may have for integration. The identification of different national patterns of integration and their analysis and comparison is what this book is about. The question of effects has been the central focus of three large surveys on children of international migrants which were done in France, Great Britain and Germany. Results of these surveys are reported elsewhere[1].

The concept of integration was defined in the project as the inclusion of new populations into existing social structures of the immigration country. Four dimensions of the process are differentiated: structural, cultural, social and identificational integration. Structural integration is the acquisition of rights and the access to membership, positions and statuses in the core institutions of the settlement society (education system, training system, labour market, housing, citizenship). Cultural integration is a precondition of participation and refers to processes of cognitive, cultural, behavioural and attitudinal change of persons. It concerns primarily the immigrants and their descendants, but is an interactive, mutual process that changes the settlement society as well. Membership of immigrants in the private sphere is reflected in peoples' private relations and group memberships (social intercourse, friendships, marriages, voluntary associations): social integration. Membership in a new society on the subjective level shows in feelings of belonging and identification, particularly in forms of ethnic, national or other forms of (multiple) social identification.

Integration in modern societies is in many ways the result of individual choices, often with motives that do not seem to be related to integration at all: "... to discuss assimilation (in the sense of integration, F.H. and D.S.) prospects intelligently, we need also to recognise that assimilation can take place despite the intentions of immigrants to resist it. Assimilation can occur as the often unintended, cumulative by-product of choices made by individuals seeking to take advantage of opportunities to improve their social situations" (Alba 1999)[2]. Besides integration as a result of individual choices and decisions there is a politically promoted process that sets conditions and gives opportunities and

---

[1] See *www.uni-bamberg.de/projekte/effnatis* or European Commission (ed.), Community Research Project Reports, Effectiveness of National Integration Strategies Towards Second Generation Migrant Youth in a Comparative European Perspective, Brussels 2001. Furthermore, see the article "The Second Generation in Germany: Between School and Labour Market" by Susanne Worbs (forthcoming in a special edition of the *International Migration Review*).

[2] Richard Alba, 'Immigration and the American Realities of Assimilation and Multiculturalism', in Münz, R. and Seifert, W. (eds.), *Inclusion or Exclusion of Immigrants. Europe and the U.S. at the Crossroads*, Demographie aktuell Nr. 14, pp. 3-16, Berlin: Lehrstuhl für Bevölkerungswissenschaft der Humboldt-Universität.

incentives for such choices and decisions: integration policies. On the one hand, there are special measures and institutions that are directly devised for immigrants, i.e. special integration policies. On the other hand, and much more so, integration is promoted by the inclusion of immigrants in the general system of nation state integration: general or indirect integration policies in the terminology of Hammar. Integration policies thus consist of special (direct) and general (indirect) integration measures. The concept does not include the effects of "positive" or "negative" external influences, like a change in the relations between the immigration and emigration countries or in the state of the economy.

On the basis of the preceding conceptual suggestions the project constructed a checklist for integration policy analysis by simply crosstabulating the four dimensions of integration with general and specific integration policies (Table 1).

Table 1: Checklist for the Analysis of Integration Policies

Dimension of Integration	General Integration Policies	Special Integration Policies
structural	1	5
cultural	2	6
social	3	7
identificational	4	8

The numbers represent different types of integration policies. Integration policies are often the subject of hot political controversies in societies and do change according to power relations. That is why we decided to discontinue a rather popular term in the integration discourse: "national integration strategy". "Strategy" implies planning and consistency, would be "pro-active", not reactive. National integration strategy would imply conscious planning, systematic and goal minded action on a national level. In that sense, integration strategy does not seem to exist in any European country.

However, there are certain consistencies and common characteristics in integration policies on a national level that are not the result of a conscious strategy, but derive from basic sociostructural principles and institutions or the *social order* of a country. Examples would be "Soziale Marktwirtschaft" in Germany, French étatism and republicanism, or the Dutch "pillarisation" of society. The ways in which a country "normally" tries to secure cohesion, conflict solution and to solve social and economic problems will also be used when integrating migrants.

11

Integration policies are also determined by what we have called *sense of nationhood* or concept of citizenship. By sense of nationhood we refer to constitutive principles of a concept of nation, especially criteria for membership and inclusion. These are of major relevance for policies of citizenship and naturalisation in relation to immigrants.

Another major influence on integration in the settlement society comes from the *"societal definition of the immigration situation"*, i. e. the understanding of major political actors of the "nature" of the ongoing immigration and integration process. "The United States is an immigration country" would be an example of such a societal definition of a "classical" immigration country. The long standing fight in Germany over the question of Germany being an immigration country or not can also illustrate the relevance of that criterion.

The complex whole of direct and indirect integration policies as they are related to the social order of the society, to sense of nationhood and to the societal definition of the immigration situation we suggest to call *"national mode of integration"*.

On the basis of these considerations the authors were asked to work with the following items in the analysis of national mode of integration:

▶ Societal definition of the immigration situation

▶ Principles of social order

▶ Sense of nationhood

▶ Checklist for integration policy analysis (Table 1)[3].

To arrive at a better understanding of the different national modes of integration the articles present a short demographic analysis for each country giving a brief account of the migrations that constitute the present migration situation. The definition of the situation can be in accordance with the demographic analysis, but in many instances is not.

To complete this introduction we briefly introduce the integration policy analyses for the countries represented.

Dominique Schnapper, Pascale Krief and Emmanuel Peignard of the Ecole des Hautes Etudes en Sciences Sociales in Paris reconstruct the French Republican model of assimilationist integration, which does not give minority cultures a place in public space. Its opposition to multiculturalism does not mean, however, that cultural differences and minority cultures are not tolerated in the sphere of personal expression and private social relations. It means that multiculturalism defined as the recognition of cultural difference in political life and in the public domain are in conflict with political tradition and national myth.

---

[3] The degree to which this checklist has been followed varies between authors.

Great effort is devoted to explore the relation between the "model" as a normative standard and how "real" integration policies work. These do not always follow the standard, but have to give in to various social needs and political pressures.

Friedrich Heckmann of the european forum for migration studies at the University of Bamberg argues in his paper on Germany that the long lasting official denial of an immigration situation which ended only at the end of the century cannot be equated with the total lack of an integration policy. Integration measures began in the mid 1970's. The main feature of the German mode of integration has been the inclusion of immigrants into the general welfare state and social policy system. Compared to that special measures of immigrant integration have much less relevance. Welfare state integration without citizenship gave integration policy in Germany an ambivalence which resulted in a lack of identificational integration of migrants.

John Rex of the Centre for Research in Ethnic Relations at the University of Warwick reports in his article about serious doubts as to the success of British "multiculturalism". Multiculturalism with its official recognition and support of ethnic minorities could be regarded as the very opposite of French republican universalism. Doubts seem to develop recently as a consequence of last year's ethnic clashes in British cities. Integration policies in Great Britain have predominantly been defined as anti-discrimination policies. The legal backbone of such policies are so-called race-relations acts. The problems which policy discussions about integration addresses are the specific problems of Black and Asian minorities, not of immigrants in general.

Charles Westin and Elena Dingu-Kyrklund of the Centre for Research in International Migration and Ethnic Relations (CEIFO) at Stockholm University report that Sweden has had a distinct immigration and integration policy characterised by a tendency to limit intake of new immigrants while allotting increasing resources to promote the integration of those already accepted. Swedish integration policies rely heavily on the general welfare policies administered by the public sector. It has therefore been considered normal that the role of the public sector in promoting integration is large in comparison with many other European countries, where non-governmental organisations are central actors.

Hans Mahnig and Andreas Wimmer of the Swiss Forum for Migration Studies at the University of Neuchâtel start with the observation that Switzerland is a multicultural society with one of the highest immigration rates in Europe. However, Switzerland does not recognise that it has become an immigration country and has no real immigration policy on the federal level. Another paradox is the fact that in spite of the absence of most of the problems of other European immigration countries, immigration and integration issues have almost uninterruptedly been on the political agenda since the 1960's. The same factors which can be considered as crucial for the political integration of the country are also responsible for the specific ways Switzerland treats its immigrants. These factors are federalism, municipal autonomy, consociational and direct democracy and the specific character of Swiss national identity.

For *Jeroen Doomernik of the Institute for Migration and Ethnic Studies (IMES) at Amsterdam University* the tradition of consociational democracy and the "pillarisation" of society have been important principles of the social order that have influenced not only the sense of nationhood, but the integration of immigrants as well. In consociational democracies conflicts are settled by pacification and compromise, leading to equal access to the state's resources for all groups involved. This principle has been extended to the newcomers and has been conducive to formulating the idea of a Dutch multicultural society. Thanks to this multicultural policy, special programmes for immigrants were started. But many special policies aimed at the integration of immigrants that were started in the 1980's have been substituted for general policies for all disadvantaged people, autochthonous and migrants alike.

In opposition to The Netherlands Finland has only recently become a country of immigration and developed an official integration policy in 1999. *Eve Kyntäjä of the Finnish Centre for Russian and East European Studies, University of Helsinki*, states that most of the immigrants are "ethnic return migrants" from the former Soviet Union. One of Finland's interesting features is the drawing up of individual integration plans for immigrants. Stimulated by the very high rate of unemployment among refugees from Third World countries a discussion has begun to introduce a system of competence assessment of migrants to support their integration into the labour market.

The recent emergence of an immigration situation is also true for Spain. *Rosa Aparicio and Andrés Tornos, Instituto Universitario De Estudios Sobre Migraciones, Universitad Comillas Madrid*, write that the immigration situation has been characterised by large numbers of illegal migrants and ensuing amnesties. Measures to support the integration of immigrants embrace the following: setting up special channels to inform immigrants about the regulations affecting them, regulating the regrouping of families and providing complementary schooling in the language and culture of their countries of origin or in their religious beliefs. Due to the fact that immigration is still a new phenomenon, much of the discourse on integration relates to questions of schooling. The children of immigrants will normally be enrolled in a school within the general education system and will be expected to follow the same curriculum as Spanish children.

It is apparent from these short remarks that there are clearly different national modes of immigrant integration. From a European perspective, however, the question of common elements is as important as that of differences. Can we identify structures and developments that are indicative of convergence and the formation of a European mode of integration? We shall come back to this question in the conclusion of this book.

Dominique Schnapper / Pascale Krief / Emmanuel Peignard

French Immigration and Integration Policy.
A Complex Combination

1. Introduction

In France, a country with a long history of immigration, there is a tradition of a so-called "assimilation" policy with regards to foreign migrants. It has been closely linked to the particular history of the integration and formation of the national population.

The nation has been historically constructed through the "assimilation" of populations from various regions (Burgundy, Brittany, Provence, for instance). All these populations had their own cultural identities and in some cases, religious identities, as well as traditional dress codes and languages. The pattern of integration has always been founded on the "assimilation" of such populations, by transforming them into French citizens, as opposed to promoting a regional identity. The same policy has generally been implemented towards migrants, or at least their children, who, as a result, have the right to participate in political life and become a part of the "community of citizens"(Schnapper 1994).

National integration is, on the whole, political in France: members of the national society are integrated by individual citizenship, following a universalistic view of the citizen. National belonging is thought to be the result of cultural belonging and the individual's political will: this is the major source of the elective ideology of the nation which has dominated the French concept. Through its universal and abstract ambitions, the Revolution implied that all those who adhered to the nation's values, in particular human rights, could all become its members. In this framework, national identity is not "biological", but rather political. Thus it is possible to refer to the notion of "right to formalise one's sense of belonging to the nation" (*droit de rattachement*) regarding those who have internalised French values, or who have fully adhered to them, as well as to the notion of "assimilation".

Universalistic principles have always been favoured over acknowledging the particular characteristics of migrant populations. The principle of French policy is to be 'colour-blind'. No "minority" policies exist, nor the very idea of minorities. According to this approach, multiculturalism or ethnic cultures should remain in the private sphere, and should not be recognised in the public domain.

15

Contemporary French integration policy (which used to be called "assimilation policy") does not imply, contrary to what was argued in the 1970s, that the specific features of the populations progressively integrated into the French nation are suppressed. This is neither possible nor desirable. Except in the colonies, what used to be called "assimilation policy" has never banned multiculturalism (or cultural difference) in the personal and social spheres, but it has not allowed for the expression of cultural difference in political life in the public domain. "Multiculturalism" – defined as the recognition of cultural specificities in the public domain – is in conflict with both political tradition and national myth.

The very term of assimilation has, for a long time, been used to refer to the colonialist policy. It implied a sense of superiority of the white man whose supposed mission was to "civilise" the colonised subjects. In the colonial context, the colonised culture can only fade away, as its society is organised on the basis of the domination of the colonisers over the colonised. This is why the authors prefer the notion of the "right to formalise one's sense of belonging to the nation" (*droit de rattachement*), when discussing contemporary society as well as the term acculturation. Acculturation can be used to imply the processes of reinterpretation, in the anthropological sense, whereby populations of immigrant origin internalise the values of the society in which they live, whilst preserving, in part at least, the cultural heritage of their parents, by means of a "cultural DIY" (do-it-yourself) process which is a general feature of modern society. If identity is to be considered as a dynamic, non-static process, it can be argued that in modern and democratic societies, loyalty to one's "culture of origin" and the internalisation of values and socialisation in the new society cannot be seen as incompatible. In the same way as the other members of the "community of citizens", children of migrants become part of an "ideological DIY process" which allows them to reconcile, more or less successfully, this double reference.

Republican universalism is understood as a principle of integration, which should ensure that all people, regardless of their origins or beliefs, are likely to be "unified to" (*rattachés*) political society, if they receive national curriculum education, through which individuals from diverse backgrounds become French citizens just as much as autochthonous persons.

Ideologies have effects on reality. They are transformed into legal and institutional measures which influence everyday life and are internalised by the population. The universal Republican idea and ideal justified the opening up of nationality laws, by liberally granting French nationality to the children of immigrants who were born and educated in France. The openness of French nationality legislation and the acquisition of citizenship is supposed to encourage individuals to internalise French norms and values as well as allowing them to mix with the general population. It legitimises the practice of state or republican schools to ignore the historical and religious backgrounds of the pupils, for their right to non-difference (*droit à l'indifférence*). It is the foundation of the political practice whereby members of parliament do not represent any specific group but rather the entire abstract body politic, all members of the nation, which excludes the idea that certain "political communities" or "ethnic groups" in particular can be recognised as such in the public domain. It is also the basis, to a large extent, for the social practices of immigrants and their children, and the attitudes of the autochthonous population towards them. The internalisation of universal values by both autochthonous and migrant populations is a major feature in the whole national integration process.

But this pattern cannot be wholly implemented, it necessitates adjustments, even departures from the ideal model. General guiding principles should not be confused with actual social practices. When it comes to the analysis of actual practices, one cannot crudely oppose universalistic and particularistic policies. Taking the example of policies carried out in Europe in order to integrate populations of immigrant origin, it can be observed that certain countries claim to have universalistic principles, but are, as a result of the actual process of the management of diversity, inevitably obliged to take into account the specificities of various populations. Other countries, more attached to differential policies, sway towards universalistic measures.

The French pattern of integration, as well, is characterised by a tension between "universalistic principles" and the (more or less unofficial) departures from these principles. The universalistic concept of nation and citizenship is a principle with concrete effects on French integration policy, on a macro-sociological level. Although the theoretical and ideological conceptions of nation and citizenship do translate into political practice, some departures from the ideological conception do exist. However, it shall also be pointed out that, even in these cases, the guiding principles still dominate the application of these adjustments.

France has been a country of immigration since the mid-19th century, unlike most of her European neighbours. However, it has never had, and still does not have any specific integration policies with regard to foreigners, in accordance with the "republican model" of citizenship, which forbids any differentiation between French nationals and foreigners except in the cases of rights and duties explicitly linked to citizenship (vote, access to civil service posts). Where French nationals are concerned, whatever their "origin", the main implicit principle of the French Republican approach to integration is that the lack of a specific integration policy is the best way to integrate children of international migrants. They are simply considered as French citizens. At school, in the workplace, in trade unions, the "ethnic" dimension has never been taken into account, even if, in practice, these principles have not always been scrupulously followed. The promotion of French nationals of foreign origin has always been carried out and continues to be carried out on an individual, rather than a collective basis. This "colour-blind policy" is supposed to favour integration, and is based on the Republican and Jacobinist model of national integration that has been in place since the IIIrd Republic (1871). Its aim is to promote a strict equal opportunities policy, which the welfare state helps to implement. It chooses to favour integration by the mixing of populations and the internalisation of French values through employment and school education.

2. Migrant Statistics and Nationality Law: How Foreigners Disappear from the Statistics

As a result of a century and a half of immigration, the French pattern of integration is based on the idea of the legal transformation of immigrants and their children into French citizens. Laws relating to nationality as well as statistics concerning the number of people of immigrant origin illustrate the French approach in this domain.

In France, statistics on foreigners do not give an accurate picture of the extent or importance of immigration. From the end of the nineteenth century until the 1950's, the foreign population probably stood at around 1 to 2 million, and this figure increased to 3 million during the second part of the 20th century. But if one tries to quantify the real demographic effect (the number of migrants and their descendants), one can estimate, as does French demographer Michèle Tribalat, that the population living in France today would be10 to 12 million less if there had not been any immigration from the mid-19th century onwards (Tribalat 1996). Until the mid-nineteenth century, immigration was mostly European and elitist, composed mainly of artists, students, courtiers and officers. Immigrant labour was rare and mostly seasonal. In 1851, only 380,000 foreigners were registered in the census. But from the middle of the nineteenth century onwards, France experienced huge demographic changes. In 1850 the number of children per woman was 3.5 (while it was between 4.5 to 6 in all the other European countries) and natural increase was at 0.4%. These rates were the lowest in Europe. French demographers in the nineteenth century and at the beginning of the twentieth century highlighted the need for immigration in order to contain this population decrease which was perceived as a serious danger by both scientists and politicians (Bertillon 1911). Indeed, at this time France was often described as a "dissolving sugarcube", or as "the country of empty places"(Bonnet 1976). During this period, immigration was perceived as the only way to re-populate the country and to maintain a large enough labour force (Schnapper 1992,41-46). In fact, France developed an active immigration policy from this time onwards, due in large part to industrialists who directly recruited manpower from abroad. Thus, after 1850, immigration can be described as labour or working class.

Most of the immigrants were European, that is, from Belgium, Italy, Spain and Switzerland. Large numbers of immigrants arrived: there were 800,000 foreigners in France in 1876 and 1.04 million in 1896 (3% of the whole population). The second wave of immigration in the 1880's was made up of Italian and Spanish immigrants, and the third wave, at the beginning of the 20th century, was mostly from Poland and Algeria. The government started to implement an official immigration policy during World War I in order to replace the lack of manpower – there were 1.4 million casualties as a result of the war – and this initiative continued until the end of the 1920's. During the war, 78,000 Algerian workers were directly recruited by the government as well as 23,000 Portuguese, 24,000 Greek and 15,000 Spanish workers (Lequin 1992,325-342). However, many of them returned to their countries after World War I. But both industrialists and the government continued to pursue an active recruitment policy of foreign labour, generally by signing direct agreements with the governments of the foreign countries concerned. This was, for instance, the case with Italy, Poland (in 1919) and Yugoslavia (in 1925). In 1925, a *"Société Générale d'Immigration"* was created by some industrialists and officials. It had offices in Belgium, Sweden, Yugoslavia, Italy and Poland. This active policy almost doubled the number of foreign workers within 10 years. In 1921, 1.5 million foreigners were living in France, and 2,7 million in 1931 (6.6% of the whole population). Italians were the largest population (808,000), followed by the Poles (508,000), the Spaniards (352,000), and the Belgians (250,000). At this time, France had the highest immigrant population rate in the world: 515 inhabitants out of 100,000 were foreigners, compared to 492 in the United States (Noiriel 1988,21). Of course, these figures do not take into account those misgrants and their children who had acquired French nationality. Despite this influx of people the birth rate and natural increase were still dramatically low.

After World War II, natural increase went up to 0.8%, as a "baby-boom" developed. But natural increase went down after 1970. Post World War II was a period of reconstruction and high growth rates of the economy. During the *Trente Années Glorieuses*, France, like other Western European countries, needed again to call on foreign workers in order to maintain a large enough labour force. Again, both the government and industrialists adopted policies of massive recruitment: an *Office National de l'Immigration* (ONI) was created, in order to recruit foreign labour. The policy toward foreigners was very open: any foreigner, whether he had a legal or illegal status, or even if he had entered the country with no more than a tourist visa, was to be accepted and regularised by the government if a company would employ him. For example, in 1968, only 18% of the foreigners with jobs who had arrived during that year had applied directly to the ONI from their own country, thus entering France already in possession of a work permit. 82% simply legalised their presence ex-post after being recruited (Schnapper 1992,35).

Between 1946 and 1975, the foreign population rose from 1.75 million to 3.4 million.From 1946 until the mid-1960s, immigration was mostly characterised by a rural and male population, from Spain and Algeria. From the mid-1960's to mid-1970's, Spanish and Algerian immigration continued, and high numbers of Portuguese immigrants arrived. During this period migrants were more often women and children and increasingly came from urban areas. In 1975, there were 498,000 Spanish, 710,690 Algerian and 759,000 Portuguese persons in France. Although birth-rate and natural increase decreased again, the government decided to bring a halt to immigration in 1974, like in other European countries.

From that date onwards only political refugees and the wives, husbands and children of residents have been allowed to come. The law of August, 24th 1993 introduced the right to family reunion (*regroupement familial*). However, since this date, it has proved to be increasingly difficult for immigrants to bring their families, because of the new legal conditions with regard to income and housing. In spite of the fact that immigration has supposedly been suspended, between 1982 and 1990 approximately 100,000 immigrants continued to arrive in France every year. This was mainly due to family reunion from Morocco and Tunisia, as well as both family reunion and the arrival of refugees from Africa and South-East Asia. According to the INSEE census (National Institute of Statistics) carried out in 1999 4,310,000 people living in France (7.4% of the population) were immigrants and 3,260,000 (5.6% of the population) were foreigners[1].

It might seem surprising that the number of foreigners should decrease or remain stable over a long period of time despite the fact that migrants generally were not returning to their countries of origin and that the numbers of new immigrants continued to be significant. If France did not recognise herself as a country partly built on immigration until only recently, this is mainly due to the fact that for more than a century a large part of former migrants and almost all their children became French citizens, thus "vanished" into the mainstream population and from the statistics. This shows to what extent the French pattern of integration has been internalised by the political, administrative and the scientific spheres as well as by the population itself. A third or fourth-generation descendant of a migrant would not consider him or herself as a foreigner but as French.

---

[1] Of course, these figures overlap each other to a certain extent, as a considerable proportion of the immigrant population is not foreign (this proportion being French nationality holders) and also because a part of the foreign population is made up of the children of migrants, who have not immigrated themselves, but who still have not acquired French nationality, or in rarer cases, having refused it.

In fact, children of immigrants are not considered as "foreign nationals" in the census, even if they have double nationality, but simply as French. Moreover, as the law states that it is forbidden to question a French national about the origin of their parents, the children of immigrants therefore do not appear in the statistics as people who are of foreign origin, and it is not even possible to quantify them. The only way to calculate the approximate number of French from foreign parents is to take into consideration individuals who live with his/her foreign parent(s) in the same household, since census data give information on the birthplace of parents. Conversely, it would be impossible to know the "origin" (and therefore to calculate the number) of children of immigrants living on their own. In political terms, we should be glad of this (considering the use of the files containing information on foreigners and those who had recently been naturalised by the Vichy government during World War II), but it should be pointed out that research on contemporary immigration and on integration of populations of foreign origin is rendered more difficult as a result. This was demonstrated during Michèle Tribalat's INED study by the huge task (and the large sum of money spent to this end) of gaining access to the children of migrants (Tribalat 1996). If one wants to compare French data to other countries' experiences, one should take into account this French specificity in the collection of data. It is estimated that nowadays one in five people living in France (whatever his/her nationality) has foreign ancestry in the sense that at least one of his/her parents or grand-parents is not French (Tribalat 1997).

Nationality Laws

Democratic nations are founded on the integration of populations into a community of citizens which transcends differences in social, religious, regional and national origins. This is even more so the case for France, due to its political ideology and its historical experience. French law is, more than other European laws, the most "open" when regarding nationality law, for reasons related to political legitimacy and demographic requirements. Indeed, France's demographic crisis meant that foreigners were needed to stem the decrease in population size and cultural centralisation led to the adoption of a policy of "Frenchification".

Since 1889, nationality laws have been very open in France, as they constitute the main political application of universalistic principles, and are considered as favouring integration. Since the nineteenth century, anyone has been able to obtain French nationality, if sufficient "assimilation" is proven, or if the claimant has been married to a French national for more than one year (this period of time was limited to six months until 1993 and then increased to two years from 1993 to 1998). In all cases, the acquisition of French nationality does not affect the maintenance of the former nationality: dual nationality is not an issue. It should be highlighted that the process of acquiring French nationality is referred to as "naturalisation" which implies, in the mind of the legislator, that the person in question who becomes French is French "in nature" – that is, he/she has adopted the French universalistic point of view to such an extent that he/she could in fact have been born French. French citizenship is seldom refused – 80% of the claimants become French – and there is no French language or civilisation "test". The simple fact that nationality has been requested is seen as ample proof of the claimant's desire to be attached to the French community of citizens.

According to article 44 of the nationality code, most children of immigrants born in France become French citizens when they reach the age of majority. Traditionally, *jus sanguinis* and *jus soli* combine, so that anyone born in France – even of foreign parents in an illegal situation – who wants to become French can do so. It is, however, not a question of the simple application of *jus soli* or territorial rights to become French: being born on French territory does not automatically lead to the granting of French nationality at birth, contrary to procedures in the United States. Already the Code Civil (1804) rejected the notion of nationality based only on the principle of *jus soli* (whereby "Any person born in France is to be considered as French"). The law of 1889 considered foreign men's children as French when they reach the age of majority, if they were resident in France.

The ordinance of October 19th, 1945 (modified by the law passed in January 1973) inaugurated the *Code de la Nationalité Française*, which amalgamates former laws. Article 44 (*acquisition de la nationalité*) stipulates that children who are born in France to foreign parents, themselves not born in France, obtain French nationality automatically when they are 18, on the condition that they have lived on French territory for at least five years preceding their majority. They can also acquire French nationality before the age of 18 if they request it (amendment of 1973). From 1993 to 1998, they had to make a special claim for nationality between the age of 16 and 21. This request system was otherwise known as the demonstration of the will (*manifestation de la volonté*). As a result of this law, each year, more and more children became French as soon as they turned 16: 32% in 1994, 43% in 1995 and 46% in 1996. Only 2.6% of the claims were rejected by the courts. This law was rescinded by the new socialist government in November 1997, the amendment coming into operation after September 1st 1998. The new article 44 abandoned the *manifestation de la volonté* clause, but confirmed the possibility of acquiring French nationality at the age of 16, or before if the parents request it. The original articles of legislation were re-confirmed in 1998. Article 17 specifies that a child born from foreign parents who themselves were born in France, is automatically French at birth. Article 23 (dating from 1962) specifies that the children of Algerian parents are automatically French at their birth, if they were born after 1963 on French territory and if their parents were born in Algeria before 1962 (as it was a French département prior to this date). In spite of these various modifications, in practice article 44 has always allowed nationality to be granted to children of immigrants.

The link between socialisation and citizenship is a special feature of the French legislation since 1889, which makes it different from the American model. The French so-called "Republican" and "Jacobinist" pattern bases nationality on socialisation. It is not a simple application of ius soli, but applies ius soli principles under the condition of schooling and socialisation in France, the topic of our next section.

3. A Pattern Based on Integration at School and in the Workplace

French integration policy has focussed on the integration of migrants' children rather than on that of the migrants themselves. School as modelled by the IIIrd Republic, along with nationality legislation, has been considered as the best instrument to translate universal principles into actual practices, and to integrate young people into the national culture, whatever their "origins". In this way, school is expected to teach, amongst other subjects, the French language, mathematics and the rights and duties of citizenship.

Numerous theoreticians of the nation – Rousseau, Kant, Fichte, Mauss – emphasised the role of the school in forming the citizen, because the school forms the citizen. In its role of socialisation, the school is an essential institution in modern societies. A nation exists only if it is translated into objective social forms. Socialisation is the means by which one becomes a member of the national society. An individual is in a position of becoming the citizen of a nation in so far as he/she has received its education at school. It is not a matter of a mere transformation of words: national belonging and sentiment are effectively born out of the internalisation of a group of cultural models and specific values, which define a personal identity inextricably linked to a collective identity. School is the institution *par excellence* of the nation. School transforms every child, whatever their origin, into a citizen. After the Revolution school teachers ceased to be called "regents" and became known as *instituteurs*, because they were now in charge of "instituting" the nation. School can be regarded as the main instrument and symbol of the French model of integration; *l'école républicaine* is supposed to produce a cohesive French nation. Teachers are expected to help in creating a homogeneous society. School has always been considered to be, and still is, the institution where socialisation into and acculturation of French culture takes place.

Due to centralisation educational programmes at primary school level (*ecoles* and *collèges*) are identical in the 36,000 French *communes*, whatever their size. Children of immigrants do not follow special curricula and there is no variation in terms of organisation and administration of different schools or *collèges*.

23

Every child has the right to an education, even if his/her parents are illegal immigrants (according to laws passed on July 11th 1975, July 10th 1989 as well as ordinance of the *Conseil d'Etat* issued on November 11th 1989). In exactly the same way as children from French families, children of immigrants attend school from the age of three until the age of sixteen, when school attendance ceases to be compulsory. Children must attend school five days a week for six hours every day (there is no school on Wednesdays and instead three to four hours on Saturday mornings). As a large proportion of pupils have their lunch at school, most of them stay at school from between eight in the morning until four or five in the afternoon, four days a week. For those young children whose mothers work, there is the *crèche*, which means that some children are socialised into a public sphere before the age of three. It should also be pointed out that the constant expansion of higher education means that more and more young people of working class or more modest backgrounds, which include those of immigrant origin, are continuing their studies beyond the statutory minimum school-leaving age and are tending to stay (and remain socialised) in the education system until they are twenty or even twenty-five years old. This is why more and more young people of immigrant origin obtain the baccalaureate and spend one or a number of years in higher education, at university or are pursuing more vocational qualifications. Education has for a long time been the very cradle of social mobility. As it is secular, compulsory and free, school has been considered as the best way to ensure equal opportunities, regardless of social, regional or national origins, in accordance with the meritocratic ideology. The French model of integration does have quantifiable effects on society. For example, school results achieved by children of immigrants and autochthonous pupils from the same socio-economic backgrounds are similar (Bastide 1982; Vallet and Caille 2000; Vallet 1996).

School contributes to the socialisation of migrants' children and allows them to share the same culture and school results as other French children from the same social background. Whatever their "origins", children take the same subjects and are supposed to be treated in the same way as any other French child and therefore mix with pupils from many different origins.

The role of the school has been traditionally continued by the army, as national military service was compulsory for all young French men regardless of social, regional or national origins. All young French men of the same age were expected to learn the same things in the same sort of environment at the same age and, above all, they were supposed to learn how to live together and internalise French values and patriotism. The civic role of the army has a tradition in France. When compulsory military service was established in 1873, it was seen as a means of extending education to the masses (Weber 1976).

Besides national institutions, the organisations of labour parties and trade unions did for a long time help to integrate the working class and foreign populations. It is first and foremost through work that the majority of individuals takes part in collective life. The Jacobinist model that has made work a central value, was founded on the notion that the socialisation of foreigners would occur through the common bond which would develop between foreign and autochthonous workers in the big industrial regions of Northern and Eastern France. The world of work had for a long time been a way of encouraging the integration of foreigners who often shared the same living and working conditions as French workers. Both French and foreign workers were often housed in *HLMs* – council housing – or *corons, cités ouvrières* – workers' residences. Adherence to left-wing parties, particularly the Communist Party and to the trade unions allowed foreign and French workers to mix, giving them a common political objective as well as sharing the myth of worker solidarity.

Political commitment and trade union activity have now diminished in popularity and thus their capacity to rally workers, whether they are French or not. Nevertheless, the notion that integration in the workplace is the most effective way for the immigrants to be integrated into French society remains. Over the last twenty years, for example, a number of measures have been introduced in order to prevent redundancies, to help young people to gain access to jobs and to help the unemployed to get back to work. None of these measures has been directly targeted at migrants or their children. However, they benefited from these measures, since a majority of migrants are unskilled workers and a large part of their children are less qualified than the autochthonous.

Since the 1980s, a number of measures have been introduced in order to help young people find jobs. From 1986 to 1989, the TUC (*Travaux d'Utilité Collective* or public works programme) and the SIVP policy (*stage d'initiation à la vie professionnelle* or a work-placement introducing young people into working life) were introduced, which allowed local authorities, associations and firms to employ young people for a modest wage and to exempt employers from paying contributions. After that the CES policy (*Contrats Emploi-Solidarité*) was launched in 1989. Throughout the duration of the contract, different measures of training are done in order to help young people find a regular job. In addition, the *contrat de qualification-jeunes* was introduced, which allowed employers to recruit young people and pay them between 30 and 60% of the statutory minimum wage (the *SMIC*). During the period of employment, employees receive training and subsequently, a qualification. Apprenticeship contracts (*contrats d'apprentissage*) are another measure encouraging employers to hire young people without qualifications and offer training. Apprentices divide their time between school and workplace. In 1992, the orientation/ professional guidance contracts (*contrats d'orientation*) were introduced which meant that young people could find jobs from six to nine months and during this period the ANPE (*Agence Nationale pour l'Emploi*) would help them to find a job. In 1997, the *emplois-jeunes* initiative was implemented which facilitated the creation of five-year contracts in the public sector (civil service), local authorities and associations.

More than 200,000 contracts of this kind were created by the end of 1999 and employees receive the minimum wage (*SMIC*). Organisations which employ young people on this basis receive a basic state allowance of 95,000 FF (15,000 Euros) per annum. Other measures were also introduced to encourage employers to recruit. For example, grants lasting for a period of eighteen months to two years are awarded to employers when they hire their first employee. Firms that are situated in urban peripheral areas, urban renewal areas or in rural renewal areas benefit from exemption from employers' contributions for a period of twelve months. The last area of intervention of the state in order to create employment concerns continuing education and career reorientation. All those who have qualifications which do not or no longer allow them to gain access to a job can retrain, within the framework of the various job schemes discussed above or by taking special leave in order to retrain (known as CIF – *Congés Individuels de Formation* or *Congé de Conversion*) in order to update their training and skills. All these programmes involve over a million people each year and they play an important role in the professional advancement and employment of youth. They are general integration measures, but are of special importance for the migrant populations.

4. Equal Rights

In accordance with European legislation, France gives the same economic and welfare-state rights and duties to foreigners. Generally speaking, legally resident foreigners have the same social and economic rights as French nationals. Although most immigrants and their children are French citizens, the government is forced to fight against discrimination. Legally resident foreigners who do not have French citizenship, benefit from the same social rights as French nationals: as employees, they contribute to and receive social security benefits such as illness and disability allowances, pensions, unemployment benefits, widow's pensions, family allowances and social assistance (especially help for children, old people and single mothers).

In the workplace, in accordance with universalistic principles, no form of discrimination, whether negative or positive (affirmative action) is permitted with regards to foreigners or their children. The only employment restriction related to nationality is that non-French nationals cannot hold all types of civil service posts. All special measures that are implemented to enhance young people's occupational and social integration are for young people in general and are not specifically aimed at immigrants and children of immigrants.

Foreigners and immigrants have the same right to council houses/flats as nationals, but practices don't always follow the law. The local authority housing policy aims to avoid the creation of ghettos by using an unofficial quota system in the allocation of housing. It is very rare that an area or an apartment building exclusively houses people from the same ethnic group. Usually, there is a tendency for one particular ethnic group to be predominant but the tenants are hardly ever all homogenous in terms of ethnicity. In most apartment buildings with a high concentration of migrants these make up between 40% to 70% of the whole population, and there is often a mix of between ten and forty different nationalities present.

Anti-Discrimination Laws

The preamble of the French constitution of 1958 refers to that of the 1946 constitution, which quotes the Human Rights Declaration of 1789. It highlights the equality of all men/women before the law, and prohibits discrimination on the basis of one's origin, "race" or religion. It also states that it respects individuals' different beliefs. As a result of its decision made in January 1990, the *Conseil Constitutionnel* applies the principle of equality to foreign nationals: all those present within the national boundaries benefit from fundamental constitutional rights and freedoms.

The first law prohibiting racial discrimination dates from July 1st, 1972. It was integrated into the penal code (*Code pénal*), the 1881 law on the freedom of the press, and was added to and further developed in 1975, 1977, 1983, 1985, 1987 and 1990. Any discrimination defined as the refusal to provide goods or services, refusal to employ an individual, unfair sanctions or dismissal, or hindering normal economic activity on the grounds of somebody's "race", religion or origins constitutes a criminal offense. Any incitation to discrimination, violence or hatred because of an individual's "racial" or religious origins in published form is also illegal. The Home Secretary can ban the publication of racist works, if their content incites to racial hatred, violence or discrimination. Recording data on people's "race" is illegal as well. Furthermore, the *Président de la République* can dissolve associations which encourage hatred, violence or discrimination against people because of their national, ethnic or religious origins. The wearing of uniforms, badges or emblems recalling those responsible for crimes against humanity (*crimes contre l'humanité*) and the wearing of symbols related to a racist ideology during sporting events can also be prosecuted.

The anti-discrimination and anti-racist laws have been reinforced during the 1990's. The law of July 13th 1990 outlaws any discrimination on the basis of belonging (or assumed belonging) to an ethnic group, nation, "race" or religion. It strengthens the type of sanctions that can be applied against such an offence which has recently been put into the category of crimes against humanity (*crimes contre l'humanité*). This same law also protects associations against racism and discrimination and grants them new rights. The law of December 1993 officially recognised what is known as an "exhibition offence" at sports events. The creation of this new offence category aims to prevent the proliferation of the wearing and display of symbols and signs that are linked to racist ideologies. In March 1994, the new penal code came into effect. This reaffirms the *délits de presse* laws, that is, special legislation that regulates what is published by the press. The new code also aims at dealing with racist infractions more effectively and has outlawed non-public racial provocations, insults and defamation. These offences are punishable by imprisonment and fines.

5. Between Universalistic Principles and Unofficial Departures: A Complex Combination

The universalistic concept of integration through individual citizenship has always been a goal, a political project, and not an empirical description of social reality. The principle of tearing away from one's particular ethnic belonging through naturalisation can never be fully realised. All nations have incorporated and reinterpreted pre-existing ethnic elements (Schnapper 1994). In France, the inevitable compromises between the ethnic elements and the civic principle take the form of a complex interlocking or combination of universal principles and more or less unofficial departures from these principles. This tension and the manner in which it is managed, on a day to day basis by individuals and institutions, constitutes one of the features of the country's approach to integration.

5.1. School and Education

School is the most important institution where universal values are founded and are applied. In this domain, as in others, the combination of universalism and unofficial departures from it can be observed in day to day practice. Even during the Third Republic at the end of 19th century the theoretical model was reinterpreted by the teachers themselves. The centralised administration of the education system masked the existence of a sense of pluralism in secondary education and a large amount of independence for lecturers at universities. The secular state has always negotiated religious holidays: for example, with the Catholic authorities a day off on Wednesdays for catechism. During the interwar period, the so-called "Jacobinism" of the system did not present an obstacle for the teachers to take into account Jewish festivals and holidays, with the permission of the school inspectors. Jewish schoolchildren attended school on

Saturdays, without writing anything down and then borrowed their classmates' notes on Sunday. Some Parisian schools situated in Jewish areas of the city closed on Saturdays and opened on Wednesdays instead. Certain modifications of the principles have always existed: institutions do not treat people as abstract "citizens", but rather as real individuals. Universal values have never excluded departures from the principles. They just took place in practice, which has not hindered the affirmation of and respect for the uniformity and centralisation of the French system. No more than it hindered Jews and non-Jews, autochthonous people and the children of migrants to frequent each other inside and outside school and to internalise the same values.

Republican universalism was also betrayed in the day to day practices at school. During the Third Republic, primary school teachers were fervently patriotic as was common at that time, and often mistreated the children of immigrants in their class. We now have access to memoirs, written by French people of foreign origin, who reveal how teachers, who supposedly embodied Republican universalism, were not immune to xenophobic reactions, in complete contradiction to the beliefs they should stand for. The civic education programmes that they were teaching led them to claim that France was the "most just, most free, the most humane of all nations" (official curriculum in the 1890s). This implied that all other nations were regarded, as a result, as less just, less free and less humane. Patriotism during the age of nationalism encouraged xenophobia and the rejection of the Other.

Thus teachers behaved in the same way as the rest of the population. Even if the children of immigrants were integrated into the French population over one or two generations, this process was not free of hostility and xenophobia. Throughout southern France, hatred and prejudice against Italian immigrants, which was often violent, as in Aigues Mortes in 1893, endured until the 1960s. During the 1930s, a period of economic crisis, xenophobic sentiment was freely expressed. In a recent book, Gérard Noiriel points out that the xenophobia of the Republic, even before the 1930s, had set the stage for the policies of the Vichy government (Noiriel 2000). Many professionals demonstrated against foreign doctors or recently naturalised doctors; a large number of intellectuals and politicians contested naturalisations which they felt to have been too easily granted in making reference to the "mother country" (la "terre nourricière"), its "truth" and its "authenticity" in defence against the foreign "métèques" or the "Levantins", which are offensive terms for foreigners used in the 30's.

Deviations from guidelines remain present in schools today, whether because of a latent racism on the side of some teachers at secondary schools (collèges) or sixth form colleges (lycées) or on the contrary, unofficial adaptations of the guidelines, such as acceptance of absences or unfinished homework during Ramadan, adjustments made to food in canteens, or as we shall see further on, the acceptance on a case by case basis of the wearing of headscarves by Muslim girls in some secondary schools and sixth form colleges. However, it is, above all, on an institutional level that certain departures from the guidelines have been gradually introduced into the school system.

The main aspect of this apparent flexibility with regards to egalitarian principles is the fact that all religious groups have the right to establish special schools, with the support of the state. So far, Catholic, Protestant and Jewish private schools do exist but there are no Islamic schools, at least partly due to the failure to organise an Islamic representative body which would act as the state's interlocutor, as is the case for the other religions. On the surface, this development may appear to be a departure from universalistic values, in the sense that not all children are obliged to attend secular public schools. The community approach seems to be taken into account instead. However, it should be noted that these schools are rarely "national" schools, (i.e intended for children from a specific country only), but rather they are "confessional" schools. In addition, pupils who attend these confessional schools are still required to take the same national examinations as other pupils in mainstream schools. The teaching program is expected to be the same as in mainstream schools and teachers must have graduated from the university system. Furthermore, the only private schools that are attended by large numbers of pupils are Catholic schools. In fact, the so-called "religious schools", especially the Catholic ones, are often perceived by the parents who choose them, as a means of avoiding sending their children to state schools in deprived areas, rather than a decision to bring their children up according to religious principles. Both Catholic and Protestant schools always accept children from other religious backgrounds, and a considerable number of pupils enrolled in these schools are children of immigrants, including Muslims. On the whole the universal model in education remains the norm, as the majority of children from practising Catholic, Protestant or Jewish families still prefer to send their children to state schools rather than to a confessional school. It is therefore reasonable to assume that similar developments will occur when Islamic schools are opened.

Another apparent feature of departure from the principle in the French education system is the provision of specific teaching programmes for the children of migrants or children who have recently arrived in France. However, these departures implemented in accordance with European directives are in practice not taken advantage of by a great number of people for whom they are made. This phenomenon can be seen as directly related to the internalisation of French pattern of integration by immigrants and their children.

The so-called programme "languages and cultures of origin" (*LCO - Langues et Cultures d'Origine*), introduced under the Giscard d'Estaing presidency in 1974, provides for the teaching of Arabic, Portuguese, Spanish, Turkish and Serbo-Croatian languages and civilisations for the children of immigrants. This complies with European regulations on education and with bilateral agreements with the countries of emigration concerned (Tunisia, Morocco, Algeria, Portugal, Spain, Turkey and Yugoslavia). But the LCO policy has failed: children of immigrants rarely attend these classes. Firstly, because immigrant families themselves often don't want their children to be marked as "different"for following a special curriculum. Secondly, because foreign teachers' methods of instruction often differ from the French teaching styles which the children are more used to and which they find more acceptable. Most of the children who attended these classes, abandoned them. Moreover, the policy of teaching in the so-called maternal language has been denounced as absurd, as, for instance, about 70% of the Algerians in France don't speak Arabic but Berber. Finally, the internalisation of the French pattern of integration means that most children of immigrants prefer to learn their parents' language and culture at home, in the private sphere, rather than at school, that is in the public sphere.

In some areas, the minister of education has implemented special measures for immigrant children, such as classes otherwise known as *classes d'accueil* for recent immigrants who speak little French. Other measures include special training and information centres concerned with the education of the children of immigrants who have recently arrived in France (*Centres de Formation et d'Information pour la Scolarisation des Enfants de Migrants – CEFISEM*). However, these initiatives are only meant to be temporary. The aim is to give these children the possibility to join the mainstream system as soon as possible. In most cases, attending theses special classes does not continue for more than one or two years.

Another public policy could be considered as a departure from the principles of universalism. The creation of "priority education zones" (*Zones d'Education Prioritaires – ZEP*) and of the category of "problem schools" (*établissements sensibles*) could be seen as a sort of affirmative action policy, since special funds, extra staff and larger budgets are allocated to establishments situated in deprived areas, particularly on the peripheries of large towns and cities, where a large proportion of immigrant children live and go to school. However, these specific policies are applied in a universal manner, which is in part due to the fact that young people of low social background live in the same housing areas and go to the same schools.

The priority educational zones scheme (*ZEP*) was introduced in 1982. It is not officially intended for children of immigrants, but one of the criteria for receiving funds, extra staff or teaching hours, is the percentage of foreigners at the school (more than 30% of the school's pupils). The socialist government (elected in May 1997) decided to give it a new lease of life in 1998. It was one of the nine projects put forward by the new minister of education. None of these projects is specifically concerned with children of immigrants and their integration. The aim of the current reinforcement of the ZEP policy is to consolidate the teaching of the core subjects (French, mathematics, foreign languages, history and geography) in order to improve the academic standards of all pupils. According to the minister of education, the ZEP policy does not intend to compensate for pupils' economic, social or cultural "handicaps" in the poorer suburbs, but instead to kick-start the whole national education system by creating a sort of exemplary model of teaching through reforms; to strengthen the partnership between schools and local authorities, local associations, families, and other relevant actors in order to create a cohesive, dynamic and non-violent educational environment which can effectively facilitate learning.

Since 1992, another measure has been in place in order to deal with problem schools (*établissements sensibles*).This involves combatting crime and violence (theft, racketeering, fights, drugs) in schools located in deprived areas. This policy is not concerned with children of immigrants in particular, either in terms of the criteria for access to supplementary staff or grants, or in the measures taken to remedy typical problems such as having less pupils per class or special educational help programmes. Yet, in practice the programme concerns many immigrants' children. The main objectives are as follows: the improvement of teaching and learning conditions; guidance of pupils through the curriculum; encouragement of academic progress; strengthening of teaching staff teams in order to create more of a team spirit; increased adult presence and authority inside the institution, facilitated by the presence of more school prefects.

In 1998 the minister of education introduced a new programme to improve the quality of schools. Its main aims are as follows: the creation of new posts for assistant teachers; wider use of information technology and communication; a campaign against violence in schools (along with educational, preventive and repressive measures); citizenship education and citizen initiatives (*éducation à la citoyenneté et initiatives citoyennes*)[2]; boosting the ZEP policy; the reorganisation of *lycées*. In this programme, children of international migrants were never cited and no specific measure was taken to favour their integration into the school system.

The "headscarves affair" (*affaire des foulards*) illustrates how the French concept oscillates between two opposite poles, and how any departures from the guiding principles are implemented on an individual, case by case basis, and never as official principles.

---

[2] The *éducation à la citoyenneté* consists of developing teaching hours devoted to human rights and citizenship issues and intends to promote a sense of personal and collective responsibility, as well as developing pupils' critical reasoning skills. The *initiatives citoyennes* consist of learning through the experience of citizenship, democratic civility, respect and solidarity.

Secularism is an essential aspect of the modern state, because it allows to transcend the diversity of religious belongings: religious beliefs and practices become private matters and the public sphere is a religiously neutral space commonly shared by all citizens, whatever religion they belong to. The general principle takes specific forms in French society for historical reasons. Since school is considered as the embodiment of equality and secularism, the debate on secularism (*laïcité*) occurs predominantly in the sphere of education.

The so-called headscarves affair received a lot of publicity when several Muslim girls were almost excluded from school for wearing headscarves, which were considered to be emblems of their religion: the "headscarf scandal" is an illustration of French "*laïcité*". It began in September 1989, when the head teacher (from the French West Indies) of a secondary school in the Paris region did not allow three young girls wearing headscarves to come to *collège* (secondary school). This decision was, as a result, widely and passionately discussed by the media. For the supporters of traditional Republican education, it was the right decision in order to protect educational establishments from religious influences, an idea which lies in the heart of French *laïcité*. French secularism also implies the notion that ostentatious signs representing the following of a particular faith should be prohibited, in order to combat fundamentalism and to help children adopt universal values. However, religious leaders (Catholics, Jews, Muslims and Protestants) and some Socialist Party politicians argued that cultural and religious differences had to be respected, and that headscarves should thus be permitted. The *Conseil d'Etat* – the highest state court – claimed that, in accordance with human rights, no one should be persecuted because of his/her opinions, even religious opinions, as long as these do not threaten public order:

> "The wearing of symbols by pupils, demonstrating their adherence to a religion is not essentially inconsistent with the principle of secularism, insofar as it constitutes the exercise of the freedom of expression and the exhibition of confessional beliefs, but this freedom should not allow pupils to wear signs, revealing adherence to a religion, which, by their very nature, by the conditions in which they may be individually or collectively worn, or by their ostentatious or conspicuous character, would constitute an act of pressure, of provocation, evangelism, propaganda, or undermine the dignity and freedom of pupils or of other members of the educational community, or compromise teaching activities and the teacher's educational role, or finally would disturb the order or the regular functioning of the public institution."

In December 1989 the minister of education (Lionel Jospin, socialist, former Prime Minister) had urged the schools' directors to negotiate with parents to discourage the wearing of headscarves. The minister stipulated that there should be no generalised prohibition of the wearing of ostentatious symbols of religious belief, as long as this was not coupled with evangelism or social disturbance. However, all subjects and classes in the curriculum should be attended. Some Muslim families wanted to prevent their daughters from going to physical education or biology classes. In September 1994, the new minister of education (François Bayrou, Christian-democrat), supporter of the French model of integration and of the Republican school, finally prohibited the wearing of headscarves or any ostentatious religious symbols. Some pupils were, as a result, excluded from schools. In his *circulaire* – a minister's decision which is circulated throughout government and published in the *Bulletin Officiel* of his ministry – François Bayrou clarified his traditional understanding of the role of schools:

> "In France, the national project and the republican project are merged into one around a certain idea of citizenship. This French idea of the Nation and of the Republic is, essentially, respectful of all convictions, particularly, religious and political convictions, as well as cultural traditions. But it excludes the fragmentation of the Nation into separate communities, indifferent to others, only concerned about their own rules and their own laws, engaged in mere coexistence. The Nation is not only a whole entity of citizens, guarantor of individual rights. It is a community of fate. This ideal is first taught at school."

However, despite this circular, the matter is always dealt with on a case by case basis in the schools where it is an issue, in accordance with the Republican tradition of unofficial adjustments and pragmatic measures which are taken, but are not codified in legislation. A ministerial mediator (a Muslim woman of North African origin) has been nominated in order to oversee the arrangements made in each case.

This example also implicitly illustrates to what extent migrants and their children have internalised the French pattern of integration, or to what extent the parents' decision to emigrate revealed an undeclared adherence to the universalistic model, as the wearing of Islamic headscarf was never an issue in France before 1989, and remains a rather marginal phenomenon for young girls of immigrant Muslim origin. It should be added that although wearing a scarf is legal in universities, this practice remains marginal.

5.2. The FAS, Immigrants' Associations and Associations for the Defence of Foreign Nationals' Rights

The FAS (Social Action Fund for Immigrant Workers and their Families – *Fonds d'Action Sociale pour les Travailleurs immigrés et leurs familles*) is another example of the complex interlocking of universalism and departures from the principles. The FAS is the main official instrument targeted at migrants' integration by providing funds for occupational training, housing and social work.

The main functions of the FAS fall into the following categories: reception of immigrant families, housing, education, employment, social and civic rights. The FAS' projects are local, based on a precisely defined area, and they are not limited to one aspect of integration. The organisation works with local partners and does not only apply government decisions in the traditional top-down manner that is common in French administration. The FAS works under the authority of the Ministry of Social Affairs and Integration and cooperates with a consultative committee, the National Board of Immigrant Populations (*Conseil National des Populations Immigrées – CNPI*). The FAS' main partners are: the OMI (*Office des Migrations Internationales*) which deals with immigrants' economic situation, housing and health, and the SONACOTRA, the National Society for the Construction of Housing for Immigrant Workers (*Société Nationale de Construction de Logements pour les Travailleurs*), which was created in 1956.

At the end of the 1990s the FAS employed 230 people, was represented by fourteen regional offices and awarded 8,000 grants to approximately 4,000 associations and partners. It donated 150,000,000 Euros to social initiatives, 40,000,000 Euros to housing policy projects and 34,000,000 Euros to training (mainly reading and writing teaching programmes). It also played a role in urban planning policies implemented in over 166 towns. The FAS is itself funded by the national family allowance contribution fund and its main task is to provide resources for local or national associations that are concerned with integration or immigration.

The main activities of the FAS, however, do not consist of implementing specific policies targeted at migrants or their children, no more than they consist of financing migrant associations set up by migrants. It usually finances associations that help integration in the wider sense of the term.

The major associations concerned with the integration of immigrants in France are run by French nationals, who are not necessarily the descendants of migrants. In fact, their salaried workers as well as their volunteers are either of autochthonous or foreign origin. For example, most associations supported by the FAS, whether local or national, which provide reading and writing teaching programmes, homework help for pupils or specific professional training for the socially marginalised in relation to employment are not only concerned with

35

helping immigrants or their children. These programs concern immigrants and their children and autochthonous individuals, who all attend the same teaching or training sessions.

In addition to FAS there are private associations created for the defence of immigrants' rights. Despite the fact that foreigners have been able to legally set up their own associations since 1981, and despite the fact that their children, due to their status as French nationals, have always been free to establish any specific associations if they so wish, the majority of these associations are not especially set up, governed, nor run by immigrants, and they are rarely devoted to one specific "ethnic minority" or "community".

The main associations in these fields are: the *Fondation France Libertés*, the *France Plus-Movement National des Droits Civiques*, the *Groupe d'Information et de Soutien des Travailleurs Immigrés (GISTI)*, the *Ligue Internationale Contre le Racisme et l'Antisémitisme (LICRA)*, the *Movement Contre le Racisme et pour l'Amitié entre les Peuples (MRAP)*, the *Movement ATD – Quart Monde, SOS Racisme*. Only *France Plus* and *SOS Racisme* are run mostly by immigrants (*France Plus*) or the children of immigrants (*SOS Racisme*), and have a majority of adherents from various foreign origins. The others are usually run by autochthonous, and have adherents either from French or from foreign origin. Their main roles are to defend legal and illegal immigrants' rights, and to struggle against discrimination and racism. At the national level, only few play a real political role. This is the case, for instance, with *GISTI*, and with *SOS Racisme*.

Some associations exist only on the level of ethnic communities. Their role can be to participate in the general integration process. They do not, however, attract a lot of descendants of immigrants. There are, for example, numerous Portuguese folkloric local associations that teach traditional dances or songs from Portugal, or the local Algerian immigrants' circle (*Amicales des Immigrés Algériens*). But these associations do not attract a large number of immigrants from the countries concerned. Most of them are only empty shells, that do not have concrete functions. Some try to attract children of immigrants. A French-Portuguese association for instance, *Cap Magellan*, exists in order to help the children of Portuguese immigrants who would like to keep some links with Portugal, to live there for a period of time or, less often, to return permanently to Portugal. Some associations dedicated to homework help are linked to Mosques in certain areas, but they are less frequented than the non-community-based ones. The latter usually provide help with homework, teach immigrants to read and write and offer occupational training for young people and adults. Some ethnic sports associations attract members from all sorts of national backgrounds. The fact is that, even if there are plenty of seemingly community based associations in the telephone directory their community support and influence is hardly relevant.

The only truly active foreign associations are religious associations. These mostly concern immigrants themselves, as religious practice is not widespread amongst their children. In a country where secularism is the norm churches or cultural-religious associations do not play an institutional role in society. Religion is considered as something to be reserved for the private sphere. Government policy only guarantees the freedom of religious practice.

The minister of the interior, who is also responsible for religions, has tried on a number of occasions to organise an official representative body for Muslims in France, on the same basis as the Jewish *Consistoire National*. However, disagreements between the various Muslim populations have made the establishment of such an organisation impossible until now. Although there are only a few large mosques in France, plans to build new big mosques have been, until now, often been thwarted by the opposition of the local population. Despite this, more than a thousand places of Muslim worship exist, which constitute the activities of most of the cultural-religious associations. For the last twenty years the only specific measures taken in favour of Islam have been the implementation of Muslim sections (*carrés musulmans*) in French cemeteries, and the introduction of hallal meat in compulsory military service and school canteens. Former interior minister Jean-Pierre Chevènement (1995-2000) has, since November, 1999, been trying to organise the institutionalisation of Islam in France, that is, to create a National Representative Islamic Council (*Conseil Représentatif National de l'Islam*). Both mosques and cultural-religious associations would participate in its establishment. The idea behind the setting up of this body is that once in place it will be able to organise or set up Muslim schools, mosques (the creation of which can no longer be opposed by the general population), and organise Islamic education for young people. In addition, Islamic religious associations would be able to have the legal status of a 1905 association, which is the case for Catholic and Protestant churches as well as synagogues and they would no longer be governed by the 1901 association law which relates to all sorts of associations. In exchange, the signatories of this body would sign a declaration relating to the rights and obligations of their Muslim followers, compatible with the laws of the Republic.

6. Racism and Discrimination

The French model of integration has not been more successful than other approaches in the eradication of xenophobia, racism and discrimination. It is more difficult for descendants of immigrants in comparison with autochthonous individuals to escape the often modest social origins of their parents (Institut National d'Etudes Démographiques 1992). Discrimination against non-European populations, especially of Maghrebian origin[3], exists, especially in the areas of private sector employment and housing, police treatment and admittance to nightclubs. This is the real failure of the French pattern of integration, and the real discrepancy between the model and social reality. One may note, however, that racism and xenophobia have been raising all over Europe again for more than twenty years. Taking that into account one could not attribute this failure merely to the "French" pattern of integration.

Social scientists and politicians usually agree that racism and discrimination in France mainly stem from economic and social problems. French society is based more upon social distinctions than ethnic ones, and the most important difficulties that immigrants or their children encounter in public life can be more attributed to social problems than to ethnicity – even if there is a mixture of "ethnic" and "social" dimensions in the expression of racism.

People who emigrated to France were mostly from rural areas, were unskilled, and a high percentage of them were/are illiterate. But huge differences may be observed from one country to another. Turks, Portuguese, Spaniards, Algerians and Moroccans are mainly from rural areas. South-East Asians and Africans are mostly urban. Differences in illiteracy rates also vary greatly: the majority of Spaniards, Portuguese, Turks and South-East Asian immigrants went to school in their countries. This is not so often the case for Algerians and Moroccans. The social origins of migrants' parents differs greatly from country to country: Algerians, Moroccans and Turks mainly had parents who were peasants or workers. At the other end of the scale, South-East Asian migrants often have parents who were mainly upper or middle class (Tribalat 1996).

Less than 30% of the French economically active population are workers, but this figure is 55 to 65% for Spanish, Portuguese or Maghrebian and other nationalities. In 1992, more than 80% of migrants' descendants aged between 20-29 of Spanish, Portuguese or Algerian origin had parents who are (or were) workers, against only 40% for the French-stock population of the same age in

---

[3] Examples of racism in France can be found in the following publication: *Xénophobie en France*, United Nations Human Rights Commission Report, special rapporteur's report on contemporary forms of racism, racial discrimination, xenophobia and intolerance, M. Maurice Glèle-Ahanhanzo, presented in accordance with Human Rights Commission resolutions 1993/20 et 1995/12. Special Rapporteur's report on the mission he carried out in France from 29 September to 9 October 1995.

1992 (ibidem). It is also significant to note that in 1995, 20% of immigrants were unemployed while the national average was 12%, and that joblessness particularly affected Portuguese and Maghrebian immigrants. This may be partly attributed to discrimination, but may also be explained by the high rate of unskilled workers within the immigrant population.

Generally speaking, African and South-East Asian emigration was mostly an emigration of the educated, urban upper or middle classes, whereas other countries' migrants, especially from the Maghreb and Portugal, are from rural, illiterate lower classes. This is due to the circumstances of emigration, as South-East Asians emigrated mainly because of the political persecution of middle and upper-classes in their countries, while the Portuguese or Maghrebian experience was mainly economic migration and labour-related. However, this has important consequences on the way these people are perceived by the population as a whole, and can partly explain why racism is more often directed against Maghrebians than against Asians or Africans. The high rate of unemployment amongst Maghrebian nationals also enforces "social racism", as unemployment is one of the most deprived social conditions, especially when it is long-term. As in other countries, social and national origins combine, and those who are not of French origin are at a disadvantage. Yet when migrants or their descendants belong to middle or upper-classes, the handicap due to "origins" or background tends to disappear. Although it is very difficult to prove that discrimination has taken place, various studies present evidence of it (Bataille 1997).

A famous example of discrimination in employment is the abbreviation "BBR" (*Bleu, Blanc, Rouge* – the colours of the French flag), or the numbers "001" on job advertisements. These codes which are placed in job offers and descriptions are supposed to let the National Employment Office (*Agence Nationale pour l'Emploi – ANPE*) know that the employers who have placed the advertisement want the agency to send only autochthonous or at least European candidates for interviews. This illegal practice was denounced in 1996 in an official report on urban integration policy (Mekachera and Gaeremynck 1996). In 1997, with the support of universities, research institutes and hospitals, the most ambitious French investigation ever into racism at work was carried out (Bataille 1997). This study showed racist practices both in the civil service and in the private sector.

One should add that a quarter of all jobs, as they are linked to the civil service, are in fact not open to foreigners. As a result of European legislation, discrimination in job recruitment can no longer be defined solely in terms of nationals versus foreigners but rather European versus non-European immigrants. With regards to social rights, France has been accused of unjustly imposing the condition of French nationality to gain access to certain benefits, such as for adult handicap allowance and supplementary allowances for old people. After the European Court of Justice ruled against French legislation in

1990 and 1991, the decisions made by the *Conseil Constitutionnel* (high-level court with jurisdiction over the legality of laws) did change. Landmark decisions were made by the *Conseil* in January 1990 and August 1993. The law on immigration passed in May 1998 (*loi Chevènement*, named after the Home Secretary) led to the abandonment of all nationality requirements with regards to social rights and benefits. Yet the claimants of these rights must still be able to show legal residence permits. In the allocation of council housing, however, there does exist an illegal but current practice by which immigrant and other socio-economically deprived populations are in practice refused housing in certain areas (Dubedout 1996).

Xenophobic attitudes exist in various sectors of French society. According to a recent nation-wide survey, it seems that 60% of French people claim that they are "not really or not at all racist", but 38% declare that they are "racist or somewhat racist"[4]. However, one should be cautious in interpreting these answers. One year later, the 1999 *Commission consultative des droits de l'homme* poll showed that 60% of the population answered that it was "racist or somewhat racist". A majority claimed there were "too many Arabs in France" or that "migrants come to France in order to take advantage of the social benefits and assistance". The *Front National*, which governs a few municipalities, and received 15% of the national vote in the 1990s elections, (in some areas this percentage went up to 40%), advocates what is known as national preference (*préférence nationale*) i.e. discrimination against foreigners in favour of French nationals in employment and the allocation of social rights.

A number of special institutions have been created or revived in the fight against racism and discrimination. An independent consultative committee for human rights (*Commission consultative des droits de l'homme*), created in 1947, was re-instated by a decree in 1984, and thus came under the control of the Prime Minister in 1989. Since 1990, one of the committee's main roles has involved the publication of an annual report on racism and xenophobia. It also exists to keep the Prime Minister up to date on national and international human rights issues. Its seventy members consist of civil servants who represent the Prime Minister, the Home Secretary and the Ministers of Justice, Social Affairs and Education. Representatives from national human rights associations, trade-unions (like *CGT, CFDT, CFTC*), experts and personalities (particularly religious leaders) are also part of the Committee.

---

[4] See for instance: Commission nationale consultative des Droits de l'Homme, *La lutte contre le racisme et la xénophobie. Exclusion et Droits de l'Homme*, Rapport au Premier Ministre, Paris, La Documentation Française, 1999.

In March 1993, the Ministry of Justice set up local cells to combat racism, xenophobia and anti-Semitism (*cellule départementale de coordination de la lutte contre le racisme, la xénophobie et l'antisémitisme*) as part of local committees established to deal with delinquency. These boards meet at least once a year to inform about and discuss racist incidents. In January, 1999, the Minister of the Interior, Jean-Pierre Chevènement, set up 115 *Commissions d'Accès à la Cito-yenneté* (CODAC). Placed under the authority of the *Préfets*, they are set up in order to ensure equal rights and to fight against racism and discriminations.

In 1998, the employment minister, Martine Aubry, claimed that special attention needed to be paid to the issue of discrimination at work, and set up a *Groupe d'étude sur les discriminations* (observators group against discrimina-tions) in order to carry out a study on the matter. Victims of discrimination were at the same time encouraged to seek justice. One of the first measures consecutive to this study has been the implementation (May, 2000) of a free phone number (*numéro vert antidiscrimination, 114*) which all victims of racism or discrimination can call in order to get psychological or legal support. Within the first four days of it implementation, 491 cases of discrimination were made to the CODAC, that studies each case and takes legal action if possible.

In 1999, *SOS racisme* set out to prove the presence of racism and discrimina-tion in the courts through special initiatives such as "testing". Two young people were sent to a nightclub, one after the other, one was autochthonous and the other from obviously foreign origin, both were accompanied by a court usher so that any discrimination would be witnessed. In the same way, two identical Curriculum Vitae were sent to various companies, one bearing a foreign first name and surname and the other bearing a French first name and surname, in order to find incidents of discrimination.

It should be pointed out that those very people who claimed in a recent poll that they are racist or racist to a certain extent, also claim that they are com-pletely against discriminatory practice, especially in the workplace. 80% of those who replied in this poll claimed that they found the notion that some-body would not be hired or promoted at work because of his/her "origins", unacceptable. Another point is that these specific polls take into account the racist categorisation and discourse promoted by the Front National. The use of abstract categories such as "immigrant","foreigner", "Maghrebian", "Black", "Jew" in opinion polls favours a racist discourse when answering. Racist prac-tice however, does not always follow as a result of attitudes and opinions. This illustrates the paradoxical nature of the French integration pattern. As it is founded on universalism, "origins" become a taboo subject. To evoke the other's "origin" is perceived as xenophobia.

This observation leads to question whether not all models of integration eventually create their own forms (hidden or open) xenophobia and whether a model exists which can avoid xenophobia, a phenomenon incompatible with the values of a democratic society.

7. Conclusion

The integration of migrants and their children is ideologically centred around a political programme linked to the values symbolised by the Revolution. National integration on the whole, is political: members of the national society are supposed to be integrated by individual citizenship, following a universalistic view of the citizen and taking into account the right to attachment (*droit de rattachement*) for those who have internalised and fully adhere to French values. This principle, stemming from the founding myth of the French Revolution, is the ideological foundation of contemporary integration policy, known as "assimilation" policy. It is through individual citizenship that this policy attempts to transform a population of foreign origin into Frenchmen and women.

This policy is often criticised by France's European neighbours, who stress that due to its voluntarist character, it may mistreat immigrants or their children, whose needs and specific aspirations are being denied. This might be partly true. But it can be argued that minority-oriented policies and encouraging "communities" to express themselves publicly as such, may be normal and perhaps desirable in other European countries, but in the French model and tradition of national integration, the minority-based approach is supposed to weaken the social fabric and cohesion. All policies have their own logic in accordance with a particular national history.

The French pattern of integration can be characterised by universalistic principles, departures from these principles and the ways in which tensions between the two are managed. It is through the internalisation of the universalistic model by immigrants and their children, by the autochthonous population and the institutions that the model inspires: far from being an abstract concept, it is present in the actual practice of institutions and actors concerned.

References

Bastide, H. 1982:

Les enfants d'immigrés et l'enseignement français, Paris: Presses Universitaires de France

Bataille P. 1997:

Le racisme au travail, Paris: La Découverte

Bertillon, J. 1911:

La dépopulation de la France, Paris: Alcan

Bonnet, J. C. 1976:

Les pouvoirs publics francais et l'immigration dans l'entre-deux guerres, Lyon: Centre Pierre Léon

Dubedout, H. 1996:

Ensemble, refaire la ville, rapport au Premier ministre du Président de la Commission nationale pour le développement social des quartiers, Paris: La Documentation française

Institut Nationale d'Etudes Démographiques 1992:

Study on Geographical Mobility and Social Integration, Paris

Lequin, Y. (ed.) 1992:

Histoire des étrangers et de l'immigration en France, Paris: Larousse

Mekachera, H. / Gaeremynck, J. 1996:

Pour une relance de la politique de l'intégration, Paris: Délégation à l'intégration

Noiriel, G. 1988:

Le creuset français, Paris: Seuil

Noiriel, G. 2000:

Les origines républicaines de Vichy, Paris: Hadette

Schnapper, D. 1992:

L'Europe des immigrés. Essai sur les politiques d'immigration, Paris: François Bourin

43

Schnapper, D. 1994:

La communauté des citoyens. Sur l'idée moderne de nation, Paris: Gallimard

Tribalat, M. 1996:

De l'immigration à l'assimilation. Enquête sur les populations d'origine étrangère, Paris: La Découverte

Tribalat, M. 1997:

'Les populations d'origine étrangère en France métropolitaine', *Population*, 1, pp. 163-220

Vallet, L.-A. 1996:

'L'assimilation scolaire des enfants issus de l'immigration et son interpretation: un examen sur données françaises', *Revue Française de Pédagogie*, n°117, octobre-novembre-décembre

Vallet, L.-A. / Caille, J.-P. 2000:

'La scolarité des enfants d'immigrés', in van Zanten, A. (ed.), *L'école. L'état des savoirs*, pp. 293-301, Paris: La Découverte

Weber, E. 1976:

Peasants into Frenchmen. The Modernization of Rural France 1870-1914, Stanford: Stanford University Press

Friedrich Heckmann

From Ethnic Nation to Universalistic Immigrant Integration: Germany

1. Introduction

Germany has experienced large scale immigration since the end of World War II. German refugees, foreign workers and their families, asylum seekers and foreign refugees, EU migrants and ethnic Germans from Eastern Europe and the former Soviet Union are among the largest groups. Immigration poses the question of integration, of how to relate to the "newcomers" in the spheres of economic, political, social and cultural life. This chapter is about the political and societal responses to the "question of integration" in Germany. Since the political perceptions and attitudes towards "returning" ethnic Germans are quite different from those relating to foreign migrants it is necessary to discern between political responses towards ethnic Germans (*Spätaussiedler*) and foreign migrants. Our analysis is mainly concerned with the latter group's integration.

We shall first give a brief overview of the forms and quantities of immigration and return migration in Germany since the end of World War II. As to integration we assume that its political determinants in the receiving society are largely influenced by the *societal "definition of the immigration situation"*, i.e. the understanding by major political and societal actors of the "nature" of the ongoing migration processes. Thus, a section on the demographics of migration will be followed by a discussion of the political and societal definition of the immigration situation in a historical perspective.

Furthermore, we assume that the responses to immigration are determined by general *principles of the social order* of a country and its *sense of nationhood*. The ways in which a country generally and "normally" tries to secure cohesion, conflict solution, to solve social and economic problems will also be used when integrating migrants. We will discuss this in section 4 in more detail. By sense of nationhood we refer to constitutive principles of a concept of nation, especially criteria of membership and inclusion. These are of major relevance for policies of citizenship in relation to immigrants. Since these policies of citizenship and naturalisation have been a main aspect of structural integration policies in which major changes have occurred in Germany in 1999/2000 we will discuss citizenship policies in a separate section (section 5). Germany has been continuously classified as an archetypical ethnic nation state. That is why the present changes to a more republican and universalistic model of nation deserve particular attention.

General integration policies and welfare state measures in Germany usually include the immigrants. The relevance of general integration policies for the integration of immigrants will be discussed in section 6. On the other side, there are special measures and institutions which are directly devised for immigrants. We shall call these special integration policies (section 7).

Integration policies, general and specific, citizenship rules and other elements of a national mode of integration set conditions for the integration of immigrants. But integration cannot be forced upon people in modern societies, it is a result of individual choices, often with motives that do not seem to be related to integration at all. Integration "can occur as the often unintended, cumulative by-product of choices made by individuals to improve their social situation" (Alba 1999). If integration is – in this sense – a kind of market process there is, on the other side, a political process that sets conditions and gives incentives for individual choices and decisions: integration policies.

We are working with a *concept of integration* that leans partly on ideas of "assimilation" as formulated by Gordon (1964) and Esser (1990), and on a general and formal understanding of integration. For pragmatic reasons we have not used the term "assimilation" because it almost immediately evokes emotional reactions and connotations of cultural suppression in many audiences.

Integration as a general and formal concept may be defined as a) forming a new structure out of single elements, or b) "improving" relations within a structure and c) adding single elements or partial structures to an existing structure and joining these to an interconnected "whole". Integration refers both to the process of connecting the elements as well as the resulting degree of interconnectedness within the "whole". In the context of immigration integration refers to the inclusion of new populations into existing social structures and the quality and manners in which these new populations are connected to the existing system of socio-economic, legal and cultural relations.

Connecting the new populations to the existing structures and the resulting kind of connectedness involve a process of acquiring a membership status in the core institutions of the immigration society (economy and labour market, education, qualification system, housing market, citizenship as membership in the political community) and the learning and socialisation necessary for participating in the new society. Thus, integration means the acquisition of rights and the access to positions and statuses in the core institutions of the receiving society by the immigrants and their descendants: *structural integration*.

Rights can be used and positions and statuses can be taken up only if the immigrants actively participate in certain learning and socialisation processes. In relation to these preconditions of participation integration refers to processes of cognitive, cultural, behavioural and attitudinal change of individuals:

cultural integration or acculturation. Acculturation primarily concerns the immigrants and their descendants, but it is an interactive, mutual process that changes the receiving society as well.

Membership of immigrants in the new society in the private sphere is reflected in peoples' private relations and group memberships (social intercourse, friendships, marriages, voluntary associations): *social integration.*

Membership in a new society on the subjective level shows in feelings of belonging and identification, particularly in forms of ethnic and/or national identification: *identificational integration.*

Thus integration means an acquisition of rights, access to positions and statuses, a change in individual characteristics, a building of social relations and a formation of feelings of belonging and identification by immigrants towards the immigration society. It is dependent on a number of conditions on the part of the receiving society which could generally be described as its "openness" to the new group of people. A "successful" or progressing integration process could also be characterised by increasing similarity in living conditions and ethnic-cultural orientations between immigrants and natives, and a decrease in ethnic stratification.

As to the discourse on national differences in integration policies the term "national integration strategy" is used quite often. The use of the term "strategy" seems to be rather problematic. "Strategy" implies planning and consistency. National strategy would imply conscious planning, consistency, systematic organised and goal minded action on a national scale. In that sense, integration strategy does not seem to exist in any European country. National strategy is unlikely for another reason: migration and integration policies are very often in the centre of political battles, and are therefore subject to serious political conflict. Content and direction of migration and integration policies change according to the political climate in the society and according to power relations.

Still there are certain consistencies and common characteristics in integration policies on a national level that derive from principles of the social order, sense of nationhood and the definition of the immigration situation that we will further describe in section 3. We propose to call the whole of integration policies and their relation to the social order of the society and to the societal definition of the immigration situation *national mode of immigrant integration.*

Before we start our analysis of national mode of integration in Germany we shall give an overview of the demographics of migration into Germany since World War II.

2. Demographics of Migration

Enormous migration processes have occurred in Germany since the end of World War II. Between 1945 and the beginning 1950's about 12 million German refugees and expellees came to the four allied occupied zones from former German territories or from German ethnic minority settlements in Southeastern and Eastern Europe and the Soviet Union. Till the building of the Berlin Wall in 1961 3.8 million people migrated from East to West Germany.

Figure 1 shows the number of cases of in-migration to Germany between 1958 and 1999, as well as the number of cases of out-migration. This is roughly equivalent to the number of migrating people, but only roughly. German migration statistics record cases of migration and count every move of a person. If a person leaves the country during a year twice and comes back each time we have two cases of in-migration and two cases of out-migration.

Figure 1: Immigration – Outmigration in Germany, 1958-1999

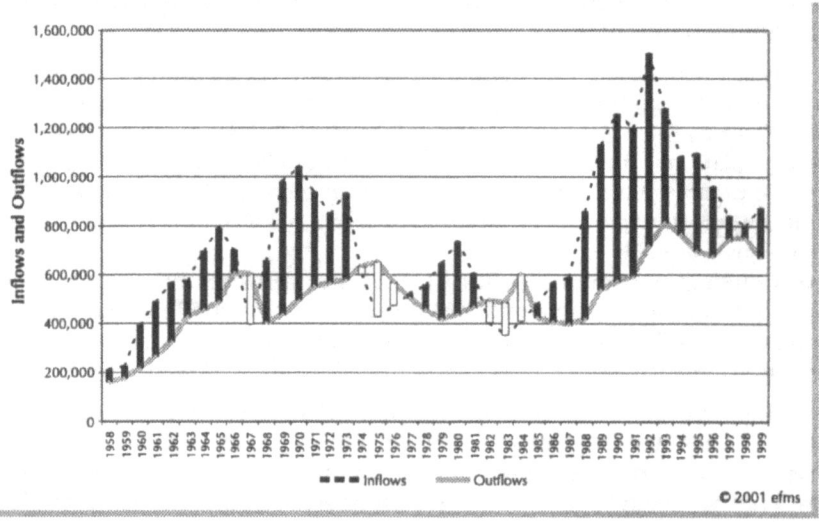

Source: Federal Statistical Office, efms

For the last 40 years there are about 30 million cases of people migrating to Germany and about 21 million cases of people leaving the country. With the exception of the periods 1967-1968, 1975-1977 and 1982-1984 there has always been a net gain of migrants. Because fertility has been below reproduction level since the end of the sixties the population increase since then has been totally due to migration gains.

Whereas migration in the late forties and early fifties was closely related to the war and its consequences, migration at the end of the fifties, in the sixties and early seventies was the result of labour market processes. The combination of high economic growth with internal labour shortages lead to a continuous and increasing recruitment of foreign workers till 1973.

After 1973 processes of family reunion occurred on a large scale and since then family reunion has become another major source of immigration to Germany. Ethnic Germans from South-eastern and Eastern Europe (*Spätaussiedler*) are a group of migrants whose migration has intensified in the 1990's after the breakdown of the Iron Curtain when more than 2 million people arrived. On the whole about four million *Spätaussiedler* came from 1950 till the present of whom very few returned to Eastern Europe (Lederer 1997 and Lederer et al. 1999).

Two other large groups of migrants are asylum seekers and refugees. About 1.8 million people have asked for asylum in Germany in the 1990's. The total number of asylum seekers from1959-1999 is 2.78 million (ibidem). War refugees, so-called contingent refugees and Jewish people from territories of the former Soviet Union form additional groups of migrants. Figure 2 shows forms of migration to Germany in the 1990's. The size of the symbols roughly represents the size of these groups.

Ethnic Germans, family reunion migrants, temporary labour migrants, asylum seekers and EU migrants are the main groups of people coming to Germany in the 1990's.

Immigration has always been accompanied by simultaneous processes of return migration or emigration. A huge "coming and going" has occurred during the last 40 years. There are about 30 million cases of people coming, and about 21 million cases of people who left the country, leading to a net gain of about 9 million between 1959 and 1999 (Lederer et al. 1999, 7). It is for those who could stay and stayed and chose to live in Germany that the question of integration is of major significance. Most asylum seekers and present day temporary labour migrants (seasonal workers, contract workers) are not among them.

A rough estimate of the size of the "integration problem" can be given by the present size of the foreign population in Germany (Table 1). The figures are imprecise and overestimate present integration needs in that they do not directly indicate kind and degrees of integration already achieved: there are foreigners who are highly integrated as well as foreigners who are little integrated. On the other side the figures underestimate integration needs because they do not record the immigrant ethnic German population whose integration requires similar efforts as that of other immigrant groups.

Figure 2: Forms of Migration to Germany in the 1990's

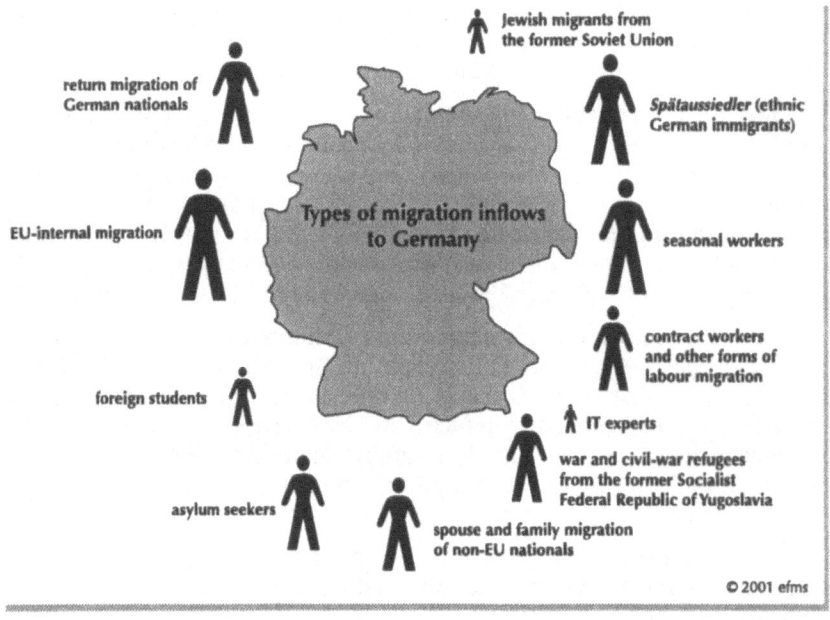

Source: efms

Table 1: Foreign Population in Germany

Year	Total Population[1]	Foreign Population[1]	Percentage of Foreign Nationals	Change in Foreign Population (in %)[2]
1991	80,274,600	5,882,267	7.3	-
1992	80,974,600	6,495,792	8.0	+10.4
1993	81,338,100	6,878,117	8.5	+5.9
1994	81,538,600	6,990,510	8.6	+1.6
1995	81,817,500	7,173,866	8.8	+2.6
1996	82,012,200	7,314,046	8.9	+2.0
1997	82,057,400	7,365,833	9.0	+0.7
1998	82,037,000	7,319,593	8.9	-0.6
1999	82,163,500	7,343,591	8.9	+0.3
2000	82,259,530	7,296,817	8.9	-0.6

Source: Federal Statistical Office; compiled by efms

[1] set date: December 31

[2] Annual change, i.e. compared to previous year

50

3. Political and Societal Definition of the Immigration Situation

Both for individual and corporate actors the "definition of the situation" is a main element for the explanation of action. Be it "objectively" true or false, or half-true and half-false, the definition of the situation constitutes and structures actor's perception of reality and determines the decision making process in social action. "... public definition of a situation ... becomes an integral part of the situation and thus affects subsequent developments" (Merton in Esser 1999, 4). The definition of the situation creates a new reality that could under certain conditions – like a self-fulfilling prophecy – change or even destroy the "other", "objective" reality.

Individual and collective definitions of the situation are – by no means – something "given" or static. As to collective definitions there is quite often a competition between different camps in society, a struggle for the power to define situations and thus influence social and societal action. Migration is a good example. For a long time there has been a struggle in Germany about the "nature" of the migration processes. *"Deutschland ist kein Einwanderungsland"* (Germany is not an immigration country) has been the slogan of the long prevailing definition of the situation. Another camp has been saying the opposite *"Deutschland ist ein Einwanderungsland"* (Germany is an immigration country). The different definitions of the situation have a determining influence on kinds and quality of integration policies. If political actors do not believe that there is an immigration process they will not – like "classical" immigration countries – create institutions and make laws to receive people from abroad as future citizens.

When active recruitment of foreign workers began in 1955 and increased rapidly after 1961 no group involved in this process perceived and defined the situation other than temporary: the employers, the unions, the state sending and the state receiving the workers, and the "guestworkers" themselves. Everyone believed in temporary employment and a kind of "rotation system" where new workers coming would substitute those who were returning. What has later been called the "myth of return" was not totally a myth. As figure 1 shows, and as mentioned before, there have been 30 million cases of in-migration (not all of whom, however, were foreign guestworkers) and 21 million cases of out-migration, most of whom were people returning to their country of origin.

The "rotation system" functioned only in part for two reasons: the employers wanted to keep workers who had been trained and socialised. They did not want to continuously have to organise processes of training, socialising to the firm and general acculturation for newly arriving foreign workers. That is, they wanted to save costs. On the part of the workers relations to German society began to develop on several levels. They kept wanting to return, but many kept postponing concrete plans for return again and again (Heckmann 1981).

During the period of guestworker recruitment that lasted till 1973, integration into German society had no place in the definition of the situation. *Partial accommodation* for a temporary stay was all that was needed. The end of worker recruitment in 1973 was meant to lead to a decrease in the foreign population, but surprisingly the opposite happened: The foreign population increased, because family reunion took place. Temporary migration began to develop into a settlement process in the 1970's (ibidem). Similar processes were happening in other European countries (Schnapper 1992, 127-134). A new definition of the situation was needed. In view of a shrinking labour demand and in view of an immigration process of family members that was not really wanted, but had to be accepted, a new formula came up: "*Deutschland ist kein Einwanderungsland*" (Germany is not an immigration country). It became, paradoxically, the official, governmental definition of the immigration situation. Basically it meant that the Federal Republic continued to regard the presence of foreign migrants as temporary and the recruitment of people from abroad for the labour market that had happened as an exception and as something of the past that should not happen again. This formula has been – with somewhat shifting meanings in the eighties and nineties – the official governmental guideline of migration policy till 1998.

If this denial of an immigration situation was one reaction to the new situation in the mid seventies, another response was the beginning of a discourse on integration and of concrete integration policies. *The denial of an immigration situation cannot be at all equated with the lack of an integration policy.* Most importantly, migrants were integrated into the welfare state system. Churches, welfare organisations as well as unions began to turn attention to living conditions and socio-economic opportunities for "foreigners". The state responded to this development by the institutionalisation of an office of "Commissioner for Foreigners" in 1978. The foundation of this office meant that integration was officially regarded and defined a necessity (Mahnig 1998, 53). A welfare state and a democracy with respect for Human Rights could not ignore the needs of an increasingly large part of its population.

Recognising the need for integration on the one hand, but sticking to the formula of Germany not being an immigration country resulted in an ambiguous definition of the situation: "Germany is not an immigration country" stands for doubts about the legitimacy of the presence of foreigners. Integration policy, particularly through inclusion into the general welfare state institutions, on the other side, reinforces relations to the country of immigration. The ambiguous character of foreigners' policy in Germany in the 1980's and 1990's with the denial of an immigration situation on the one side, and concrete measures of integration on the other, expressed itself in the official guidelines of the Federal Government's policy: "*Integration, Begrenzung des Zuzugs, Hilfe bei der freiwilligen Rückkehr*" (integration, restriction of access, support for voluntary return) (see for example Bundesministerium des Innern 1997, 5).

When the new Federal Commissioner for Foreigners of the newly elected Socialdemocratic/Green Federal Government took office in 1998 and lateron made a programmatic statement on integration policy one of the headlines of her statement read "The immigration situation has to be recognised" (Beauftragte 2000, 3). This statement clearly reflected the ongoing dispute over the definition of the immigration situation. What had changed, however, was that the new government had accepted the definition of an immigration situation in Germany. Previous governments had always denied this. The coalition treaty reads: "We recognise that an irreversible immigration process has taken place and we support the integration of migrants ..." (ibidem, 2).The citizenship law of 1999 that was one of the first projects of the new government (see section 5) can be understood as a result of the new "official" definition of the immigration and integration situation in Germany.

The years 2000/2001 saw another major change in the societal definition of the immigration situation. While in 1999 the new red-green government had given up the old formula *"Deutschland ist kein Einwanderungsland"* it was the conservative opposition of CDU/CSU who undertook a major revision of their positions (see for the following efms migration report 2000/2001, *www.uni-bamberg.de/efms*). The CDU published a paper of a commission on migration that outlines a need for controlled immigration to Germany. The CSU, who had been the most ardent opponent and critic of immigration, changed its position somewhat as well and started saying that "Germany is not a classical immigration country", but recognised that Germany needs a limited amount of *"Zuwanderung"* (in-migration) for demographic and labour market reasons.

Two interconnected developments were responsible for this change. Firstly, an improvement of the labour market with less unemployment and increasing labour shortages in some branches, particularly in the IT sector. It was Chancellor Schröder who suggested a so-called "Green-Card" for recruiting IT specialists from abroad in his opening speech at the Cebit computer fair in Hannover in March 2000. This suggestion received strong support from business leaders and the media and contributed to changing the "climate" of the immigration discourse. The other influence upon the definition of the situation was the publication and high media profile of two demographic studies: The UN study *"Replacement Migration: a Solution to Declining and Aging Populations?"* and *long term population projections* by the Federal Office of Statistics. Both studies showed a dramatic aging and shrinking process of the native population in the next 30 or 50 years and stirred a broad and ongoing debate on the possibilities of "replacement migration". Immigration is regarded as one (among many others) strategy to cope with the social and economic consequences of the demographic changes.

This process of a broadening consensus on the definition of the immigration situation was much promoted by the official installation of an independent commission for immigration reform in the fall of 2000. It was headed by the CDU Member of Parlament and former President of the Bundestag Rita Süssmuth. Apart from a few politicians and experts commission members were largely representatives of the most powerful organisations of German society: employers' organisations, unions, churches and NGOs. The installation of the commission by the government had an interesting effect upon the political parties: they, too, in a competitive process, installed their own commissions for migration. Thus, in 2001, not only did the Süssmuth Commission publish its report, but the CDU, CSU, SPD and FDP also published their own position papers. The first sentence of the Süssmuth Commission reads: "Germany needs immigrants" and the whole report is a paradigmatic change in that direction. The surprising result of the other parties' papers is that they are objectively quite close to the official commission in many crucial respects and also, compared to past conflicts, quite close to one another. Only the CSU has certain reservations, but, in a historical perspective, has changed her position quite a bit as well.

This development has clearly broadened the basis for a new societal definition of the immigration situation. The burden of immigration had been the dominant theme of the immigration debate till 2000. During the year the tone of the public debate changed and increasingly (qualified) immigrants were seen as a resource. With federal elections approaching in 2002 and deteriorating labour market data, however, the public debate in 2001 and 2002 again has shifted to controversy. In a comparative perspective, however, there is still more consensus on immigration and integration among relevant societal forces at the beginning of the 21st century than ever before in the history of immigration to Germany after World War II. The recommendations of the commission for immigration and the draft of an immigration law were not only supported by the government parties (SPD, Greens) and the Free Democrats, but also by employers' associations , unions and churches. In 2002 the new immigration law has been passed by the *Bundestag* and, in a controversial vote, by the *Bundesrat* (federal chambre) as well. We will come back to this law, as it relates to integration in section 7.

4. Social Order and Sense of Nationhood as Conditions of Integration

Societies have certain basic ways of securing macro-social integration and of defining and tackling social problems and tensions. These derive from fundamental principles of the social order. *Soziale Marktwirtschaft* as a system of economic, social and political relations is a basic element of the social order in

Germany. The state is a welfare state and its role is understood in an interventionist sense, i.e. to help provide social security, social justice and to improve opportunities for disadvantaged groups. The most important aspect of the welfare system for immigrant integration is that non-citizen residents are generally included in it.

Federalism as another basic element of the macrosocial structure of Germany gives federal states a strong role, particularly in education and culture. One implication for integration policies is that there has been no uniform way in educational policies for immigrant children. Bavaria, for instance, has had a system of bilingual education, which other federal states do not have. And, to give another example, there are different ways of approaching the question of religious instruction for Islamic children in different states.

The socio-political order in Germany is no longer solely structured by traditional nation state sovereignty. *European integration* and the respect for *Human Rights* demand the recognition of rights of migrants that a policy strictly geared by a traditional sense of national interest would not accept. The recognition of a right for family reunion is a case in point for the importance of Human Rights. European integration signifies that migrants from EU states have the same rights as German citizens, with exceptions only in political participation on the federal and federal states' levels.

Sense of nationhood: Although an ethnic vs. a political nation concept is clearly an idealtypical, heuristic juxtaposition which cannot be found in empirical reality as Dominique Schnapper (1994, 178 pp.) rightly argues, the traditional concept of nation in Germany has been mainly determined by the idea of an ethnic community. Ethnic nationalism stands for common ethnicity as a basis for state organisation. Ethnic and state borders should be the same. The ethnic nation concept defines nation as a people with its own state. Since the nation defines itself as a community of descent with a common culture and history, belonging to the people and legal membership in the political community, that is citizenship, are closely connected to one another. One of the consequences of this principle is that the inclusion into a nation that understands itself as a community of descent and culture is difficult or defined as an exception to the rule.

Nation as a cultural concept (Schulze 1994) and nationalism as social and political movement are not constant phenomena, but change historically in relation to their contents and goals. After the catastrophe of National Socialism there was a tendency to regard the concept of nation as superfluous and dangerous. The philosopher Karl Jaspers wrote in 1960: "The history of the German nation state has ended. What we can do for the world and for us is the recognition that the nation state today has been the cause of Europe's catastrophe and the cause of catastrophes in other continents. The nation state concept is the most destructive force on earth today and we should begin to completely do away with it" (Jaspers in Mommsen 1990, 265). This, however, was not a majority view, but the judgement of a critical intellectual observer. The delegitimation and deconstruction of the old concept of nation and nation state became a broader cultural movement in the 1960's and 1970's: a major influence on this was the intellectual reflection of and reaction to totalitarian Naziism with its extreme forms of nationalism.

A second major factor that put pressure on the old concepts of nation and citizenship was Germany's integration into the Western world. Democracy and constitutionalism as political principles of the "West" could be related to the early national and democratic movement at the beginning of the nineteenth century in Germany, but were in total opposition to the aggressive nationalism that developed afterwards. To become an integral part of the Western community the concept of nation that had dominated for the past hundred years had to be changed.

Thirdly, a pressure for change resulted from migration itself. Migration not only evokes the question "Who are they?", but also "Who are we?" In addition, the assertion of being a democracy and at the same time excluding large parts of the population from full political participation questioned the legitimacy of citizenship based on descent.

What I have described so far are pressures for change, for deconstructing the old concepts. From the very beginning of the Federal Republic there were attempts at a reconstruction of the nation concept, which co-existed with a position of refusal to ever again consider nation and nation states as valuable ideas. One of the key terms for this reconstruction process was and is *Verfassungspatriotismus* (constitutional patriotism). It means to identify with nation and nation state because of its constitutional order, because of the rule of law, to feel pride in one's democratic institutions. For an increasing part of the public that believes in the continuing relevance of nation and nation state *Verfassungspatriotismus* has been expressing a new kind of political identification with Germany. Apart from this new kind of patriotism economic success and the quality of institutions in Germany became sources for a new kind of national identification.

The historian Mommsen described this new national consciousness in the year of German unification as follows: "A new kind of national consciousness has developed in the Federal Republic. It is no longer under the influence of political and legal traditions of imperial Germany. This new national consciousness relates primarily to economic success and to a democratic and liberal political system. It is no longer in conflict with the political cultures of Western Europe and the USA, as has been the case for so many years" (Mommsen 1990, 272). This new concept of nation was a precondition for the reform of the citizenship law, since concepts of nation and citizenship are closely related.

5. Legal Integration: Citizenship Policies

The ethnic nation state concept that was most influential in Germany till the end of the 1990's had a clearly exclusive tendency regarding legal integration. What are the implications of an ethnic nation concept? Who are the Germans in the sense of belonging to the German nation? The consequences of an ethnic nation concept are far reaching and they mean:

1) The descendants of German citizens are also Germans, even if they are not able to exercise their rights as citizens, for instance during the existence of the German Democratic Republic.

2) Germans in an ethnic sense, particularly German minorities in several states of Eastern Europe, are entitled to the same rights as German citizens; if they come to Germany as *Spätaussiedler*, they receive their citizenship almost automatically.

3) The inclusion into a nation via naturalisation that understands itself as a community of descent and culture is difficult or defined as an exception to the rule.

As a consequence of the ethnic nation concept and the *Reichs- und Staatsangehörigkeitsgesetz* (citizenship law) based on it, Germany had small numbers of naturalisations in comparison with other European countries (Lederer 1997). The 1990's saw important changes in the concepts of nation and citizenship. The historical surprise of German reunification immensely stirred the interest in the topic of nation. On the one hand reunification was a success of the old ethnic nation principle: bonds of ethnic solidarity had remained strong despite political separation and had helped to overcome the Iron Curtain. On the other hand, reunification was the founding phase of a new republic: it was a time to once again reflect on the basic constitutional and societal organisational principles. What kind of nation and society did the new Germany want to be?

The other source of interest in nation resulted from a continuous discourse about the improvement of conditions for the integration of immigrants. Political parties, unions, churches, immigrants' organisations, social scientists, jurists, educators, intellectuals, journalists and many other representatives of an intellectual public stimulated a debate on the necessity of changing the citizenship law. The debate put forward a critique of the ethnic concept of nation that was increasingly seen as a major obstacle to the integration of immigrants. *Ius soli* should be added to the principle of descent, naturalisation should be eased and double citizenship should be tolerated. It was a vivid debate in the nineties, but the discussion had already begun in the eighties. The process can be roughly described as one in which the camp of reformers slowly but steadily gained ground. There had been a majority in the parliament in favour of a radical reform of the citizenship law already during the *Bundestag* legislative period from 1994-1998, only so-called coalition arithmetics hindered the reform from being realised. "Coalition arithmetics" meant that the Free Democrats (F.D.P.) who were in favour of a new citizenship law would not vote with the opposition parties against their own coalition partner in the government (CDU/CSU). In 1993 the *Bundestag* – with a conservative majority – passed a reform of the foreigners' law creating a right for naturalisation for children of immigrants (16-23 years old) with eight years of residence and six years of schooling in Germany. This was the first major deviation from the ethnic nation and *ius sanguinis* principles. Naturalisation figures have begun to rise since then, though not dramatically.

In May 1999 a new citizenship law has been passed by the *Bundestag*. It has come into effect on January 1, 2000, with the beginning of the new millennium. This symbolism underlines the almost revolutionary character of the law: it has introduced *ius soli*, it eases naturalisation and, to some degree, tolerates double citizenship. This means that a new principle of belonging to the nation has been introduced: not only descent, but living in the same society and on the same territory are recognised as rules of inclusion.

There has been a big fight over this law. A first version of the law foresaw a broad acceptance of double citizenship, against which the conservative opposition launched a successful public campaign which gathered millions of signatures. The campaign was successful, partly because of a mobilisation of prejudice, but also because of a feeling among Germans of privileging the foreigners over the natives. The campaign led to the restriction of double citizenship according to which children who receive German citizenship through *ius soli* in addition to their citizenship by descent must opt for one of these citizenships between the ages of 18 to 23. The big rouse over double citizenship has actually left the truly "radical" part of the law almost unnoticed, namely the introduction of *ius soli*. Interestingly enough, what the conservative opposition was suggesting as an alternative to *ius soli* was not far remote from this territorial principle either. Their concept was called "*Einbürgerungs-zusicherung*" which meant to give newly born children of "foreigners" a paper guaranteeing them citizenship at maturity and giving them an unconditional right to live in the country until then. The non-ethnic and republican content of the new law is also implied in the definition of the content of citizenship as adherence to the constitutional order. Naturalised persons have to sign a declaration of that content.

Finally, whereas the ethnic nation concept tends to see ethnic-national belonging as a kind of primordial tie, the new law explicitly understands its regulations as an instrument for integration of immigrants. The old view, still propagated by the opposition, viewed naturalisation as the concluding act of a successful process of integration.

The new spirit of the law became evident in the final parliamentary debate on May 7, 1999. Otto Schily, minister of the interior and responsible for the new law, said: "It is very interesting to remember what the French philosopher of religion Ernest Renan had to say in his lectures at Sorbonne University in 1882 about what constitutes a nation. He proceeded methodologically in his inquiry. He first looked into the question whether a nation is constituted by an ethnie. He concluded that this could not be true. The French have Celtic, Iberian and Germanic ethnic origins. The Germans have Celtic, Slavic and Germanic origins and Italy is a total ethnic mix which one cannot decipher any more" (Schily 1999). Schily continues: "How true this is" and then proceeds with long quotations from Renan. Whereas historians and social scientists again and again have been confronting the German and French opposite understandings of nation and citizenship, quoting Renan as the key witness for the French position, the German minister of the interior has been quoting "the other side".

At the beginning of the 21st century not only has the definition of the immigration situation changed, but the traditional concept of nation as well. The implication of this development for integration is that it creates new possibilities for the inclusion of immigrants into society and nation.

6. General Integration Policies and the Inclusion of Immigrants

General integration policies are those policies that the modern welfare state "normally" applies for the integration of its population as they affect natives and immigrants. *Clearly the most important single aspect of integration policies towards migrants is that migrants are usually included in these general integration policies.* We shall first discuss aspects of structural integration (labour market, education, vocational training), will then proceed to cultural integration and briefly to social and identificational integration. Structural integration policies are policies for easing the access to the core institutions of society.

6.1. Structural Integration Policies

6.1.1. Labour Market and Self-Employment

The first treaty for the recruitment of Italian guestworkers was signed in 1955. It implied a major decision the relevance of which for the inclusion of migrants cannot be overestimated: in a corporatist agreement the Federal Labour Office, employers and unions decided to employ the workers to be recruited under the same conditions of pay, health insurance, unemployment and pension benefits as native workers. Wage dumping or dumping of social security standards was to be avoided by including the foreign workers in the welfare state system (Heckmann 1988). The other recruitment treaties with Spain, Greece, Turkey, Morocco, Portugal, Tunisia and Yugoslavia followed the same line.

Thus, from the very beginning, integration into the labour market has been the prime area of integration. Today there are practically no legal barriers to the labour market for foreigners who are in Germany. Exceptions to this general rule apply to asylum seekers and to husbands and wives of foreigners who come to Germany from non-EU countries under family reunion regulations. Asylum seekers were until recently allowed to work only after they had been recognised and had received an asylum status. A new regulation of January 1, 2001 allows asylum seekers to work after one year of the duration of their asylum case. Husbands and wives of foreigners who have come to Germany get access to the labour market after a waiting period of three years. Another employment restriction is that foreigners normally cannot hold civil service positions (*"Beamtenstellen"*). With *ius soli* and the easing in naturalisation conditions this restriction will gradually loose some of its impact.

Despite a labour market that is generally open to foreign residents the unemployment rate for foreigners of around 20% is about double the unemployment rate of natives. Foreigners thus are one of the "problem groups" of the labour market. For such problem groups Germany has huge programmes of training and retraining and the law on employment promotion (*Arbeitsförderungsgesetz/SGB III*). In addition, there are special programmes like the present federal government "Jump"-programme of two billion DM for 2000 which is designed for young people under 25 (*www.sofortprogramm.de*). All these programmes of training and retraining are open to people on the basis of criteria that do not include citizenship.

Guestworkers came to Germany to be employed. Their visa documents stated explicitly that self-employment was not permitted. Gradually, the legal barriers to self-employment for foreigners – including citizens from non-EU states – were removed. While there were very few self-employed among the migrants in the first 20 years of migration to Germany the last 20 years have seen a dramatic change. Today the rate of self-employment among migrants in the economically active population in Germany is approaching that of the native population (Interministerielle Arbeitsgruppe 1999, 155).

Against the background of a modest economic growth and a high rate of unemployment a political and economic discourse on the constitutive elements of *Soziale Marktwirtschaft* and its possible reform is under way. This controversial discourse has direct implications for labour market policies and the position of immigrants in it. An American economist observer, Philip Martin, has clearly described the present challenges by way of a German-American comparison.

"Globalisation as well as demographic changes have forced a restructuring of some of the major institutions developed over the past century, including the expectation that many workers would have lifetime jobs with one large company. Many Germans continue to expect such lifetime careers, and they receive an extensive and long term assistance while waiting for 'good' jobs to become available. There are too few such good jobs ... Germany is discussing creating more good jobs by encouraging early retirement and restricting overtime. However, creating good jobs in this manner will not move foreigners forward in the queue ... The alternative is to deregulate the labour market so that employers create more jobs, even though some of the new jobs created may pay lower wages, offer fewer benefits, and not be career options. In the more flexible US labour market unskilled immigrants have little trouble finding jobs or beginning small business, but they may find it hard to earn sufficient wages to achieve above poverty level incomes" (Martin 1999, 11).

In an official report to the Bavarian *Landtag* (parliament) the Bavarian government argued in a similar way: a low wage sector would increase employment opportunities for migrants (Interministerielle Arbeitsgruppe 1999, 153).

6.1.2. Educational System

The federal states are the main actors in educational policy. Coordination efforts on a national level are regularly undertaken by the *Kultusministerkonferenz*. This conference of ministers for culture in 1964 took basic decisions for the educational policy affecting migrants' children. One major decision was that the children of guestworkers were obliged to attend school. There is no such obligation, neither for citizens nor for foreigners, however, for pre-school attendance. The significance of pre-school or kindergarten attendance for school performance of children of immigrants has been shown in several studies (Esser 1990). It has been the policy of the state on all levels of government to increase the number of kindergarten. At the moment Germany is approaching a situation in which statistically every four to six years old child could attend.

According to the 1964 decisions the children of guestworkers should be integrated into the regular school system. Preparatory and parallel German language training should be given to them, if necessary. They should be offered training in their mother languages on a voluntary basis in special courses after the regular classes. The rationale behind these decisions was to avoid social problems with a population that would temporarily live in Germany. An exception to the system are the so-called national or bilingual classes in Bavaria and the rather large system of private Greek schools in several German cities (see section 7.1.).

Germany has – in the past – not understood itself as an immigration society, giving schools, like in classical immigration countries, the explicit job of integrating ("assimilating") the children of immigrants. The rationale for educational policies towards migrants in Germany was to avoid social problems. The *"latent curriculum"* of the schools, however, always has been and is today the same as in classical immigration countries, namely *acculturation and integration.*

There has been a rather continuous improvement of educational achievements of migrant children over time, but "foreign children" – the statistics use citizenship as indicating migrant or son or daughter of migrant status – remain in a structurally disadvantaged position. Looking at different degrees with which students leave school the following picture emerges for the year 2000: on the whole 77.908 "foreign" children finished school. Of these 19.9 % left school without any degree, for Germans this figure is 8.3%; 40.2% finished school with a basic school degree ("*Hauptschulabschluß*"), for Germans this figure is 24.1%; the middle level degree was achieved by 28.9% of the "foreign" students and by 40.8% of the Germans; the highest school degree enabling to go to college or university was achieved by 11.0% of the "foreign" children and 26.9% of the Germans. Table 2 gives achieved school degrees by foreign and German children and youth from 1995 to 2000.

Table 2: Achieved School Degrees by Germans and Foreigners from 1995 to 2000 (in percent)

School-leaving certificate	1995		1996		1997	
	Germans	Foreigners	Germans	Foreigners	Germans	Foreigners
Without any degree	7.7	19.7	7.5	19.7	7.7	19.4
Basic school degree	25.7	43.8	24.8	43.6	25.2	42.7
Middle level degree	40.1	26.8	41.2	27.5	40.9	28.1
Highest school degree	26.5	9.6	26.5	9.2	26.3	9.7
Total	100.0	100.0	100.0	100.0	100.0	100.0

continued on page 63

School-leaving certificate	1998		1999		2000	
	Germans	Foreigners	Germans	Foreigners	Germans	Foreigners
Without any degree	7.9	19.5	7.9	19.3	8.3	19.9
Basic school degree	25.0	41.9	24.2	41.0	24.1	40.2
Middle level degree	41.2	28.9	41.3	28.9	40.8	28.9
Highest school degree	25.9	9.7	26.6	10.8	26.9	11.0
Total	100.0	100.0	100.0	100.0	100.0	100.0

Source: Federal Statistical Office; compiled by efms

6.1.3. Occupational and Vocational Training

There are two major qualification systems in Germany: the college-university system of higher education and the vocational training system. Both systems are open to non-citizens. Increasingly, the children of international migrants have been moving into the higher levels of the educational system, but their proportion is still much below that of their German age mates.

The large majority of first generation migrants is a working class population (with a rural background) in positions that demand few or only basic qualifications. It is realistic to assume that only a minority of their children will move directly into higher education. It is essential for the large majority of their children to get access to the vocational training system, since labour markets of the future will have fewer and fewer positions for unqualified people.

The vocational training system has as its major element the so-called dual system, i.e. apprenticeships and parallel to that schooling in special vocational schools. Besides the dual system there is a system of vocational schools without apprenticeships. When comparing integration policies of several European countries in 1990 Entzinger wrote: in Germany "special efforts have been made to attract more second generation youth to apprenticeships" (Entzinger in Faist 1993). The efforts to increase the number of apprenticeships were and are made in a corporatist arrangement. "Since the early 1970's state representatives, unions and employers have cooperated to regulate issues such as the number of apprenticeship occupations, pay rates, and revisions of curricula ... The strength of the corporate arrangement is that it has coped rather successfully with the under supply of training slots in the dual system from the late 1970's until the mid-1980's" (Faist 1993, 317).

In the 1990's it has remained difficult for young people to find apprenticeships, since most employers not only want a school diploma but also decent grades. With the new century and a changing demographic picture the situation is improving for young people. Due to the still disadvantaged position of immigrants' children in the educational system there are, however, still substantially fewer migrants' children in apprenticeship positions compared to Germans. Disregarding the students in higher education 65% of the Germans in the age-group of 18-20 against 33% among the non-Germans are in an apprenticeship training (Jeschek 1998, 4).

The data that Jeschek reports are from the Socio-Economic Panel, i.e. they are survey data. Official administrative statistics indicating the proportion of youth aged 15-18 who are in vocational training give a similar picture. Whereas the figure in1998 is 65.9 % for Germans it is 37.8 % for non-Germans (Bundesministerium für Bildung und Forschung 2000, 63).

For youth with a nationality of the guestworker recruitment countries of the 1960's figures are higher: for Spanish youth it is 73.3 %, for Portuguese 48.4 %, for Italian 47.7 % and for Turkish youth 42 %. Compared to Germans large differences remain. Looking at these data of 1998 in a time series perspective, however, it is evident that vocational training participation has been extremely low in the 1970's and has almost continuously improved.

To evaluate the data and the success or failure of integration policies with regard to education and occupational training an additional argument must be added. Official administrative statistics only differentiate between Germans and non-Germans. This means to put youth that has been born and socialised in Germany into the same category as those who came to Germany at a later stage in their lives through family reunion, as asylum seekers or refugees with their families. Introducing migration generation status into the analysis changes the picture (Straßburger 2001, 141-145).

What are the others doing, those that are not in the "regular system"? Are they working in jobs that demand no occupational training or are they unemployed? The majority of them is neither working nor registered as unemployed, but is trained in publicly financed training courses and institutions. Based upon the law on employment promotion (*Arbeitsförderungsgesetz/SGB III*) there is a series of measures designed for people who did not succeed in receiving an apprenticeship position. This system is designed for disadvantaged youth in general, German or with foreign citizenship, but is of particular importance for migrant youth, since many are in a disadvantaged position.

One type of measure is organised within the vocational schools that also train people who are in the dual system. There are two basic courses, lasting for 12 months each: *"Berufsvorbereitungsjahr"* or pre-apprenticeship programme is designed to improve basic general skills; *"Berufsgrundbildungsjahr"* or basic vocational training is more specific in terms of vocational training and can be counted as an apprenticeship year after an apprenticeship position has been found. Another type of measures ("*Ausbildungsvorbereitende Maßnahmen*") consists of courses from 2-11 months that prepare for vocational training: motivation courses, courses for basic skills (including language), courses for handicapped people and support for employers who employ and train people. Vocational training in publicly financed training firms ("*außerbetriebliche Berufsausbildung*") and supportive measures for people in apprenticeships to help them pass their exams are further examples of measures to train young people among whom are many children of international migrants. The training programmes that are specifically designed for migrants will be described in the section on special integration policies.

6.1.4. Welfare State Policies and the Inclusion of Migrants

From the very beginning of their recruitment foreign workers and their families have been fully integrated into the welfare state social security system with the same rights as natives: pension funds, health insurance, unemployment and accident insurance, and recently insurance for intensive care (Bundesministerium des Innern 1998, 64). Migrants are entitled to tax reductions for children and receive benefits for each single child. Depending on parents' income citizens and non-citizens are equally entitled to student loans and financial support for other forms of education and occupational training. Most foreigners are also entitled to welfare benefits in case of poverty. As a matter of fact, out of 1000 Germans 30 receive such benefits, out of 1000 foreigners the figure is 90 (Interministerielle Arbeitsgruppe 1999, 214).

6.2. Cultural Integration Policies

The cultural dimension of integration is a process that encompasses the acquisition of cognitive abilities and knowledge of a society's culture. Language is of prime importance here. Cultural integration also includes the internalisation of values, norms, attitudes and the formation of belief systems. Since the children of immigrants are usually incorporated into the general school system in Germany they are subject to the socialising and acculturation effects of the general school system. And this has been a conscious decision from the very beginning. In that sense there has generally been a policy of acculturation up to the present. The first generation of migrants has mostly not participated in the major general socialising institutions of society. Special measures of cultural integration which have been developed for them will be discussed in section 7. Most of their (partial) acculturation has happened on the workplace.

65

Policies of religion also play a part in the cultural and "ideological reproduc-tion" of society, despite Germany defining herself as a secular state. The Chris-tian churches and Judaism play a role in public life that is defined legally and by tradition, including a role in the educational system with an institutionali-sation of religious instruction in the school curriculum. No such role has been established as yet for the most prominent religion of the immigrants, namely the religion of Islam.

The traditional general mode of collective cultural-religious integration in Germany would be a treaty with a representative body of a religious group. The problem on the side of Islam is that there is no institutionalised centre which could legitimately act as a partner of the state. There are 2,200 Islamic Mosque organisations in Germany and at least 13 federations of whom several claim to represent the interests of all Moslems (Zentrum für Türkeistudien 1999, 119). A process is under way, however, which could result in an institutionalisation of Islam according to general patterns. Already since 1985 the state of Nord-rhein-Westfalen is teaching Islam in schools by Islamic teachers under super-vision from the state government. Hessen is proceeding in a similar way. Re-cently, a high court in Berlin ruled that Islam should be treated analogously to the Christian churches and to Judaism and has allowed an Islamic federation to start organising the teaching of religion in the public schools of Berlin. On the whole, however, it is safe to say that the relationship between the German State and Islam is still in a state of search for clarification and definition.

6.3. Social Integration Policies

The modern democratic nation state, of course, does not rule the structure of private relations in a free society, but certain basic political decisions and state structures do have an influence on private relations. For the first genera-tion of migrants the vast majority of private social relations is centred within the ethnic group. In relation to children of international migrants the most relevant influence as to social integration is the structural decision by the state for common schooling and common occupational training of migrants and natives, since common schooling and occupational training are a major oppor-tunity for establishing social relations and friendships among young people. Up to fifth grade this policy is reenforced by a territorial principle obliging parents to send their children to the elementary school in their residential area. People have to use tricks to evade this rule.

Ethnic housing segregation could counteract the integrating effect of the territorial principle. Despite prominent examples to the contrary (like Kreuz-berg in Berlin or Wilhelmsburg in Hamburg) it has been the mostly rather successful policy of urban communities to avoid large ethnic concentrations and "ghettos". Cities are obliged by law and government orders to avoid concentrations of migrants in public housing (Interministerielle Arbeitsgruppe 1999, 211/212). Seen in an internationally comparative picture ethnic housing segregation seems to be rather low in Germany.

General mode of integration in a society includes both state and private actors. The area of social integration is a field where private actors play the major role. As to memberships in clubs and associations a complex picture emerges. On the one hand, these are the very central elements of the ethnic communities and an expression of the ethnic groups' motives for cultural and social "autonomy". On the other hand, if private associations of the receiving society are open to migrant membership and if immigrants are using this opportunity for common interaction in such structures these may contribute to reduce social distance between groups.

Sports clubs are by far the most relevant category of private organisations in German society. The Federation of German Sports Organisations, the *Deutsche Sportbund* (DSB) with more than 20 million members decided already in 1981 to recommend to its members to work for an individual membership of "foreigners" in "regular" sports clubs and not to favour ethnic organisation in sport (Bammel and Becker 1985). This does not mean, however, that ethnic sports clubs would not be accepted in the *Deutsche Sportbund*. The integration into sports clubs, particularly soccer clubs has made these a most important field of establishing social relations between children of international migrants and native children and their respective parents.

6.4. Identificative Integration Policies

Identificative integration policies as part of the general mode of nation state integration includes a variety of practices to arrive at subjective feelings of belonging to the nation and nation state. Political socialisation, the teaching of history, the celebration of certain historical events, the internalisation of symbols and the development of particular emotions can be given as examples of general practices to achieve identificative integration within the population. A head of state's role in modern nations is also quite central for identification processes.

In Germany, the dominant tendency to define national belonging has been via common ethnicity. This, of course, is exclusive toward foreign migrants. The official denial of the de facto immigration situation in Germany has been regarded by immigrants as a continuous denial of the legitimacy of the "presence of foreigners" in the country. This has not been an invitation for identification. Survey research shows very low degrees of identification with Germany among migrants (Schmidt and Weick 1998, 4). Münz et al. report a figure of 11% of all migrants in the Socio-Economic Panel who identify as Germans (Münz, Seifert and Ulrich 1997, 101).

What has been lacking until recently was a model of national belonging, a model of becoming and being a German based on continuously living and working there and thus including migrants as well. The general mode of identificative nation state integration has not included the foreign migrants. It has only included one large group of migrants: those defined as ethnic Germans (*Spätaussiedler*).

There has been, however, no total consistency in identificative integration policies. The line that we have described is that of the Federal Government till 1998. Some federal states, cities, welfare organisations, churches and NGOs have actively been leading campaigns for an increase in naturalisation rates. The Federal Government and the *Bundestag*, however, have most authority and influence in this area. Even in the *Bundestag* of 1994-1998, there was a majority for a change in naturalisation rules, but "coalition arithmetics" hindered this majority to come through. The new citizenship law of 1999 that we have described in section 5 has not only brought about substantial legal changes, but wants to be seen as well as an invitation to identify with a German nation that perceives herself no longer as an ethnic nation but is redefining herself in a more universal way. The present public campaign of the Federal Government for the new citizenship law (*www.einbuergerung.de*) demonstrates this: a "foreign looking" couple, for example is shown on a poster with a text "typical German", or there is a poster with a young boy of Turkish origin who is saying "*Ich bin ein Berliner*" (I am a Berliner).

7. Special Integration Policies

Special integration policies refer to measures and institutions that are explicitly and directly designed for immigrants and their children. Special integration policies imply the creation of new institutions or the differentiation and/ or expansion of existing institutions.

Some of the special measures and institutions can be clearly related to one of our central dimensions of integration, others relate to several dimensions. The institution of "Commissioner For Foreigners" (*Ausländerbeauftragte/r*) is an example of the latter kind. It exists on the federal, the single federal state and the single city levels. Commissioners can be addressed by individuals and groups for information and support. The commissioners may act on their own and take initiatives for the improvement of migrants' opportunities. Commissioners also collect data relating to immigration and integration and inform politicians and the general public. The Commissioner for Foreigners of the Federal Government has been particularly active in this respect. Starting with the first Federal Commissioner Heinz Kühn in 1978 and his courageous analysis ("Germany has become an immigration country") the commissioners have also played a noticeable role in the political discourse and definition of the immigration situation. Geiß has impressively described the work of the different Federal Commissioners (Geiß 2001).

"Foreigners' commissions" (*Ausländerbeiräte*) are elected bodies that work as a kind of substitute for the lack of political participation of non-citizen residents. In some federal states these commissions exist on a state level and have been appointed, but the large majority has been elected – usually with a low voter turnout – in cities. They are devised to represent the migrants' interests and advise the mayor, the city councillors and the administration on matters relating to immigration and integration.

Germany's six large welfare organisations (AWO, Caritas, Diakonie, DPWV, DRK, ZWST) are all engaged in the integration of migrants. Different welfare organisations have been responsible for different nationalities and social workers relatively often are of the same nationality and/or ethnic background as their clients or speak their language. Their work is relevant for all four dimensions of integration and encompasses a large range of services, including general counselling, language training, labour market integration, health services (including mental health), social work for youth, families and for elderly migrants. The welfare organisations are private associations, but receive most of their funding from federal budgets. In the year 2000 the six welfare organisations spent more than 300 million marks for the integration of migrants (Unabhängige Kommission Zuwanderung 2001, 211). Among others, the Federal Government and the federal states have been continuously financing since 1970 around 600 counselling offices with about 900 social workers (Bundesministerium des Innern 1998, 45). With the new immigration law of 2002 the state is taking a direct and active role in the integration of immigrants. The Federal Agency of Asylum has been changed into an Agency for Migration and Refugees with a strong role in the integration process. Integration of new immigrants has become a major task of the redefined agency, not leaving the job solely to NGOs anymore. Integration and orientation courses with 600 hours of language training and 30 hours of civics and history shall be organised, starting in 2003. The courses will be obligatory for new immigrants without a knowledge of German and are open for foreigners already in the country for a few years.

In the following sections we shall discuss special measures in the areas of structural, cultural and social integration. We shall not have a section on specific identificative policies, because little has been done in this respect. One measure, however, that is worth mentioning is the campaign for the new citizenship law by the Federal Government that we discussed in 6.4. It aims not only at the ethnic German population but could also be regarded as an invitation for identification. Similar intentions can be attributed to ceremonies for new citizens at the occasion of their naturalisation in some cities (Berlin, Frankfurt, Bamberg).

7.1. Structural Integration: Special Measures

Special measures relating to structural integration have been developed in education and vocational training. "Transitory classes" (*Übergangsklassen*) are intensive German language classes that prepare children for participating in the regular school system.

On the level of single municipalities as well as federal states a multitude of programmes exist to support the children of immigrants who attend regular classes. They receive additional language training and are given special tutoring for their homework. The state of Nordrhein-Westfalen has installed a network of more than twenty educational tutoring institutions ("*Regionale Arbeitsstellen zur Förderung ausländischer Kinder und Jugendlicher*") that are spread all over the state.

Whereas the aforementioned measures support children of international migrants in the regular school system the so-called national or bi-lingual classes in Bavaria and the rather large system of private Greek schools are outside that system. Instruction in these systems is given in the respective national languages: in the bilingual Bavarian system the concept is to start with the mother language and then introduce instruction in German progressively. In relation to the size of the migrant school population of over 1 million in Germany only a very small proportion of students does attend these schools. In Bavaria only 4% of the migrant student body is in the bilingual system at present; figures were, however, much higher in the past. While the Greek private school system clearly originates from forces within the Greek community in Germany – supported by the Greek government – the Bavarian national classes were installed to enable migrant workers' children to easily return to their "home countries". The labour market concept lying behind this structure was that of a labour rotation system.

As to the training of teachers chairs were created in most universities for research and teaching in German as a second language, for the pedagogy of migrant children and for "intercultural relations".

In the field of special policies in vocational training the Federal Government has continuously offered a set of measures for children of international migrants that are coordinated with labour market policies of the Federal Labour Office. The measures consist of language courses, general courses to prepare for vocational training and vocational training programmes (Bundesministerium des Innern 1998, 37). Other specific measures are:

▶ special programmes to train migrant women;

▶ "*Pro-Qualifizierung*", a training programme for people between 25 and 45 to adapt to technological changes;

- ▶ incentives for employers of migrant background to create apprenticeship positions for migrant youth;
- ▶ regional and local initiatives to increase apprenticeship positions for migrant youth.

7.2. Cultural Integration

Cultural integration has a cognitive side, but also includes the internationalisation of values, norms, attitudes and the formation of belief systems. Understanding cultural integration, however, not as one-sided assimilation, but as a mutual and interactive process, cultural integration policies will include policies that give the immigrants' cultures a place in the receiving country.

With more and more guestworkers and their families settling in Germany in the 1970's the Federal Government made a coordinated effort to systematically support language training for the migrants by helping to found the *"Sprachverband Deutsch für ausländische Arbeitnehmer e.V."* in 1974. This is a federation of about 500 institutes offering German language training, who have coordinated their programmes, their teaching methods and certificates (Beauftragte 1997, 45). From 1975 to 1998 more than 1.32 million people took part in these courses and 484 millions of DM have been given by the Federal Government for the support of these courses (*www.uni-mainz.de/sprachverband*).

Cultural integration measures in schools that are geared to cultural needs of immigrants are called "mother-tongue instruction". These courses are offered to children of international migrants on a voluntary basis in afternoon classes. They are mostly financed by the federal states and are organised in cooperation with the respective national consulates. It is estimated that about one third of all migrant children take part in these classes (Kupfer-Schreiner 1996).

Public broadcasting corporations have offered special radio and television programmes since 1964, mostly in Italian, Greek, Spanish, Turkish, Croatian and Serbian. With the development of cable and satellite television these programmes find it more and more difficult, however, to reach their prospective audiences (Beauftragte 1997, 80/81).

Seeing cultural integration as a mutual process, it includes those policies that are directed towards the native population. It is impossible to describe the many cultural activities that are related to migration and the culture of the different immigrant groups. We only mention the public media of radio and television that inform about or broadcast products of the culture of immigrant groups, immigrant cultures in school curricula and the many "multicultural programmes of cities" that are not only produced for the migrant population but for a general public.

71

7.3. Social Integration

Special policies of social integration refer to measures of the state and of non-governmental organisations in relation to the development of "positive" personal social relations between natives and immigrants, often called "intercultural relations", and to the increase of migrant membership in private associations. The reduction of prejudice and discrimination is part of this work. Churches and unions have made many efforts for this purpose. In 1997 the Catholic and Protestant churches published a common memorandum about migration and integration that aims – among others – at the improvement of social integration of migrants (Kirchenamt 1997). The Federation of German Union (DGB) and most single unions have offices and employ special staff for questions of integration of migrants. A lot of NGOs were founded whose activities centre around social integration. Youth organisations are supported by the state for integrating migrant youth organisations in their federation (Interministerielle Arbeitsgruppe 1999, 182). Many organisations including the Federal Ministry of the Interior have lead campaigns or are presently campaigning against xenophobia, ethnic prejudice and racism. Since the beginning 1990's the police and the judiciary have strongly intensified their efforts against right wing extremism and racist crimes (ibidem, 228).

7.4. New Equality Promoting Policies

Equality promoting policies like affirmative action or anti-discrimination measures have gained weight in a European discourse on special integration policies. Anti-discrimination measures, for instance, are foreseen by § 13 of the Amsterdam treaty as a model for future policies.

The political discourse on anti-discrimination laws is still in a starting phase. Article 3 of the German Constitution forbids discrimination on the basis of ethnic origin, "race" or religion. "This article, however, creates directly binding obligations only for state authorities. In the area of private relations and private law the meaning and relevance of this article has to be clarified and needs to be formulated into a concrete law" (Beauftragte 2000, 5). Since article 3, however, is part of the catalogue for basic rights in the constitution there are reasons to assume that its binding obligations extend beyond the actions of state authorities. Support for this interpretation can be derived from a case in the insurance field, where an effective measure against discrimination in car insurance was taken. An extra charge for foreigners – who have indeed a higher accident rate – was forbidden by law (Beauftragte 1997, 108).

Affirmative action policies have been practised on basis of gender within the SPD and Green parties, but have as yet not played a role into the discussion of opportunities for migrants.

8. Acculturation or the Formation of Ethnic Minorities?

Is it the task of kindergarten and school to transform foreign children into young Germans or should they reinforce the ethnic identity of the family? What guidelines should be followed in language policies in the educational system? Is membership in ethnic associations and clubs desirable or should it be regarded as problematic? Are the ethnic colonies that first generation migrants have formed an institution of transition, or are they the foundation for durable ethnic minority structures?

The common core of these questions concerns the alternative between a policy of acculturation versus a policy of minority formation. There are some indicators for the preference of an acculturation policy on the part of the past Federal Government: Paraphrasing integration as "adaption to German circumstances", for instance (Bundesministerium des Innern 1993, 5), or refusing to grant the status of a national minority to immigrant groups under the European national minority protection charter (Bundesregierung 1996, 47/48). It has to be mentioned that the status of a national minority has been granted to Danes, Friesians, Sorbs, Sinti and Roma in Germany. Some ethnic organisations of immigrants as well as the Green Party were claiming the same status for immigrant groups. Recently the government of the state of Bavaria has explicitly formulated the concept of a *"Leitkultur"* ("orienting culture") in the integration process (Interministerielle Arbeitsgruppe 1999, 74).

Other official documents do not propagate acculturation, but define integration as involving ethnic minority reproduction. In the document of 1996 quoted above, the Federal Government states: "The goal (of our policy, F.H.) is integration and the preservation of cultural identity" (Bundesregierung 1996, 37). In an elaborated official document on intercultural learning the conference of ministers of culture (of the federal states) talks about "meeting foreign cultures" in the school, meaning the presence of children of international migrants in the classrooms, and recommends this as an opportunity for learning tolerance and mutual understanding towards ethnic minorities (Kultusministerkonferenz 1996).

Thus, on the level of government, an ambivalent picture of policy goals seems to emerge. Be it for "burden of the past", particularly the persecution of minorities under Naziism, be it for a lack of conceptual clarity, the question of acculturation or minority formation as a policy goal has not been resolved in Germany. In practice, however, a policy of acculturation prevails. The document of the conference of ministers of culture is one thing, what actually happens in the schools is something else: the "latent curriculum" of the schools clearly is acculturation.

73

On the city level there are some large cities who claim to follow a "multicultural policy", Frankfurt is the best known example. To give another example, Nürnberg, the site of our regional survey in the EFFNATIS project (see footnote 1 in the introduction), also has been supporting and organising a rich programme of "multiculture" for the past 30 years: films, theatre, music, dance, exhibitions, lectures from the country of origin or from the context of the migration experience. Supporting migrant associations' cultural activities is another aspect of that "multicultural" policy. The philosophies and objectives of such "multicultural policies" on the level of urban communities, however, are not ethnic minority formation and reproduction, but intercultural understanding and exchange.

9. Conclusion: Welfare State Integration as German Mode of Integration

In the first fifteen years of large scale migration into Germany from the beginning 1960's to the mid 1970's there was consensus in society and within the polity that due to the supposed temporariness of guestworker employment integration could only be temporary and partial. What follows in the mid 1970's is a gradual recognition of the fact that not all guestworkers would go back, that families were coming and that a settlement process was under way.

The long lasting official denial of an immigration situation which ended only at the end of the century cannot be equated, however, with the lack of an integration policy from the mid 1970's onwards. The main feature of the German mode of immigrant integration has been and is the inclusion of migrants into the general welfare state and social policy system. Compared to that special measures of immigrant integration have much less relevance. The effects of welfare state inclusion on overall integration have been somewhat counteracted in the past by a lack of legal integration. Welfare state integration without citizenship gave integration policy in Germany an ambivalence which resulted in a lack of identificational integration of migrants. With a gradual change of the concept of nation and a new citizenship law in 1999 there is a chance that this ambivalence will disappear and make way for a more coherent and non-ethnic pattern of universalistic immigrant integration. Despite a lack of conceptual clarity and consistency as to cultural integration, a policy of acculturation is clearly dominant in practice. Lastly, there is broad consensus that a control of further immigration is a precondition for the successful integration of those immigrants who are already in the country.

References

Alba, R. 1999:

'Immigration and the American Realities of Assimilation and Multiculturalism', in Münz, R. and Seifert, W. (eds.), *Inclusion or Exclusion of Immigrants. Europe and the U.S. at the Crossroads*, Demographie aktuell Nr. 14, pp. 3-16, Berlin: Lehrstuhl für Bevölkerungswissenschaft der Humboldt-Universität

Bammel, H. / Becker, H. (eds.) 1985:

Sport und ausländische Mitbürger, Bonn: Friedrich-Ebert-Stiftung

Beauftragte der Bundesregierung für Ausländerfragen 1997:

Bericht über die Lage der Ausländer in der Bundesrepublik Deutschland, Bonn

Beauftragte der Bundesregierung für Ausländerfragen 2000:

Anstöße zum Thema Integration (www.bundesauslaenderbeauftragte.de)

Bundesministerium für Bildung und Forschung 2000:

Berufsbildungsbericht 2000, Bonn

Bundesministerium des Innern 1993:

Aufzeichnungen zur Ausländerpolitik und zum Ausländerrecht in der Bundesrepublik Deutschland, Bonn

Bundesministerium des Innern 1997:

Aufzeichnung zur Ausländerpolitik und zum Ausländerrecht in der Bundesrepublik Deutschland, Bonn

Bundesministerium des Innern 1998:

Ausländer und Asylpolitik in der Bundesrepublik Deutschland, Bonn

Bundesregierung 1996:

Antwort der Bundesregierung auf die Große Anfrage der Fraktion Bündnis 90/Die Grünen "Situation der Bundesrepublik Deutschland als Einwanderungsland", Deutscher Bundestag, 13. Wahlperiode, Drucksache 13/5065, Bonn

Esser, H. 1990:

'Prozesse der Eingliederung von Arbeitsmigranten', in Höhn, C. and Rein, D.B. (eds.), *Ausländer in der Bundesrepublik Deutschland*, pp. 33-53, Boppard am Rhein: Boldt Verlag

Esser, H. 1999:

Soziologie. Spezielle Grundlagen. Band 1: Situationslogik und Handeln, Frankfurt: Campus Verlag

Faist, T. 1993:

'From School to Work: Public Policy and Underclass Formation among Young Turks in Germany during the 1980's', *International Migration Review,* 2, pp. 306-331

Geiß, B. 2001:

Die Ausländerbeauftragten der Bundesregierung in der ausländerpolitischen Diskussion, in Currle, E. and Wunderlich, T. (eds.), *Deutschland – ein Einwanderungsland? Rückblick, Bilanz und neue Fragen,* pp. 127-140, Stuttgart: Lucius und Lucius

Gordon, M. 1964:

Assimilation in American Life. The Role of Race, Religion and National Origin, New York

Heckmann, F. 1981:

Die Bundesrepublik: ein Einwanderungsland?, Stuttgart: Klett-Kotta

Heckmann, F. 1988:

'Gewerkschaftliche Migrationspolitik', *Migration,* 3, pp. 79-95

Interministerielle Arbeitsgruppe Ausländerintegration 1999:

Ausländerintegration in Bayern, Bericht für den Bayerischen Landtag, München

Jeschek, W. 1998:

'Integration junger Ausländer in das Bildungssystem kommt kaum voran', *DIW Wochenbericht,* 24, pp.1-13

Kirchenamt der Evangelischen Kirche in Deutschland und Sekretariat der Deutschen Bischofskonferenz 1997:

"... und der Fremdling, der in deinen Toren ist." Gemeinsames Wort der Kirchen zu den Herausforderungen durch Migration und Flucht, Bonn-Frankfurt-Hannover

Kultusministerkonferenz 1996:

Empfehlung "Interkulturelle Bildung und Erziehung in der Schule", Beschluß vom 25.10.1996

Kupfer-Schreiner, C. 1996:

Schule braucht Kulturen. Ausländische Schülerinnen und Schüler in Nürnberg im Schuljahr 1995/96, Broschüre Stadt Nürnberg

Lederer, H.W. 1997:

Migration und Integration in Zahlen. Ein Handbuch, Beauftragte der Bundesregierung für Ausländerfragen (ed.), Bonn

Lederer, H.W. / Rau, R. / Rühl, St. 1999:

Migrationsbericht 1999. Zu- und Abwanderung aus Deutschland, Bericht im Auftrag der Beauftragten der Bundesregierung für Ausländerfragen, Bamberg

Mahnig, H. 1998:

Integrationspolitik in Großbritannien, Frankreich, Deutschland und den Niederlanden, Forschungsbericht Nr. 10 des Schweizerischen Forums für Migrationsstudien, Neuenburg

Martin, Ph. 1999:

Germany and the United States: Searching for 21st Century Migration Policies, IGCC Policy paper 50, Washington

Mommsen, W. J. 1990:

'Die Idee der deutschen Nation in Geschichte und Gegenwart', *Gewerkschaftliche Monatshefte*, 5/6, pp. 263-273

Münz, R. / Seifert, W. / Ulrich, R. 1997:

Zuwanderung nach Deutschland – Strukturen, Wirkungen, Perspektiven, Frankfurt – New York: Campus Verlag

Schily, O. 1999:

'Was heißt eigentlich "Nation"?' Bundestagsdebatte zur Reform des Staatsbürgerschaftsrechts am 7.5.1999, *Das Parlament*, 21-22 (21./28.5. 1999), p. 16

Schmidt, P. / Weick, St. 1998:

'Starke Zunahme von Kontakten und Ehen zwischen Deutschen und Ausländern', *Informationsdienst Soziale Indikatoren*, 19, January, pp. 1-5

Schnapper, D. 1992:

L'Europe des immigrés. Essai sur les politiques d'immigration, Paris: Francois Bourin

Schnapper, D. 1994:

La communauté des citoyens. Sur l'idée moderne de nation, Paris: Gallimard

Schulze, H. 1994:

Staat und Nation in der europäischen Geschichte, München: Beck Verlag

Straßburger, G. 2001:

Evaluation von Integrationsprozessen in Frankfurt am Main, Stadt Frankfurt: Amt für Multikulturelle Angelegenheiten, gedruckter *efms*-Forschungsbericht

Unabhängige Kommission Zuwanderung 2001:

Zuwanderung gestalten – Integration fördern, Berlin: Bundesministerium des Inneren

Zentrum für Türkeistudien 1999:

Türkei Jahrbuch, Münster-Hamburg-London: Lit Verlag

John Rex

Integration Policy in Great Britain

1. Introductory Note

This chapter will seek to give an account of the British experience of integrating immigrant ethnic minorities and their immediate descendants in terms which makes this account comparable with that given for other countries. At the same time it must be emphasised that policy arguments about integration in Britain do not fit easily into these categories. It is therefore necessary to precede what is reported here under each of the comparative categories with an account of the way in which the problem appeared in Britain.

There are certain features of the process of policy formation which we should notice at the outset. First it should be noted that it has always been partly pro-active but also partly reactive. The pro-active part has depended upon a group of individuals in a position to influence political parties and the civil service. They had dealt with the problem first of overcoming class conflict and creating a concept of citizenship and secondly with the integration of sub-national and immigrant minorities. It has, however, always to be remembered that although such policies were being pushed through they did encounter opposition and the underlying philosophy of integration did not enjoy universal support. All of these points will be evident in what follows.

2. The Ethnic Minority Population in Question

Getting a clear idea of the numbers of ethnic minority people in Great Britain[1] is difficult because the categories used in the census and in other surveys have changed. Prior to 1981 the census simply recorded an individual's country of birth. Since, however, there was some desire to know the numbers of children and grandchildren, the 1981 census recorded the numbers of those living in a household headed by an individual with a particular country of birth, while in 1991 individuals were asked, regardless of generation, to say to which ethnic group they belonged. Between these dates numbers are derived from the Labour Force Survey which studies a sample of individuals and households.

---

[1] The figures given here are for England, Scotland and Wales combined. They do not include Northern Ireland. The percentage of ethnic minorities in the total population is actually higher in England than in Scotland or Wales. See OPCS 1991 Census.

There has been some argument about the desirability of having a so-called ethnic question in the census at all. The categories used are somewhat surprising. An individual is asked to say whether he or she belongs to the following categories: White, Black (Caribbean, African or Other), Asian (Indian, Pakistani, Bangladeshi, Chinese or Other Asian) and Other Other. The main aim appears to have been to classify the non-White minorities and the term ethnic minorities is usually assumed to refer to these. On this basis it is claimed that the ethnic minority population has increased between 1991 and 2001 from 7.6 per cent of the total in 1991 to 10 per cent in 2001.

These minority percentages do not of course include any immigrants from the Irish Republic, from continental Europe, or from the Mediterranean territories of Cyprus, Malta and Gibraltar. For the purposes of this chapter this is unfortunate because each of these groups may have special problems of integration. The problems which policy discussion about ethnic minority integration addresses are the specific problems of Black and Asian minorities. In 1991 the number in thousands of those identifying as Black was 890.8 (Black Caribbean, 500, Black African, 212.4, Other Black 178.4), the number of those identifying as Indian was 840.3, as Pakistani 476.6, as Bangladeshi, as Chinese 156.9, as Other Asian 197.5[2].

There was no question about religion in the 1991 census. There were, however, known to be a very large number of religions present. Some of their variety has been recorded in a multi-faith directory entitled *Religions in the UK*, published by the University of Derby and the Interfaith Network (Weller 1993). Apart from the main groups such as Roman Catholics and Protestant Christians, the three major South Asian religions of Hinduism, Sikhism and Islam and the various West Indian Pentecontalist and Holiness sects, there are many others, some of them being breakaway sects from the main religions. There are many varieties of Islam and there are Buddhists, Jains, Parsees and Bahais.

The fourth survey conducted by the Policy Studies Institute (Modood et al. 1997) carried out sample surveys amongst all their White respondents and amongst half of those from ethnic minorities. This showed that 68% of the Whites (excluding the Irish) were Christian and 31% had no religion, and 1% other religions; amongst the Irish 85% were Christian and 14% had no religion; amongst Caribbeans 69% were Christian, 28% had no religion, 1% were Muslims and there were another 1% claiming other religions; amongst Indians 50% were Sikhs, 32% were Hindus, 6% were Muslims, 5% were Christians, 3%

---

[2] Source OPCS 1991 Census, *Ethnic Group and Country of Birth, Great Britain*. There are a number of difficulties involved in interpreting these figures. The various ethnic groups having white skin colour are not differentiated from one another; there is no category of Black British and no way of distinguishing East African Asians from Indians and Pakistanis. This has to be kept in mind in relation to any statement referring to the experience of "Ethnic Minorities".

belonged to other religions and 5% had no religion; amongst African Asians 58% were Hindu, 19% Sikhs, 15% were Muslims, 3% were Christians, 3% belonged to other religions and 2% had no religion; amongst Pakistanis 96% were Muslims, 2% had other religions and 2% none; amongst Bangladeshis 95% were Muslims, 2% Hindu, 1% Christian, 1% had other religions and 1% none; finally amongst the Chinese 58% had no religion, 23% were Christian and 19% had other religions[3].

Table 1: Numbers in Thousands and Percentages of Different Ethnic Minorities in Great Britain

	Numbers	Percent of Total Population
Black	890.8	1.6
Black Caribbean	500.0	0.9
Black African	212.4	0.4
Black Other	178.4	0.3
Indian	840.3	1.5
Pakistani	476.6	0.9
Bangladeshi	162.8	0.3
Chinese	156.9	0.3
Other Asian	197.5	0.4
Other Other	290.0	10.5

Source: This table has been constructed from the numbers and percentages to be found in the Fourth PSI survey (Modood et al. 1997)

The census of 2001 did have a religious question but the results of this are not yet available. Modood has been active in urging that religious discrimination should be recognised and prevented under a reformed race relations act.

---

[3] These data are taken from Table 9.5 on page 298 of the Fourth Survey. It is not clear what being classified as a member of any of the religions actually meant although Modood does make the point that New Protestant West Indians and Muslims took part in religious services much more frequently than other groups and also claimed much more frequently that religion was very important in their lives.

3. Debates on Integration

In the nineteen fifties there were two separate debates about immigrant minorities in the British Parliament. One concerned the restriction of immigration from the Commonwealth, the other the prevention of racial discrimination. The first of these led to the passage of the Commonwealth Immigrants Act of 1962 which restricted the number of Commonwealth immigrants to 7,000 per annum although it still allowed for family completion. Such restrictions became even more severe in the following ten years, with new immigrants being required to show that they had skills which the British economy required or jobs to which they could come, and, with increasingly narrow definitions of the dependants who were allowed to join primary immigrants. Control was also extended to United Kingdom passport holders In East Africa. Moreover eventually in 1981 the British *nationality* was redefined so that instead of its being shared equally by subjects of the Empire, it was divided into different categories with unequal rights of settlement in Britain.

Such immigration controls were deemed necessary by leading politicians on the grounds that too large numbers would make integration impossible. On the other hand measures were gradually developed to prevent discrimination against immigrant minorities. As one leading Labour politician put it, "Without (immigration) control integration is impossible, but without integration (immigration) control is morally indefensible". In other words, every effort should be made to reduce the numbers of incomers while seeking to ensure fair and equal treatment for those actually admitted (Rex and Tomlinson 1979).

The integration of these populations was seen as having two main elements. On the one hand integration would require equal access between incomers and the host population to opportunities in employment, housing, education and other services. On the other there was the question of how far the incomers preserved their own culture or adopted that of their hosts. Thus the Home Secretary in 1966 sought to deal with the problem by defining "integration" "not as a flattening process of uniformity but as cultural diversity coupled with equal opportunity in an atmosphere of mutual tolerance" (Rex and Tomlinson 1979). Unlike some definitions of multicultural societies this definition included the notion of a common and equal citizenship. This had been the theme of T.H. Marshall's important book *Citizenship and Social Class* (Marshall 1951). Marshall had argued that class identification and consciousness would only be superseded by identification with citizenship when the working class had attained not merely legal and political but also social rights. This was the basis of the post 1945 Welfare State in which a minimum of entitlements was guaranteed to all citizens. Marshall, however, did not deal specifically with ethnic minorities and the problem today is that of how far immigrants and their hosts will attain equal citizenship rights.

4. Surveys of Disadvantage and Discrimination and the Race Relations Acts

So far as access to opportunities and the use of resources was concerned the degree of equality attained was monitored in four successive surveys by the organisation called Political and Economic Planning which later became the Policy Studies Institute (Daniel 1966, Smith 1974, Brown 1982, Modood et al. 1997).

The fact that these four surveys of ethnic minorities' experience were made is an indication that some non-governmental organisations were concerned to discover degrees of inequality between ethnic groups and that itself is an important political fact. So was much of the work of the unofficial Runnymede Trust which promoted a series of investigations which led to the setting up of a "Commission for a Multi-Racial Britain" which produced a report (Runnymede Trust 2000) which was submitted to the Home Secretary. A comment on the weight which should be attached to them is given below. First, however, we should report the findings of these studies.

The first PEP survey (Daniel 1966) occurred at a time when discrimination against individuals in the fields of housing and employment was still legal and as a consequence of the information provided by the survey the new Race Relations Act of 1967 sought to counter discrimination in these fields. Even when it was illegal, however tests using actors to apply for jobs and houses, a technique first used in the 1966 PEP survey, showed that discrimination against Black applicants was still occurring.

The 1974 study by David Smith (Smith 1974) turned attention to the problem that, even when there was no proof of deliberate acts of discrimination, ethnic minorities might disproportionately suffer disadvantage. Such disadvantage was clearly shown to occur in the fields of employment and housing. This sometimes resulted from indirect discrimination where criteria for success of an application made no direct reference to race or colour but gave those of certain minority groups less chance of success. These findings contributed to the shaping of the comprehensive Race Relations Act of 1976. The report's handling of the themes of disadvantage and indirect discrimination to some extent foreshadowed the discussion of *institutional racism* which was central to the findings of the MacPherson Report which enquired into the murder of the Black teenager Stephen Lawrence.

The third national survey (Brown 1982) found the disadvantage of minority groups continuing, but detected some upward mobility in employment. The survey, however, also showed that different minority groups had different levels of success and increasingly thereafter all studies broke down the crude categories in terms of which minorities were classified. The 1991 census, as we have seen, classified the non-white minorities as Black Caribbean, Black African, Other Black, Indian, Pakistani, Bangladeshi, Chinese, Other Asian and Other Other. Using a different procedure in the fourth survey Modood et al. (1997) classified the population and chose samples described as White, Caribbean, Indian, African Asian, Pakistani, Bangladeshi and Chinese[4].Within these groups moreover new tables, much more sophisticated than in any equivalent study of discrimination and disadvantage in Europe, were set out. Tables are given, for example, which differentiate between the experience of men and women, of different age groups, of groups with differing lengths of stay in Britain, of groups in areas with differing degrees of immigrant concentration and segregation, of groups with differing degrees of education, and of groups with different religious affiliation.

This detailed specification of all of these different sub-groups makes it difficult to make any simple summary statement about the integration of immigrant minorities[5]. We may, however draw attention to some of the overall features of immigrant minority integration under the headings of economic, residential and educational integration, the last of which we deal with most extensively.

It was expected by policy makers after 1976 that the main agent of change so far as ethnic minorities were concerned would be the *Commission for Racial Equality.* It should be noticed here that the setting up of this body had followed a number of visits to the United States by a cross party group who had the power to influence the policy makers. The recommendations which followed these visits placed great emphasis upon *race, racial disadvantage and racial discrimination.* This emphasis was very different from that in continental Europe where the very concept of race had become discredited, but it followed from the fact that British thinking was more influenced by the United Sates than it was by Europe. However it presented a problem to the New Commission for Racial Equality. The main way in which Asian immigrants would be dealt with would be to see them as different in terms of race and colour, even though their processes of settlement had a different trajectory from those of the Black Afro-Caribbeans. Some like Modood have argued that being classified in this way did positive harm to British Asian minorities.

---

[4] The rationale for classifying the population in this way is described in the First Chapter of the Fourth Report, pages 8-12.

[5] For a full account readers of this chapter are referred to the fourth survey, *Ethnic Minorities in Britain* itself (Modood et al. 1997).

5. Economic Integration, Housing and Residential Segregation

5.1. Economic Integration

Policies of integration which were pursued in the late sixties and through the seventies, eighties and nineties underwent considerable change both with regard to social classes and with regard to ethnic minorities The title of a government policy paper in the late sixties, *In Place of Strife*, (Department of Employment and Productivity 1969) signaled the aim of successive governments to get rid of the conflicts engendered by totally free collective bargaining and to produce a system in which trades unions and employers were encouraged to collaborate by government. At the same time the integration of ethnic minorities was promoted through the Commission for Racial Equality a large part of whose work dealt with questions of employment.

The simplest index here is that of the percentage of those in manual and non-manual work in the various ethnic minority groups compared with Whites. In 1982 the majority of males in all groups were in manual work though the percentage was lower amongst Whites, but by 1994 51% of Whites were in non-manual work, but 57% of African Asians and 67% of Chinese were. Amongst the other groups only 31% of Caribbeans, 32% of Pakistanis and 29% of Bangladeshis were non-manual. The percentage of female employees in non-manual work is much higher in all groups but this raises the question of what the manual/non-manual distinction means. Possibly amongst men it involves a degree of status attainment.

Looking at these figures in more detail 30% of white males were in the category of Professional, Managerial or Employers. The percentage for Chinese was 41%, African Asians 26% and that for Indians 19%. In the semi-skilled and unskilled occupations compared with a White percentage of 18%, Caribbeans had 32%, Indians 29% Pakistanis 32%, Bangladeshis 69%, Chinese 28% and African Asians 20%. Once again one has a picture of Whites and African Asians pulling clear of the less desired and arduous occupations. Amongst women Whites with 21% and African Asian with 14% do best in the Professional/ Managerial/Employer category. In the intermediate and junior non-manual categories all groups are well represented with Caribbeans getting the highest percentage score of 76%. These categories, however, are probably misleading unless taken in conjunction with the occupational figures. Many minority women are in clerical work and nursing.

So far as industrial categories are concerned one finds amongst male employees higher concentrations of Whites (14%), Indians (13%) and Asian Africans (17%) in Banking and Finance. In metal extraction, manufacture, metal goods, engineering and vehicles one finds that Caribbeans have 22% of their number, Whites, Indians and Pakistanis 15 or 16%, Bangladeshis 13% and African Asians only 9%. Bangladeshis (60%) and Chinese (23%) have much the highest proportions in hotels and catering, no doubt because of the restaurant trade. Amongst women African Asians and Whites have the highest proportions in Retail distribution and in Banking and Finance (17% of Whites and 22% of African Asian women are in retail distribution and 15% of Whites and15% of African Asian women in Banking and Finance). Caribbean (39%) and Chinese (30%) women score highest for the proportion of their members working in hospitals.

A general impression can be gained from these figures of the position of the various minorities. Indians and African Asians seem to be doing as well as Whites, or perhaps in the case of African Asians, even better. Caribbeans, Pakistanis and Bangladeshis do much worse than any of these groups and probably in the order Caribbean, Pakistani and Bangladeshi. Caribbean men tend to be concentrated in the manufacturing industries and Bangladeshis and Chinese in catering. Amongst women Caribbeans and Chinese were commonly employed in nursing.

To complete the picture of ethnic minority employment one should consider the question of self-employment and the distinction between employment in the public and private sector. So far as the first of these is concerned it is clear that self-employment is far more common among all the ethnic minority groups than it is amongst Whites and this is true for both men and women. So far as public sector employment is concerned comparing Whites, Caribbeans and South Asians[6] the percentages in the public sector for males are 26%, 33% and 27%, and for females 38%, 61% and 39%.

The Fourth PSI survey also makes comparisons between 1982 and 1994. Its conclusion from this comparison is that all groups have improved their position but that the gap between the successful groups (White, Indian and African Asian) and the relatively unsuccessful ones (Caribbean, Pakistani and Bangladeshi) has probably widened. The position of the less well off groups might best be described by the old-fashioned term "relative deprivation".

The survey has also sought to measure the income of various groups in complex ways, looking at such questions as the number of earners in a household, the household's age structure, the qualifications of its members and so on. According to Berthoud (Chapter 5, Modood et al. 1997), White households with at least one earner had an average income £395, such Chinese households £413, African Asians £380, Indians £367 and Caribbeans £327. The least well off in terms of income were the Pakistanis and Bangladeshis. The average income of these two groups taken together was only £245. This is a useful set

---

[6] It is not clear why the authors of the survey group ethnic minorities differently in relation to this question. It would in fact have been interesting to know what differences there were between the larger number of groups used at other points in the survey.

of statistics since it is the income of the household as a whole which is important for most people rather than the earnings of individuals[7].

5.2. Housing and Residential Integration

Policy on the housing of ethnic minorities was part of the general policy of seeking to overcome discrimination after the mid sixties. In this area, however, it created an important dilemma. Should the aim of policy be to facilitate housing mobility especially to better forms of ownership and tenure in the suburbs or should the value of maintaining residential ethnic communities be recognised?

Evidence from the Fourth PSI Survey showed the following: 67% of Whites were owner-occupiers. Indians (85%) African Asians (84%) and Pakistanis (79%) exceeded this percentage. Caribbeans at 58%, Bangladeshis at 48% and Chinese at 54% had lower percentages than Whites. 23% of Whites were in social housing (either Council Houses or Housing Association houses). The equivalent percentages for the various ethnic minorities were Caribbean 47%, Bangladeshis 45%, Chinese 24%, Pakistani 15% African Asian 12% and Indian 9%. Private tenancies were 9 % in the White group and between 5 and 9% in the main ethnic minority groups with the exception of the Chinese who had 22% and mixed Asian/White households who had 17%.

Ethnic minorities were concentrated in certain regions and in certain parts of cities. Looking at regional concentrations fewer than 10% of Whites lived in the Greater London area, but more than 50% of Caribbeans, African Asians and Bangladeshis and more than 40% of the Chinese and a third of Indians. Substantial proportions of Pakistanis lived in Yorkshire and Humberside, in the West Midlands and the NorthWest. Indians outside of London were concentrated in the West Midlands.

Quoting Robinson's work comparing 1981 and 1991 census figures Lakey says "far from becoming dispersed more widely across different areas of the country, ethnic minority groups have become more concentrated into urban areas in (this) decade. Caribbean, Indian and Bangladeshi groups became more concentrated in the South East; Indians and African Asians became more concentrated in the East Midlands and Pakistanis in the North West Region" (Modood et al. 1997).

An indication of segregation within urban areas is provided by the percentage of ethnic minorities in wards where particular ethnic minorities lived.

---

[7] There are of course enormous problems in assessing the contribution of separate individuals to the household, including not only earnings but various social security benefits which are thoroughly discussed by Berthoud (Modood et al. 1997, Chapter Five).

In wards where White respondents to the Fourth Survey lived the proportion of ethnic minorities was less than one in 20, whereas Caribbeans and Indians lived in wards where ethnic minorities represented a quarter of the population, while Pakistanis and Bangladeshis lived in wards with one third of the population from the ethnic minorities.

There was a considerable debate arising partly from my own work with Robert Moore (Rex and Moore 1967) which had suggested that segregation was the result of racial discrimination. Dhaya (1974) criticised my work claiming that segregation was a matter of choice rather than the result of discrimination. Subsequently this became a debate amongst social geographers about the relative effect of constraint and choice as causes of segregation.

In more recent times due largely to the occurrence of rioting involving Asians and Whites in Northern cities questions have been raised about the desirability of segregation. The common view is that segregation leads to the emergence of ethnic minority wards which become no-go areas for Whites and for other groups. These areas become the targets for White racists and law and order passes from the police to vigilante groups. As a result there has been pressure on policy makers to develop policies of housing dispersal and opposition to segregated schools. There is no doubt that ethnic conflict now seems to have set in in British cities between wards and between groups. Against this there are some who would still argue that predominantly ethnic minority areas are not incompatible with the development of a sense of shared local citizenship between groups.

6. Integration and Segregation in the Educational System

There are at least six elements involved in dealing with this dimension of structural integration: first there is the question of language; secondly there is that of cultural difference; thirdly there is that of equality of opportunity in attaining educational success; fourthly there is that of occupational and vocational training, fifthly that of education in citizenship; and, finally there is the question of religion in education.

6.1. Questions of Language and Language Policy

The language question itself breaks down into two. The first is the question of the medium of instruction. In England the assumption is that this should be English although support will be given to children whose home language is not English without necessarily involving the employment of interpreters. This clearly has involved some difficulty for the children of early Asian immigrants who inevitably find understanding their first teachers difficult and can be held back by this in educational terms. One alternative also explored has been to take children out of the mainstreams or classes and concentrate on teaching them English, in which case their reinsertion in the main classes is difficult, in that they will not have had the other lessons which their peers have had.

The surprising thing is that many Asian children do in fact quickly acquire a good knowledge of English from their contact with their peers outside school as well as from listening to their teachers. In principle it might be thought that these problems are not so acute for Afro-Caribbean children since their home language is thought to be English. For many Afro-Caribbean children from working class homes, however, their home language is a Creolised form of English. They seem to face in a more acute form the problems which Bernstein (1961) noted as facing English working class children whose home language is slightly different from that used in school and for whom language has other purposes than the conveying of knowledge. Native working class children and Afro-Caribbean working class children share this experience, though for Afro-Caribbean children the problems are more serious and may be at the root of the problems of discipline which they present to their teachers.

In any case, whatever consideration is given to the difficulties involved in the early acquisition of English the objective of all schools has to be that of enabling children to be able to cope with English as the main medium of instruction later on. The remaining question is that of how far schools should attempt to maintain mother tongues. There are some local education authorities and individual schools which have attempted this but the overall picture is one in which mother tongues are not taught in schools. Jennifer Williams has pointed out that where there is any attempt to maintain mother tongues, (or, for that matter, minority cultures), it is located in the low status uncertificated parts of the syllabus. There have been a few attempts to teach Asian languages in the high status certificated parts of the syllabus, but the Asian languages are far less likely to be taught at this level than West European languages.

One should note here that there has been some demand on the part of immigrant communities for separate schools. There is an opening for this in English practice because the state has supported separate Protestant (especially Anglican), Roman Catholic and Jewish schools and there is always the possibility of the communities establishing their own schools without state support. Most recently the government has suggested increasing the numbers of faith based schools which should be publicly supported and for the first time a few Muslim state supported schools have been established. The existence of this diversity involves more issues than those of language but does have implications for language policy. Clearly non-English faith schools are more likely to foster mother tongue teaching.

The Linguistic Education of Adult Immigrants

Immigrant workers face two problems. On the one hand they must learn sufficient English to cope with their work situation; on the other they have to deal with a world outside working hours. So far as the first is concerned a minimal English is usually acquired to enable them to understand what is required of them and they may learn this with the aid of voluntary organisations or through those of their own number who have been in England longer or simply know more English, the latter having been called "pivots" by some social scientists (Brookes and Singh 1979, 19-30).

In dealing with the wider world outside work immigrants may often be helped by their children especially in dealing with local and national bureaucracies in filling in their forms. In large areas of life, however, they may have their own associations or sports clubs in which they speak their own language and remain to a large extent segregated. An enhanced power of children in the family results from this. But, if children have enhanced power, in linguistic matters non-working wives have less. In fact women are often dependent on both their husbands' and their children' s English. Voluntary organisations have thus come into being to promote the linguistic education of these women.

Present Changes in Government Language Policy towards Immigrants[8]

Recent events have led to a renewed emphasis on linguistic questions in relation to immigrants. The disturbances amongst Asians in Northern cities have led government ministers to demand that all members of the immigrant communities should learn and be helped to learn English and also the values of British citizenship. This has been urged even more strongly as Britain became part of the American led coalition against terrorism after the attacks in New York and Washington on September 11, 2001.

This change of emphasis in language policy results from an overall belief that any kind of segregation is necessarily undesirable and the cause of ethnic conflict. A minority view as that suggested in the earlier part of this paper, holds that the maintenance of strong ethnic communities at least for several generations is not incompatible with the existence of a single national or urban society. Included in what does need to be maintained is the maintenance of community languages. Moreover, if as we said one of the reasons for sustaining

---

[8] There was a considerable shift in government thinking about policy towards the end of 2001. a whole range of reports emphasising the dangers of segregation and seeing it as the source of threats to British society. How far this will remain on the level of rhetoric remains to be seen. All this debate takes place within a wider discussion of social inclusion and exclusion, but that itself could easily be a matter of rhetoric.

separate minority communities is that they should have the means of collective action, even the existence of vigilante groups such as have been seen in Northern cities can be seen as part of this process.

The mainstream view at the moment is essentially an assimilationist one fuelled by fears of violence. Not surprisingly there are more and more positive references to the French example.

6.2. Questions of Cultural Difference

A wider question than that of linguistic differences is that of cultural differences. Here there has been much discussion of the desirability of multicultural education. At one extreme there are those who suggest that the schools can be used in a project of social engineering through which an originally unitary culture is replaced by one in which several cultural traditions coexist. This diverse culture is regarded as being the likely culture of Britain in the future. Theoretically such a view has derived support from the work of the Canadians Charles Taylor (1994), Will Kymlicka (1995) and from the British Indian political theorist, Bhiku Parekh (2000). It is, however, not a majority view and is opposed by those like Brian Barry (Barry 1999) who insist upon the importance of shared political values as well as, in the present political climate, those who have come to believe in assimilation. A leading British Conservative, Lord Tebbitt, has repeatedly argued that the British people have never accepted the idea of a multicultural society.

Many of the arguments for and against multicultural education in schools have been discussed above in relation to language, but there is more to it than this. There is a widespread commitment to the belief that education should be multicultural. This is apparent in numerous statements by local education authorities. If, however, this is thought to involve little more than rhetoric, there have been attempts to introduce special classes devoted to propagating a variety of cultures and it is also suggested that the teaching of all subjects should be revised to give recognition to a variety of cultural perspectives. The most obvious cases are those of history, geography and literature. In the case of history, instead of a simple British history dealing mainly with the history of the monarchy and the British Empire, history is required to be more international taking account of other countries and other empires. In the case of India it is now widely recognised that Indian history in the past has been written from an essentially British imperialist point of view. Now it is suggested that it should be rewritten to take account of Indian views and of the later development of Indian culture in what is seen as an Indian diaspora. Geography, it is suggested, should be focussed on different countries and different topics of concern to minorities. A literary education which used to rest upon a specific English canon will now be required to be based upon a range of other literatures, albeit in translation.

So far as the simpler question of holding classes on multiculturalism is concerned little has actually been done except in the discussion of religion, which will be considered below, to acquaint all students with a variety of cultures. What has been suggested instead is that minority children should receive education in their own cultures to raise their self-esteem. Some supplementary schools have been started by minority communities with this in mind. There is, however, another view argued for by the Black school teacher, Maureen Stone (Stone 1985) that the connection between low self esteem and low performance has not been established and that supplementary schools should be devoted to teaching basic literary and numeracy skills lack of which holds children back in their main classes.

Another source of opposition to multicultural education derives from the work of radical educational sociologists like Troyna (1987). They would argue that multiculturalism in any case involves little more than token recognition of minority cultures represented, Troyna believes by the images of "Saris, samosas and steel bands" as giving the essence of Asian and West Indian culture. Instead of the syllabus being made more multicultural he argues that in should be "anti-racist"[9].

6.3. Equality of Opportunity and Level of Educational Success

Central to any argument about integration through education is the question of the relative educational success of children from different backgrounds. Even the case for multicultural education is argued for on the ground that it can promote higher levels of achievement for otherwise disadvantaged minority children.

The underachievement of Afro-Caribbean children in schools became a matter of concern during the seventies and a government committee was appointed to investigate the matter. The members of this committee were divided on the question of whether this underachievement was due to the school system or to the homes and communities from which the children came, so that any recommendations which it made about alterations to the school system were weakened by doubt (Department of Education and Science 1981). The Chairman of this committee, Anthony Rampton, then resigned and Lord

---

[9] I have suggested in an obituary note on Troyna's important work (Rex 1997) that Troyna offers an oversimplified view of multiculturalism in general and that my own notion of egalitarian multiculturalism which emphasises equality of opportunity as well as cultural diversity involves a commitment to anti-racism.

Swann was appointed to move the committee's work along[10]. The Swann Report as it came to be known had to look at several new problems. On the one hand it had to deal with the fact that Asian minority children were not doing as badly as Afro-Caribbean children, and that some, indeed, were doing better than their White peers. It also had to deal with the question of cultural diversity. Its recommendations were therefore inevitably complex. It concluded that minority children suffered from racism in society at large but also within the schools themselves. In the schools, however, racism was seen as expressed through a failure to understand cultural diversity rather than any malign intent. Thus, ignoring the view represented by writers like Stone discussed above, it suggested that a more multi-cultural syllabus would lead to higher achievement. On the other hand it also called for clear policies in schools to prevent racial discrimination. The Report also adopted the slogan "Education for All" as its title thus abandoning the notion that it was simply about, and for, minority children (Department of Education and Science 1985).

What a central government Department of Education could achieve in bringing about change was, however, limited by the fact that Britain does not have a centralised educational system so that much depended upon policies adopted by local education authorities or even by individual schools. Troyna and I discussed the variety of local policies in a submission to the Swann Committee. Some of these local authorities emphasised the need to respect cultural diversity, others the need to combat racism. Some of the variety of responses is also well reflected in a collection of essays entitled *Multicultural Education: The Interminable Debate* (Modgil, Verma, Mallick and Modgil 1986). Verma, however, went on to give his strong support to the Swann Report dedicating his edited volume *Education for All: A Landmark in Pluralism* (Verma 1989) to Lord Swann.

The actual levels of achievement of children from the various minorities were considered in some detail by Modood in the Fourth PSI study in 1994 (Modood et al. 1997) and he compared the position in 1994 with that in the mid seventies and in 1982. In 1982 he tells us that "Caribbean and Pakistani men were less qualified than their white peers, while Indians and African

---

[10]The original committee was unusual in its composition. Usually such committees' members were drawn from what were called "the great and the good". In this case, however, Anthony Rampton the Chairman had had considerable experience of community relations work in South London and he was joined on the committee by members of the ethnic communities themselves who were thought to be representative. When the committee reported however its recommendations were largely dismissed on the ground that troublemakers had taken control. At this stage a new chairman Lord Swann was appointed with a background in the BBC and as a University Vice-Chancellor he was manifestly one of the great and the good. A rare criticism of the Rampton Committee's work from another point of view came from Reeves and Chevannes who suggested that if statistical controls of third variables such as parent's occupation, parent's level of achievement were introduced, the apparent difference between Afro-Caribbean and other children disappeared (Reeves and Chevannes 1981).

Asians were the best qualified" and that "South Asian women, especially the Pakistanis were much less qualified than the men". West Indian women, however, were better qualified than West Indian men. In 1982 it was clear that while in the older age groups earlier patterns held, among the 16-24 year old South Asian men had higher qualifications than Whites. Subsequently the Labour Force Survey showed that African Asians and Indians had higher average qualifications than Whites, the position of Pakistanis and Bangladeshis was much worse. Finally Modood goes on in great detail to explore the position of various minorities as revealed by the 1991 census. As a generalisation it can be said that the Fourth PSI survey finds that while in the sixties and early seventies the main problem of underachievement was seen to be that of the West Indian children, the present position is that, while Indians and African Asians are doing better than Whites, the least successful are the Pakistanis and Bangladeshis, who are now worse off than West Indians.

How far these changes are due to policies adopted in schools is difficult to say. What does seem to be clear, however, is that most local education authorities have made statements and implemented policies which commit them to both multiculturalism and anti-racism. Thus while it was possible in the mid seventies to find as Tomlinson did in reporting her school based research (Rex and Tomlinson 1979, Chapter Five), that there was still much prejudice and racism in schools, this was no longer the case by the nineties when all teachers had learned that they had to work within a framework of multiculturalism and anti-racism. This is not to say that racial prejudice ceased to exist or that there were never acts of discrimination. What had happened was that the institutional framework set up by policy had changed.

A final comment on the question of the relative attainment of ethnic minority children should also be added. This was made by Smith and Tomlinson (1989) who pointed out that whether children did well or badly depended on how good or bad the school they attended was. This, however, seems to divert attention away from the effect of racism and ordinary anti-racist and multicultural policy in schools to a simple consideration of educational issues. It is similar to the implication of the Swann Report's work which had held that the problems of ethnic minority children had to be solved by good education for all.

6.4. Vocational and Occupational Training

The discussion of vocational and occupational training has already been implicit in the discussion of economic integration. Nonetheless it is an important topic in this section on educational integration and a specific concern of the EFFNATIS study conducted by Penn in the Northern British towns of Rochdale and Blackburn (Penn et al. 2000). Its major conclusions may be stated summarily as follows:

1. Ethnic minority students are likely to stay in full time education rather than entering the labour market at the age of 16+.

2. This can be partly explained by the very poor opportunities for them in the sphere of employment and industrial training.

3. Occupational Training Schemes outside the schools include Modern Apprenticeships, National Traineeships and other Youth Training. Modern Apprenticeships cover a wider range than traditional apprenticeships, but if one looks at engineering and construction, they are very similar to them. Those who did not get these apprenticeships either went into National Traineeships which were valued less, but the least valued forms of training were those referred to in the EFFNATIS study as "Other Forms of Training". These other forms of training might well involve what Willis has called in his provocative study "learning to labour" (Willis 1977). In the highly valued Modern Apprenticeships 98% of those entering were White while Asians were proportionately more likely to be in the residual category of Other Youth Training.

4. The New Deal was designed to get young people off relying on unemployment benefit for more than six months by putting them in jobs with government subsidised wages. During 1998 and 1999 380,000 entered the scheme and of these 50,000 were from ethnic minorities. However, while it was easy enough to enter the scheme the finding of the EFFNATIS study was that for ethnic minority entrants participation was less likely to lead to permanent employment. This was the case even though ethnic minority entrants were better qualified than Whites[11].

---

[11] In the immediate post-war period Britain established a tripartite system of secondary education. Students went to Grammar, Technical or Modern Schools, but there were few technical schools as compared with other European countries and it was not clear what the secondary modern students were supposed to be like; they were simply a residual category. Public dissatisfaction with this system lead to the introduction of comprehensive schools for most of the state system and within these schools there was supposed to be a wide range of student ability and a wide range of courses, some of them of the grammar and technical type and some vocational. Some grammar schools in some local authorities survived outside the comprehensive system and there were still a few schools calling themselves technical or modern. None of this of course refers to fee-paying schools outside the state system and some parents fearing the comprehensive system paid the necessary fees to go there.

6.5. Citizenship Education

On the question of citizenship the first thing to be pointed out is that there is a considerable difference between the way in which the question of citizenship or education in civics has been handled in France and in Britain. In the centralised educational system in France it is possible to ask what education in civics is being given nationally. In the decentralised British educational system each local educational authority has its own system. Nonetheless there has been some discussion of education in citizenship at a national level. A Commission headed by Bernard Crick (Advisory Group on Citizenship 1998) former editor of the journal *Political Studies* recommended that there should be such education in all schools. Moreover there has been some element of political education in the syllabus of most schools going under a variety of titles such as Personal and Social Development, albeit not as part of the compulsory national curriculum.

The sort of political education or education in citizenship recommended nationally and actually practised in schools was in the eighties very much influenced by the debate about multicultural and anti-racist education. No doubt in earlier times it had reflected the views of a White-governed society and of imperialism and colonialism. The new emphasis in the eighties was on the education of White children, whether in mixed schools or in overwhelmingly White ones, so that they would accept an inclusive society. This contrasted with the French view that the children of immigrant minorities should be the prime target of such education. They had to learn the French concept of citizenship.

This situation is now undergoing change. It was noted above that in linguistic and cultural matters there had been a move in Britain towards the French model. So also this was the case on the question of citizenship. Faced with disturbances amongst Asians in Northern cities and with the new fear of terrorism what the Home Secretary was suggesting in the latter part of the year 2001 was that immigrants and their descendants should be the target of education in citizenship. These policies on the other hand drew criticism from the ethnic minority communities themselves who argued that the emphasis upon educating them in citizenship drew attention away from the fact that they suffered from discrimination and disadvantage. They said that this was typical of the tendency to blame the victim.

One final point to be noted is that debate about citizenship underwent a further important change. In the discussion of the concept in the work of Marshall the emphasis had been on the *rights* of citizenship. But even before the political anxieties of 2001 a new emphasis was placed upon citizenship's duties. Such a notion appealed to conservatives but it crept into a wider debate especially when discussing ethnic minorities, the working classes, or hooligans.

6.6. Religion in Education

There are three aspects to the question of religion in education. The first is that of what are now called faith schools. The second is that of religious assemblies and worship. The third is that of religious education.

On the question of faith schools the longstanding policy of the British government was to provide the great bulk of the finance for Catholic, Anglican, Non-Conformist, and Jewish schools subject to their carrying out national policies and being open to inspection. In the last few years, however, this policy has been extended to place two or three Muslim schools in a similar position. Of course nothing could stop any religious community from establishing its own independent schools for which finance had to be found from the community or from parents. There are a number of such schools in London and in the North. Some of these schools introduced different religions into the assemblies so that children might take part in Christian, Hindu, Sikh and Muslim services on different days. Not surprisingly White Christian parents resisted these experiments.

On the question of religious assemblies the independent schools and the state financed state schools organised religious assemblies and worship in accordance with their faith. In other state schools Christian assemblies were common but there were also many authorities like the Inner London Education Authority in which it was thought sufficient simply to introduce morally uplifting ideas to the pupils. Where there was Christian worship non-Christians were given the option of leaving and occasionally having their own forms of worship financed by their communities.

Religious education might be of two kinds. One was that which sought to teach pupils to practise their own religion. The other was to teach them *about* religion either that of their own community or that of other communities. There has been considerable change in the Religious Education curriculum in the eighties and nineties. Most commonly children learn about Christianity in its Catholic and Protestant forms and about Islam, Hinduism and Sikhism. There have also been attempts to introduce Humanism and even Marxism into this syllabus but they have not been widespread. One other development has been the provision of religious education outside school hours in Muslim madrasa and similar places. Such activity receives no support from public finances.

Both religious assemblies and religious education have been part of the political debate in Britain. One conservative and traditional approach has been to try to retain Christian assemblies and religious education of a Christian kind although this might take the form of calling for assemblies and religious education to be "predominantly" Christian. Radical opponents of this traditionalism claim that the formula "predominantly" Christian actually means excluding any multi-faith approach in either sphere.

The whole debate about religion in schools reflects the uncertainty about whether there should be segregation or integration. In the new climate generated by the disturbances in the Asian population and by the fear of terrorism there has been a move away from any toleration of segregation. By the same token it is becoming accepted that religion in schools should only be tolerated if it does not threaten a unified civil society.

7. Social Order, Nationhood and the Integration of Minorities

The various social institutions in Britain in the immediate post war period were established through the implementation of the Beveridge Report (Beveridge 1942). This called for the payment of benefits in times of unemployment and ill health financed by compulsory contributions from employers and employees. There was also to be assistance for those who had not been able to make these contributions. Insurance benefits were to be paid as of right and not on the basis of a means test. The implementation of the Beveridge Report was accompanied by establishment of a National Health Service paid for out of general taxation involving medical treatment free at the point of delivery. This system came under strain in several ways. A minority suggested that such a state welfare system undermined the family and private charity and it was clear in any case that there was a new category of people in poverty who slipped through the welfare net, including many from the ethnic minorities. While some like T.H. Marshall whose work we referred to earlier sought to go beyond Beverage to establish a social citizenship involving the right to a minimum standard of provision in housing education and employment matters while permitting free collective bargaining over wages. Others sought to confine state activity to the provision of social insurance only while encouraging self-help and enterprise. This was the essence of what came to be called Thatcherism.

The Labour opposition to Thatcher remained for a long time wedded to the idea of national control of the means of production, distribution and exchange set out in Clause Four of its constitution and to the Marshallian concept of the Welfare State but these ideas were radically changed by the New Labour Party led by Blair. Clause Four has been abolished. Many existing public services have been privatised or opened to public/private partnerships. Considerable restrictions have been placed upon trade union activity and the older forms of collective bargaining.

This new social order adopts a new language, shared with many other European countries, which talks about social exclusion. It is recognised that the new economic and social order does not automatically include all individuals and special policies have to be devised to overcome those who are excluded. This is the most comprehensive language within which all problems of disadvantage and discrimination are to be discussed and the position of ethnic minorities has to be set within this framework.

The British sense of nationhood rested in the nineteenth and first part of the twentieth century on the fact that Britain was an imperial power. It was also independent of control by any other European nation and within it the various sub-nationalities, the Welsh, The Scots and the Northern Irish were subject to the rule of a Parliament which operated from Westminster in England. All of these elements are now undergoing change. The empire no longer exists: the so-called United Kingdom is subject to various forms of control by the European Union. Policies of devolution have passed power from Westminster to Wales, Scotland and Northern Ireland[12]. There are many respects in which these subordinate sub-nations also have a distinct culture. For the first time the English have had to consider whether they should have a separate culture and identity.

There is now considerable argument over how far the Westminster government should control the assemblies in Scotland Ireland and Wales and, so far as Europe is concerned, there is a division between those who favour the surrender of power to Europe and those who resist it (commonly referred to as Europhiles and Eurosceptics).

One general question which remains is that of how far the British or English sense of nationhood includes ethnic minorities as British. The reply to this must be very complex. Clearly those who have designed the ethnic question for the census assume that the difference between Whites and the ethnic minorities is a significant one. The advertising industry and the visual media increasingly represent the typical British as including people with different physical and cultural appearance. To treat ethnic minority individuals as other than British is also tabooed in much of the quality press. On the other hand the underlying assumption in the popular tabloids seems to be that only White people are really British and they may reflect strong widespread emotional attitudes. There are also different attitudes to the presence of a variety of cultures. Some see these cultures as enriching, others as threatening. Full integration of ethnic minorities would only be achieved if they were accepted as fully part of the British nation and their cultural differences were celebrated as enriching. This is a separate question from that which has been dealt with at length in earlier parts of this chapter of the degree to which different minorities suffer disadvantage and discrimination.

All these attitudes seemed to be affected at the end of the year 2001 by two issues in the public mind. One was the fear of terrorism and the fact that some of those arrested because of their alleged connection with the Al Quaeda

---

[12]In the case of Northern Ireland this process is delayed by the fact that after years of civil war devolved power depends upon the maintenance of a "peace process". Involving the parties in Northern Ireland, relations with the Irish Republic in Ireland and a Council of the Islands involving other parts of Britain.

network lived in British cities with large immigrant communities. The other was the fact that there had been disturbances, riots and an increased vote for racist parties in cities with predominantly Asian minority populations. The government has responded by emphasising the dangers of segregation and the importance of training in the English language and English citizenship, while local minority leaders have alleged that this draws attention away from the real problems of racial discrimination and disadvantage. The attitudes of members of government, politicians and ethnic minorities are all in a very volatile state. We cannot say what the outcome of this will be. The optimistic view is that a longer-term trend towards integration, incorporation or assimilation will predominate and that the present highly charged political situation is essentially temporary. The more pessimistic view is that we are entering a period of increasing polarisation and ethnic conflict.

References

Advisory Group on Citizenship (Chairman B. Crick) 1998:

Education for Citizenship and the Teaching of Democracy in Schools: Final Report, London: Qualifications and Curriculum Authority

Barry, B. 1999:

Culture and Equality: An Egalitarian Critique of Multiculturalism, Cambridge: Polity Press

Bernstein, B. 1961:

'Social Class and Linguistic Development : A Theory of Social Learning', in Halsey, A., Floud, J., and Anderson, C. (eds.), *Education, Economy and Society*, pp. 288-314, Glencoe (Illinois): Free Press

Beveridge, W. 1942:

Social Insurance and Allied Services (The Beveridge Report), London Cmnd 6405

Brookes, D. / Singh, K. 1979:

'Ethnic Commitment versus Structural Reality: South Asian Immigrant Workers in Britain', *New Community*, Vol VII, 1, London: Commission for Racial Equality

Brown, C. 1982:

Black and White Britain, London: Policy Studies Institute

Daniel, W.W. 1966:

Racial Discrimination in England, London: Political and Economic Planning

Department of Education and Science 1981:

West Indian Children in Our Schools, Interim Report of the Committee of Enquiry into the Education of Children from Minority Groups (Chairman Mr Anthony Rampton), Cmnd 8273, London: HMSO

Department of Education and Science 1985:

Education for All, Report of the Committee of Enquiry into the Education of Children from Minority Groups (Chairman Lord Swann), Cmnd 9453, London: HMSO

Department of Employment and Productivity 1969:

In Place of Strife : A Policy for Industrial Relations, Cmnd 3888, London: HMSO

Dahya, B. 1974:

'The Nature of Pakistani Ethnicity in Industrial Cities in Britain', in Cohen, A. (ed.), *Urban Ethnicity,* pp. 77-118, London: Tavistock

Kymlicka, W. 1995:

Multicultural Citizenship, Oxford: Oxford University Press

MacPherson, W. 1999:

Stephen Lawrence Inquiry: Repost of an Inquiry by Sir William Mac Pherson of Cluny, 2 volumes (CM 4262-I and II), London: HMSO

Marshall 1951:

Citizenship and Social Class, Cambridge: Cambridge University Press

Modgil, S. / Verma, G. / Mallick, K. / Modgil C. 1986:

Multicultural Education: The Interminable Debate, Brighton: Falmer Press

Modood, T. et al. 1997:

Ethnic Minorities in Britain: Diversity and Disadvantage, London: Policy Studies Institute

Office of Population, Census and Statistics (OPCS) 1991:

Census 1991, London

Parekh, B. 2000:

Rethinking Multiculturalism: Cultural Diversity and Political Theory, Cambridge (Mass.): Harvard University Press

Penn, R. / Perret, J. / Lambert, P. 2000:

Policy Responses to International Migration in Britain since 1945, Annex Volume I to EFFNATIS Project (SOE2-CT97-3055) Final Report, pp. 79-129, Bamberg: european forum for migration studies

Reeves, F. / Chevannes, M. 1981:

'The Underachievement of Rampton', *Multiracial Education,* Vol 10, 1, London/Balham: National Association for Multiracial Education

Rex, J. 1997:

in Sikes, P., and Rivzi F. (eds.), *Research Race and Social Justice in Education: Essays in Honour of Barry Troyna,* Stoke: Trentham Books

Rex, J. / Moore, R. 1967:

Race, Community and Conflict, Oxford: Oxford University Press

Rex, J. / Tomlinson, S. 1979:

Colonial Immigrants in a British City: A Class Analysis, London: Routledge and Kegan Paul

Runnymede Trust 2000:

The Future of Multi-Ethnic Britain: The Parekh Report, London

Smith, D. 1974:

Racial Disadvantage in Britain, London: Political and Economic Planning

Smith D. / Tomlinson S. 1989:

The School Effect: A Study of Multiracial Comprehensives, London: Policy Studies Institute

Stone, M. 1985:

The Education of the Black Child: The Myth of Multicultural Education, London: Fontana Press

Taylor, C. 1994:

'The Politics of Recognition', in Gutmann, A. (ed.), *Multiculturalism: Examining the Politics of Recognition*, pp. 25-73, Princeton: Princeton University Press

Troyna, B. (ed.) 1987:

Racial Equality in Education, London: Tavistock

Verma. G. (ed.) 1989:

Education for All: A Landmark in Pluralism, Brighton: Falmer Press

Weller, P. (ed.) 1993:

Religions in the UK: A Multi-faith Directory, Derby: University of Derby and Interfaith Network

Williams, J. 1967:

'The Younger Generation', Chapter X in Rex and Moore, op.cit. 1967

Willis, P. 1977:

Learning to Labour: How Working Class Kids get Working Class Jobs, Farnborough: Saxon House

Charles Westin / Elena Dingu-Kyrklund

Immigration and Integration of Immigrants and their Descendants: The Swedish Approach

1. Introduction

Sweden has a history of immigration since World War II. The first phase of refugee migration in conjunction with the war was soon replaced in the post-war period with labour migration. This continued uninterruptedly until 1972 when the authorities put a stop to it. It was not until the final years of the labour migration that the authorities started to look into the long-term effects of the past twenty-five years of immigration. Commissions were set up in the late 1960s, policies were drafted and research was gradually established. From the early 1970s through the 1980s migration to Sweden mainly consisted of refugees and their families from countries in the Middle East and Latin America. In the 1990s migration of refugees continued, and like many other countries Sweden accepted a large number of refugees from Bosnia and Kosovo.

The primitive view of assimilation in the 1950s was replaced by a radical multicultural policy in 1975. Sweden was the first European country to take this step. Although the new policy gained international recognition as being foresighted, it never gained full recognition with the domestic public opinion. Sweden has had to contend with an increasingly negative public opinion, the establishment of a racist and neo-Nazi underground, and unsolved problems of discrimination on racial and ethnic grounds. Today the political aims are captured by the terms integration and diversity.

This paper concentrates on two aspects reflecting the Swedish integration policy: the general demography of migrations to Sweden, with special focus on children of international migrants, and policy aspects as they are reflected through legislation. The information contained has been collected through official documents, legislation, national statistics and research reports.

2. Demography

2.1. The National Population

The total registered population of Sweden was 8,861,426 persons on 31st of December 1999. This figure includes Swedish citizens as well as foreign citizens residing permanently in Sweden. The birth rate (the number of births per 1,000 individuals) has decreased dramatically just over a few years. From being exceptionally high in the early 1990s it dropped to 10.1 for 1998, its lowest level since 1809. In 1997 the number of deaths exceeded the number of births for the first time since 1809. This natural decrease of the population has now continued for the third year running. The slight increase of the total population is entirely due to in-migration.

Migration flows for Sweden are given for the years 1995, 1996, 1997 and 1998 in table 1.

Table 1: Migration Flows 1995-1998

	1995			1996			1997			1998		
	in	out	net	in	out	net	in	out	net	in	out	net
Nordic countries	8,760	11,020	-2,260	8,082	12,074	-3,992	8,113	13,965	-5,852	9,854	14,242	-4,388
Rest of Europe	18,956	9,413	9,543	13,370	10,014	3,356	16,264	11,755	4,509	7,782	2,152	5,630
Africa	2,912	934	1,978	2,842	895	1,947	3,050	901	2,149	2,995	809	2,186
North America	2,925	4,132	-1,207	3,325	4,030	-705	3,174	4,505	-1,331	3,627	4,540	-913
South America	1,707	1,168	539	1,614	1,080	534	1,681	1,116	565	1,696	1,011	685
Asia	10,078	3,289	6,789	10,003	3,270	6,733	11,881	3,459	8,422	14,027	3,248	10,779
Oceania	450	750	-300	568	691	-123	536	669	-133	710	662	48
Unidentified	99	3,278	-3,179	91	1,830	-1,739	119	2,173	-2,054	503	2,436	-1,9
TOTAL	45,887	33,984	11,903	39,895	33,884	6,011	44,818	38,543	6,275	49,391	38,518	10,873

Source: Statistics Sweden

The migration to Sweden in 1998 was of 49,391 persons. This continues the trend of a slight increase for the most recent years. In a longer perspective, however, the figures remain lower than for the first half of the 1990s.

Sweden is losing to neighbouring Nordic countries. To a large extent, this is the result of a return migration of labour that came to Sweden within the framework of the common Nordic labour market. The flows back and forth in relation to other European countries consist partly of movements of professionals, students and company officials within the European Union labour market, but mainly it consists of refugees from Bosnia, Macedonia, Croatia and Kosovo, family reunifications and some return migration. Although some refugees are gradually returning to their home countries, family reunions in Sweden account for most of the movements to Sweden. In-migration from Europe (excluding the Nordic countries) is comparatively large, but so is return migration. Immigration from Asia, although increasing, is lower than that for Europe, but so is also return migration, thus leading to a higher net immigration for Asia than for Europe.

2.2. The Immigrant Population

Different classifications of immigrants are used in the Swedish statistics. In recent years the concept of *immigrants* has been criticised that when used in statistics, policy documents and official contexts, it perpetuates an outsider status to people of foreign background who reside permanently in Sweden. Basically two categorisations are employed in the statistics, namely *country of birth* and *citizenship*.

Table 2: Stocks of Foreign Nationals and Foreign Born by Continents and Naturalisation Rate, by 31st of December 1998

Continent	Foreign citizens 1998	Foreign born 1998	Foreign born or/(and) foreign citizens including born in Sweden	Foreign and Sweden born with (an/both) immigrant parent(s)	Naturalised Swedish citizens	Naturalisation rate 1998
Europe	326,095	602,318	666,707	1,216,659	516,797	0.46
Nordic countries	159,717	282,634	324,155	654,845	339,847	0.43
EU 15 - less the Nordic countries	52,177	93,243	102,722	212,454	51,852	0.44
Rest of Europe (-EU 15 & Nordic)	114,201	226,441	239,830	349,360	125,098	0.50
Africa	27,734	52,080	56,291	86,073	27,625	0.47
North America	14,747	23,122	24,833	48,955	10,477	0.36
South America	17,932	49,292	49,691	73,217	31,362	0.64
Asia	100,469	231,094	243,888	334,546	131,835	0.57
Oceania	2,112	2,659	-	4,330	742	0.21
Former Soviet Union	876	7,984	8,014	-	6,011	0.89
Stateless/unknown	9,966	158	2,186	-	60	-
TOTAL	499,931	968,707	1,058,142	1,746,921	731,909	0.75

Source: Statistics Sweden

The total population of *foreign citizens* residing in Sweden was by 31ˢᵗ December 1999 approximately 500,000 or 5.6 percent of the population, which represents a stagnation in comparison to the previous year. This may partly be explained by an increase in the number of naturalisations during 1998 (46,090 as compared to 28,864 in 1997).

When classified by country of birth, the number of foreign-born persons amounted in 1999 to about 969,000 persons or 10.9 percent of the population.

The national origins of the migrant population are given in table 2 by continents. The largest groups are given in table 3. Overall the foreign-born population may be divided into three groups: Nordic (282,634), other European (319,684), and non-European (366,389)[1].

Table 3: Stocks of the Largest Groups of Foreign Nationals and Foreign-Born Respectively; Naturalisation Rate by 31ˢᵗ of December 1998 Compared to Same Period in 1997

Country of citizenship/ birth	Foreign citizens 1997	Foreign citizens 1998	Foreign-born 1997	Foreign-born 1998	Naturalised 1997	Naturalised 1998	Naturalisation rate 1997	Naturalisation rate 1998
Lebanon	3,372	3,503	21,424	20,243	18,052	16,740	0.84	0.83
Ethiopia	3,407	2,894	13,306	13,108	9,899	10,214	0.74	0.78
Germany	14,467	15,124	36,053	37,237	21,586	22,113	0.60	0.59
Poland	15,842	15,925	39,575	39,737	23,733	23,812	0.60	0.60
Yugoslavia	33,568	25,971	70,867	70,876	37,299	42,525	0.53	0.55
Chile	11,860	11,376	26,745	26,615	13,885	15,239	0.52	0.57
Finland	101,333	99,902	201,025	198,848	99,692	98,946	0.50	0.50
Iran	26,238	19,793	49,818	50,252	23,580	30,459	0.47	0.61
Turkey	18,404	17,396	30,642	30,950	12,238	13,554	0.40	0.44
Denmark	25,388	24,962	38,874	38,187	13,486	13,225	0.35	0.35
USA	9,436	9,515	13,974	13,963	4,538	4,448	0.32	0.32
Norway	31,021	30,610	42,734	41,937	11,713	11,327	0.27	0.27
Iraq	24,800	26,600	32,692	37,902	7,892	11,302	0.24	0.30
UK	11,711	12,098	13,339	13,666	1,628	1,568	0.12	0.11
Somalia	13,122	13,450	12,012	12,498	-	-	0	0
Bosnia	54,771	44,461	48,309	49,987	-	-	0	0
All others	135,169	126,351	289,587	272,695	154,418	146,344	-	0.54
TOTAL	522,049	499,931	954,231	968,707	432,182	468,776	0.45	0.48

Source: Statistics Sweden

---

[1] 1998 figures.

The Finns are by far the largest group of immigrants, and Finnish has recently been recognised as a national minority language in Sweden. The Nordic Labour Market Treaty in 1954 and the Nordic Passport Union in the mid-1950s made the free movement of labour between the Nordic countries possible.

The immigrants of (other) European origin broadly consist of two categories, labour migrants (from the 1960s and early 1970s) and refugees. The most numerous group of labour migrants of non-Nordic origin were the Yugoslavs who came in the 1960s. Greeks and Turks also joined the forces of labour migrants. The number of different migrant groups was limited, a factor that had implications for the integration policies.

A third and most inclusive classification includes all foreign-born persons and their children. Looking at the general trends, one should note the number of persons with an immigrant background may be given as about half a million, one million or 1.7 million persons, representing either 5.8 percent, 10.9 percent or 19.7 percent of the total population of Sweden.

Table 4: Official Residents of Sweden According to Background by 31st of December 1999

Country of birth	Number*	Percent
1. Foreign born	969,000	10.9
Residence time in Sweden: 0-4 years	186,000	2.1
5 or more years	779,000	8.8
2. Born in Sweden	7,886,000	89.1
2.1. With two foreign parents	265,000	3.0
2.2. With one Swedish-born and one foreign-born parent	514,000	5.8
2.3. With two Swedish parents	7,107,000	80.3
Total:	8,854,000	100.0
Citizenship	Number	Percent
1. Foreign citizens	500,000	5.6
2. Swedish citizens	8,354,000	80.3
Total:	8,854, 000	100.0
Generic/Comprehensive populations	Number	Percent
1. Persons with immigrant background (Foreign-born + born in Sweden, with two foreign-born parents)	1,233,000	13.9
2. Persons with both Swedish and immigrant background (Born in Sweden with a Swedish-born and a foreign parent)	514,000	5.8
3. Persons with Swedish background (Born in Sweden with two Swedish-born parents)	7,107,000	80.3
Total:	8,854,000	100.0

* Figures presented available in thousands, thus rounded

Source: Statistics Sweden/Åke Nilsson: 'Invandrare – 500 000 eller 1,7 millioner?' ("Immigrants – 500 000 or 1.7 millions?"), *Välfärds Bulletinen* Nr.4 1999

Refugee waves date back to World War II with large numbers of refugees from neighbouring countries (see table 5). About 45,000 refugees from the German concentration camps also came to Sweden at the end of World War II. Conflicts and political persecution linked to the uprisings in Hungary and following the Prague Spring led to a relatively large number of refugees from these countries. Wars and oppression in non-European countries (Eritrea, Iran, Iraq, Chile etc.) brought a large number of refugees to Sweden.

The largest flow of asylum seekers to be accepted since World War II fled from Bosnia in the 1990s. The numbers were so large that the government introduced visa requirements for Bosnians and other peoples coming from ex-Yugoslavia in 1993.

Non-European immigration is linked to conflicts in various parts of the world. The most important groups are from Chile and countries in the Middle East (most notably minority groups such as Kurds and Assyrians/Syrians), groups that established themselves in Sweden in the 1970s. Chain migration processes have continued since then. In the 1980s, Iranians became one of the largest refugee groups. Iraqis, many of whom are Kurds, have become an increasingly important refugee group during the 1990s. From the African continent Eritreans and Somalis are the principal groups.

The social origins of the migrants in their native countries are very different. The labour migrants from the 1960s and early 1970s were clearly of working class background and, in the case of Finland, even of rural background. Later refugee migrants have rather mixed social backgrounds. Many tend to belong to the well-educated strata of the sending society, in some cases with clear links to labour unions and radical political organisations. A large share of the Latin American and Iranian refugees had university training. Refugees from Turkey on the other hand don't tend to have academic backgrounds. The Assyrians/Syrians are a clear example of an entrepreneurial middleman minority with their economic base in small business, trades and crafts.

There is a wide range of birth rates for different nationalities, from high figures for migrants from Somalia and Iraq, and the extremely low figures for Chilean migrants. The exceptionally high rate for Somalia relates to cultural attitudes to family structure, gender, birth control and sexuality predominant in Somalia, attitudes that migrants from Somalia have not basically changed. Another factor is of course the age structures of the groups concerned, which in turn relates to the period in time during which the group primarily established itself in Sweden. The exceptionally low rate for Chilean citizens reflects an increasing naturalisation among young persons of Chilean origin (see table 3). The low figure for Chileans could also reflect a gradual "return" migration of young Chilean citizens since the amnesty was issued.

Table 5: Major Influxes of Refugees in Sweden

1939-1945 About 122,000 Nordic refugees	About 60,000 Finnish child evacuees, plus 18,300 Danes and 43,000 Norwegians
1944-45 About 35,000 Baltic nationals	During the final years of the Second World War
1945-1949 About 45,000 refugees	From concentration camps in Germany
1956 and the 1970s and 80s About 15,000 Hungarians	The 1956 uprising and political persecutions during the 70s and 80s
1968 and the 1970s and 80s About 6,000 Czechs	The 1968 Prague invasion, political persecutions in the 70s and 80s
The 1970s About 11,000 Eritreans*	War in Eritrea since the end of the 1970s
The 1970s About 20,000 Kurds	War, oppression and genocide in Turkey, Iran, Iraq and Syria since the beginning of the 1970s
1973 - present About 25,000 Chileans	Following the 1973 military coup
The 1970s About 10,000 other Latin Americans	Political persecution in various countries of South America
1975 - present 20,000 Assyrians and Syrians*	Conflicts between Christians and Moslems in Turkey and the Middle East, emigration from 1975 onwards
The end of the 1970s 9,000 "Vietnam Chinese"	Persecution of boat refugees
1979 - present About 40,000 Iranians	Following the Iranian revolution of 1979 and the war between Iran and Iraq
The 1980s and 90s About 25,000 Iraqis	Oppression in the 1980s and 90s
The 1980s 13,000 Palestinians	War in Lebanon
The 1980s and 90s 9,000 Somalis	War in Somalia and Ethiopia
The 1950s, 60s and 90s About 93,000 from the former Yugoslavia	Yugoslavs, Bosnians and refugees from the Federal Republic of Yugoslavia etc.

* Number uncertain, due to immigrants' in Sweden not being registered by ethnic identity

Source: The Swedish Immigration Authority – *Statens invandrarverk*, SIV– September 1999

Table 6: Birth Rates for Foreign Citizens Residing in Sweden, 1997[2]

Country of citizenship	Population	Number of births	Birth rate per thousand
Somalia	13,122	429	32.7
Iraq	24,800	732	29.5
Ethiopia	3,407	67	19.7
Turkey	18,404	347	18.8
Yugoslavia	33,568	567	16.9
Bosnia-Herzegovina	54,771	690	12.6
Norway	31,021	364	120
Denmark	25,388	276	11.7
Finland	103,333	1,013	9.8
Poland	15,842	154	9.7
Germany	14,467	135	9.3
Iran	26,238	219	8.3
UK	11,711	65	5.5
USA	9,436	37	3.9
Chile	11,860	12	1.0

Source: Statistics Sweden

The authorities closely monitor the population of Sweden. Although it may be possible to live outside the confines of society, it is extremely difficult to do so in actual practice. Illegal immigrants exist. An increasing number of peddlers, street musicians and prostitutes from Russia and other parts of Eastern Europe have found their way to Sweden. They lack residence and work permits. Another category of illegal aliens is persons who have been denied asylum and who escape into hiding. A third category is people who enter the country on regular tourist visas and overstay their visit. It is difficult to assess the number of illegal aliens. Official assessments of the number of denied asylum applicants in hiding and of permanent residence permits issued on false grounds are in the range of 5,000 persons. It is generally assumed that the real figures are higher. Illegal immigrants and their children are not entitled to any social rights. Their children are not entitled to schooling. There are no economic or social benefits for them. Authorities are expected to report illegal migrants to the police.

---

[2] Birth rate is defined as the number of births per thousand of the population. The birth rate for Swedish citizens was 10.2 for 1997. The figures for 1998 were still not available to us by the time the final revision of this work was completed.

Medical care in cases of severe emergency is the only right an illegal immigrant has. Even then the immigration authorities will intervene in order to locate the whereabouts of the person or family in question.

Table 7: Residence Permits Issued 1994-1999, by Categories

	Family reunion	Refugees	Labour	Student	Adopted children	EEA/ EU Treaty	Other	Total
1994	25,975	44,875	127	1,086	884	6,040		78,987
	32.9	56.8	0.2	1.4	1.1	5.9		
1995	19,707	5,642	190	1,504	794	4,649		32,486
	60.7	17.4	0.6	4.6	2.4	14.3		
1996	18,816	4,832	274	1,771	807	5,184		31,664
	59.5	15.2	0.9	5.6	2.6	16.3		
1997	18,910	9,596	433	2,376	694	4,556	49	36,565
	51.7	26.2	1.2	6.5	1.9	12.4	0.1	
1998	21,673	8,193	363	2,665	804	5,735		39,433
	55.0	20.8	1.0	6.7	2.0	14.5		
1999	21,744	5,582	6,166	2,866	914	6,183		43,455
	50.0	12.9	14.2	6.6	2.1	14.2		

Source: National Board of Immigration

Table 7 shows the current proportion of residence permits issued. Family reunification has been the main reason for granting residence permits. Labour has not been a significant category in the immigration statistics until 1999, reflecting the current upturn of the economy. The EEA/ EU treaty represents mostly a sector of professionals. Although an average of five thousand persons have moved to Sweden since it came into force, a slightly larger number have left Sweden at the same time.

	1970	1980	1990	1997	1998
Live births	110,150	97,064	123,940	90,383	89,028
Deaths	80,026	91,800	95,161	93,278	93,271
Immigrants	77,326	39,426	60,048	44,872	49,391
Emigrants	28,653	29,839	25,196	39,074	39,518
Increase of population	79,034	14,769	63,583	2,903	6,697*

*Increase of population 1998 is the difference between 31 December 1998 and 31 December 1997

Source: Statistics Sweden

Table 9: Preliminary Population Changes During 1998 Compared to 1997

	Jan-Nov 1997	Jan-Nov 1998
Population by period's end	8,848,728	8,855,524
Population increase	+4,229	+7,899
Population surplus by birth	-1,040	-1,773
– Live birth	84,200	82,754
– Deaths	85,240	84,527
Immigration surplus	5,584	+9,589
– Immigrants	42,159	45,522
– Emigrants	36,575	35,933
Adjustments	-315	+83

Source: Statistics Sweden

Children of international migrants 0-19 years old totalled 503,705 persons in 1998. A total of 126,151 or 25 per cent of the international migrant children of were foreign citizens in 1998. By the end of 1998, a majority of the children of international migrants i.e. 373,080 persons or 74 per cent out of a total of 503,705 were born in Sweden. That also implies that 377,554 or 75 per cent of the total amount of children of international migrants between 0-19 years of age were Swedish citizens by the end of 1998. This is in accordance with the intentions of Swedish integration policy. Although citizenship follows the principle of *ius sanguinis* Sweden, has encouraged permanent settlers to naturalise. For this reason, requirements to get Swedish citizenship are comparatively liberal by European standards. Citizenship is recognised as a principal means of incorporation into society, especially important for children of international migrants born in the country.

3. Policies Towards Immigrants

3.1. General Policy Objectives

The main objectives of Swedish integration policies are *equality, freedom of choice* and *partnership* (Westin/Dingu-Kyrklund 1997).

Equality is the central objective. Immigrants, including children of international migrants, are to enjoy the same social, educational, cultural, and in a restricted extent, political rights as native-born Swedish citizens (Hammar 1985, Ålund/Schierup 1991, Westin 1996).

The *freedom of choice* clause implies that individuals have the right to identify culturally and ethnically as they wish. This is an *individual* right, not a *collective* right. Sweden is not prepared to recognise ethnic or cultural minority communities resulting from immigration, but Sweden does accept and respect ethnic and cultural rights to identification. Freedom of choice may be seen as a parallel to the freedom of religion. It is something belonging to the private sphere. It implies that specific measures need to complement the general rights following from the equality clause. Specific measures apply in particular to language training, educational programmes, naturalisation rules and anti-discrimination legislation.

The *partnership* clause seeks to encourage participation and interaction with Swedish political institutions and organisations at all levels. Integration policy aims to incorporate immigrants into the polity. Taken together, these clauses represent a specific Swedish brand of the divide and rule strategy – extend cultural rights to the immigrants, but only on condition that they organise their affairs according to accepted Swedish principles, i.e. adapt to the host society's requirements. There is no contradiction in accepting the individual right to ethnic and cultural identification on the one hand and a policy of inclusion in the polity on the other.

Sweden encourages naturalisation as an essential vehicle for full participation in society. Nordic citizens only need to have two years of residence in the country to be eligible for Swedish citizenship. Other nationalities have to fulfil five years of permanent residence. Even persons whose identity is not possible to establish beyond doubt are entitled to apply. No requirements of language proficiency or knowledge of the country's history or political institutions apply. However a good conduct clause implies that applications are rejected if the applicant has been sentenced for criminal offences or found guilty for certain misdemeanours. In order to encourage naturalisations the acceptance of dual citizenship is being considered.

In the following pages, the Swedish citizenship policy is outlined in some detail as it is codified in the Swedish Citizenship Act.

3.2. Nationality Law and Citizenship

The main law regulating citizenship is the *Swedish Citizenship Act* (1989, 529), recently revised, and the *Citizenship Ordinance* (1989, 547). In principle Swedish legislation does not distinguish between Swedish and foreign citizens. There are some specific exceptions. Swedish citizenship is based on *ius sanguinis*. Citizenship cannot be acquired automatically by residing in the country though the time of effective residence in the country is an important element in the naturalisation procedure. Citizenship may be acquired. Table 10 shows 6.6 percent of the population have naturalised.

Table 10: A Typology of Inclusion in the Swedish State, Population 1999

Not included	Foreign-born	Born in Sweden	Total
Permanently residing foreign citizens	400,085 4.5%	87,090 1.0%	487,175 5.5%
Swedish citizens	581,548 6.6%	7,792,703 87.9%	8,374,251 94.5%
Total	981,633 11.1%	7,879,793 88.9%	8,861,426

Of the 581,548 persons 61,036 are in the age brackets 0-18 years of age, that is children who are born in another country and who have received Swedish citizenship through their parents naturalising.

Persons acquire Swedish citizenship automatically

▶ *through birth* through the mother's citizenship i.e. when she is a Swedish citizen;

▶ *through adoption* of a child under 12 years of age by a Swedish citizen;

▶ *through legitimisation*: An unmarried child under 18 years of age is granted Swedish citizenship when the child's mother marries the child's father who is a Swedish citizen;

▶ as *a dependent to a parent becoming a Swedish citizen*: An unmarried child under the age of 18 acquires Swedish citizenship when the child's parent(s) becomes a Swedish citizen(s) and the child is domiciled in Sweden.

A foreigner may acquire Swedish citizenship through naturalisation, if s/he is 18 years of age, has been domiciled in Sweden for five years (two for Nordic citizens), and fulfils the good conduct requirement. The National Board of Immigration has a discretionary right to decide. Becoming a Swedish citizen is not a guaranteed right, even if the requirements are met. Naturalisation can also be granted as a matter of exception from the conditions above if it is considered to benefit the country if the applicant becomes a Swedish citizen as for instance in the case of some sportsmen. There are some other exceptions. But they hardly come into consideration.

3.3. The Educational System and Integration

Since practically all children of international migrants either attend day nurseries, pre-school, compulsory school or upper secondary school, it is essential to analyse the educational system in some detail.

The educational system is society's principal instrument of socialisation and thus the most essential tool for integration of children of international migrants. Swedish language courses are considered an important part of the basic introduction programme for migrants. It is a two-year programme during which migrants are expected to learn Swedish and then either continue labour market training or apply directly for a job. Throughout this period of time, migrants will receive economic support meant to cover all expenses, from rent and transportation to living expenses for the entire family.

All immigrants are entitled to receive free instruction in the Swedish language. In practice, however, *children have more extended rights than adults*. Children of international migrants are required to study the Swedish language with the aim of reaching the same proficiency as their native-born peers. They are entitled to receive intensive special classes in Swedish, but they are also entitled to study their mother tongue. This is a right that only applies to immigrant children as a means to maintain their cultural heritage. It should be mentioned that Sweden has recently recognised the existence of *five minority languages*, – Finnish, Meänkieli (Tornedal-Finnish), Saami, Yiddish and Romani, conferring a special status to the respective groups and granting them increased rights to language education.

The Swedish model of encouraging bilingualism, providing children of international migrants with specific classes in their mother tongue as well as Swedish language training has its roots in domestic experiences and in internationally adopted guidelines. In 1953, UNESCO underlined the importance of providing children with basic education in their mother tongue in order to benefit from the educational process. Children of international migrants are entitled to mother tongue instruction throughout the first seven years of elementary school. The only real requirement is that the language is used as a communication means at home, that there are at least five applicants applying for mother tongue instruction in the same language and the local municipality is in a position to grant the requirement.

As early as in the 1960s it had become clear that school results for pupils having a language of instruction other than their mother tongue were closely related to their degree of linguistic competence. This observation applied both to children of international migrants as well as to children of ethno-linguistic minorities (Saami and Meänkieli/Tornedal-Finnish). Studies conducted by linguists and educationalists showed that children of international migrants often had notable difficulties to cope with the requirements of the school curriculum

117

when having only received a brief introductory course in Swedish (Hyltenstam 1996, 31). An insufficient knowledge of the mother tongue proved to hamper the ability of these children to learn a second language properly, with the double disadvantage of not having a thorough command of any of them. The problem has been discussed from various points of view by a number of scholars. Malmberg (1964) drew attention to the inadequacy of the official approach on minority languages and its socio-political implications. Hansegård's study (1968) raised the question of the risks occasioned by an insufficient command of two languages as basic communication means. He introduced the concept of "semi-lingualism", a controversial concept that is still debated to this day. Spokesmen for minority language education see semi-lingualism as one of the most serious threats to international migrants and most specifically to their children.

Immigrant children began to receive some instruction in their mother tongue gradually from the early 1960s. As from 1966, the local administrative authorities started to receive state support for providing foreign children special classes in Swedish as a second language and to provide counselling in their mother tongue, a recommendation which was expanded to cover all children of international migrants in 1968. However, municipalities were not obliged to comply with these requests until the so-called home-language reform made it compulsory. In 1969 the municipalities were required to assess the number of pupils having other mother tongues than Swedish as well as their need and willingness to participate in special tuition in Swedish and their respective mother tongue (Hyltenstam/Tuomela 1996, 44). These structures were broadly preserved over time, with some variations as regarding the extent of the obligation to provide such classes and the limitations of these rights.

A good command of one's mother tongue is normally a prerequisite for preserving one's cultural, ethnic and personal identity, functioning as an important communication and relation factor among kin. On the other hand, a comparable command of the language of the new country is a must for a young person who will need to be admitted as a student at various levels of education, and afterwards to find employment in an increasingly competitive society with higher rates of unemployment than before.

With the so-called home-language reform enforced as from July 1st 1977, the obligation to organise these classes meant that the municipalities were required to estimate the extent of the need, plan and reserve the necessary resources required, organise and inform those concerned on the possibility to ask – and have a say in how these classes were to be organised. Until 1985, the unconditional right to benefit from these classes was only limited to pupils whose mother tongue was spoken within the family, which may imply varying levels in their language proficiency (Hyltenstam/Tuomela 1996, 46). After 1985 this right was limited according to a new definition, which meant that only pupils having at least one foreign parent who uses that language as a means of communication with the child on a daily basis were entitled to classes in that mother tongue. Only children speaking 'traditional' minority languages i.e. Saami, Finnish, Meänkieli (Tornedal-Finnish), Yiddish or Romany as well as foreign adoptees were exempted from this condition (ibid.).

By the end of 1997 there were 3,406 schools with pupils entitled to special classes in their mother tongue and Swedish as a second language. However, only 2,287 schools had pupils who took part in such instruction with a total of 62,100 participants in mother tongue classes, and 59,930 participating in Swedish classes. The ten main languages groups receiving special mother tongue instruction are: Albanian, Arabic, Bosnian /Serbian/Croatian, English, Finnish, Kurdish, Persian, Polish, Spanish and Turkish. Another 110 languages are taught. Most of these classes are taught in regular elementary schools. They are integrated into or appended to the normal curriculum.

There are a number of independent schools, established since 1991, with a certain ethnic language profile. Most of these are Swedish-Finnish and very few others provide a curriculum directly associated with children of international migrants.

It is commonly assumed that students of immigrant origin do less well in the educational system than Swedes. Data published by the National Board of Education from 1996/97 supports this view. Table 11 shows that average grades for students of foreign origin are significantly below the national average. Male students in general have lower grades than female students, and this applies as well to students of foreign origin. Thus male students of foreign origin have the lowest average grades after having completed nine years of compulsory school.

Table 11: Grades for 9th Year of Compulsory School 1996/97

	All students	Male	Female	Students of foreign origin	Male	Female
Total	96,866	49,492	47,374	13,763	7,069	6,694
Average grade*	3.25	3.1	3.41	3.06	2.94	3.19

*Grades 1 (lowest) to 5 (highest)

Source: National Board of Education

Table 12 shows the same trend that students of foreign origin are significantly behind the average levels, and what perhaps is even more important, that foreign students are massively over-represented among students with incomplete grades. Frequent absence from school is one factor that explains this situation.

119

Table 12: Final Grades for Students from 9th Year of Compulsory School 1996/97

	All students	Thereof students of foreign origin	Students with complete grades	Thereof students of foreign origin	Students with incomplete grades	Thereof students of foreign origin
Total number	97,399	14,013	91,519	11,541	5,347	2,222
Average grade*	3.25	3.06	3.30	3.17	2.40	2.50

*Grades 1 (lowest) to 5 (highest)

Source: National Board of Education

Upper secondary school (the gymnasium) is not compulsory, but a majority of all youth attend educational programmes within this level, either theoretical or vocational. Table 11 shows that students of foreign origin are below average on the distribution of grades (4 alternatives) for three subjects that are taught in all programmes and courses: Swedish grammar, Swedish literature and English.

However, the evidence is inconclusive. Quite a few studies show on the contrary that certain groups of students of immigrant origin do quite well in the school system and are on the whole not worse off than Swedes as far as school achievements are concerned. It is clear that many are ambitious, and that parents place a high value on education. Olkiewicz (1990) found this in a study of children of international labour migrants in the 1980s. The data collected by Virta and Westin (1999) on more recent arrivals support the same conclusion. A good education is regarded as a passport to better jobs and a means to ascertain social mobility for the next generation. A methodological problem is one of doing the correct comparisons. Virta and Westin compared students of migrant origins with Swedish students in the same form. When controlling for social class, students of Turkish, Kurdish and Chilean origin came out on top in comparisons with Swedish and Finnish students. However, if students of migrant origins were to be compared with Swedish students from more homogeneously middle-class neighbourhoods the outcome was different.

A follow-up study from 1995 (Arvemo-Nostrand/Theorin 1996) concluded that 25 percent of the persons with an immigrant origin hadn't completed any other form of education after seven years of elementary school. By comparison, the same figure amounted to 16 percent for the youth in the Swedish-born group. The relative unemployment among immigrant youth was 26 percent, as compared to 16 percent in the control group. Also, the possibility of getting a job in the field they were educated for was 10 percent lower for the immigrant group. Also, among the low-educated unemployed youth with an im-grant background, a majority considered their chances to get a (steady) job within the next five years as low, while those having completed high school were more optimistic.

By way of conclusion, young people of migrant origin have the same rate of participation in school up until lower secondary school. There is a certain over-representation of ethnic minority and migrant students leaving school without complete grades after the ninth compulsory year. Since grades are not given until the 9th year performance is not possible to establish before the age of 16 through broad surveys. The overall evidence points to lower achievement in terms of lower average grades for ethnic minority and immigrant students as compared to majority students. The same trend is evident for students of upper secondary school.

It is hard to determine whether discrimination exists when it comes to access to schooling and education. There is no evidence of hard, systematic discrimination, but we cannot rule out that subtle forms of discrimination can be at work in the classroom. Students of immigrant and minority background may do well at school and be highly competitive. On the other hand there is also evidence of an over-representation of early school dropouts among students of migrant and minority origin.

3.4. Employment and Occupation

Working rights are limited to permanent residents in Sweden with the exception of Nordic and EU/EEA-citizens, for whom special rules apply. This is due to the reciprocal freedom of movement of workers. Permanent residents have an unlimited legal right to work in Sweden, with exception of a few classified jobs that require Swedish citizenship. The Swedish Constitution states in ch.11 § 9 that Swedish citizenship is required for holding a position as a judge, as a civil servant directly subordinated to the government or as a being a member of an authority directly subordinated to Parliament or the government. These cases relate to The National Secrecy Act stating the limits of access to classified information for national security reasons. EU/EEA-citizens have the right to work in Sweden for three months without any permit, but they need a residence permit (no work permit) in order to work for a longer period of time. For all other resident aliens entitled to work the same limited restrictions apply as above. No comprehensive list exists of public positions only accessible to Swedish citizens.

The migrant population as a whole has serious problems of finding jobs that correspond to their qualifications. Unemployment rates are exceptionally high, especially for non-European migrants – even among the Iranians, a group which in general is highly qualified in terms of academic degrees –, and for recently arrived refugees from ex-Yugoslavia. The unemployment rate for Somalis is well above 75 per cent. Refugees with academic qualifications can very rarely find jobs according to their skills. It is a fact that all too many children of international migrants grow up with at least one parent constantly unemployed.

Various studies indicate that immigrants are more likely to be hit by unemployment than other groups. At the same time entering the labour market is considered an important step in the process of integration. Special forms of support for integration on the labour market have been developed recently. An example is "trainee positions for immigrants" where the state subsidises employment of immigrants for a limited period of time, in order to give them the opportunity to come into direct contact with the Swedish labour market and its demands. For resident asylum-seekers, a two-year "introduction programme" is designed in co-operation with the labour market authorities. It includes Swedish language training, various vocational programmes and a plan to find effective employment.

To our knowledge, there does not exist any data on qualification and occupation by national or ethnic origin for children of international migrants. Ethnicity or "race" are not registered officially or statistically. However, the Discrimination Ombudsman has recently advocated that such a classification may be justified as a first step to demand a certain positive discrimination in favour of immigrants on the labour market. The proposal has provoked a variety of reactions, both sceptical and enthusiastic. The final result is still to be expected[3].

A study from 1998 regarding foreign citizens on the labour market notes that the situation for foreign citizens of non-European origin remains most problematic. Non-Nordic citizens in general have a lower degree of occupation, a higher degree of unemployment, poorer working environment and they suffer more frequently health from problems than average Swedish citizens. Persons coming from Eastern Europe and countries outside Europe have the weakest position on the labour market. For these groups more than a third of those registered in the labour force were unemployed during the second half of 1997. A partial explanation of their weak position is their weak educational background. More than 40 percent of the non-Nordic citizens registered with the unemployment offices have barely completed secondary education. However, there is a great variation between the different sub-groups.

---

[3] Statistics on qualification and occupation of children of international migrants can be ordered from the National Bureau of Statistics – Statistics Sweden.

Table 13: Swedish and Foreign Citizens in the Labour Force Respectively Unemployed in Sweden in 1998, in Thousands

| | Swedish citizens | | Foreign citizens | |
	Natives	Naturalised	Non-Nordic	Nordic
Population*	4,765	494	252	120
% in the labour force**	77.7	67.0	52.0	70.0
Degree of occupation**	73.2	59.1	37.3	63.6
Unemployment***	5.7	11.8	28.3	9.3

* in 1000 ** per cent of the total population *** per cent of the labour force

Source: SCB/Red. G. Lindberg – Tema 'Utländska medborgare i arbetslivet' ("Foreign citizens on the labour market"), *Arbetslivsfakta* Nr.2, Sept.1998

Insufficient command of Swedish among non-Nordic citizens may also explain high unemployment rates. The quality of Swedish language courses for (adult) immigrants needs to be improved. Statistics confirm that less than half of those having started language classes during 1993/94 had completed the course after two years. However, a rather large proportion of the non-Nordic citizens do have a good formal education level. More than 16 percent of those registered with the unemployment agency have university education, as compared to less than 12 percent of the Swedish citizens. Almost 30 percent have a longer high-school education, as compared to 23 percent of the Swedish citizens. Normally, a higher education is more likely to lead to employment. However, as a rule Swedes stand much better chances to getting employed. A good command of Swedish is obviously an important requirement for white-collar jobs. Yet this does not exclude that manifest and subtle forms of ethnic discrimination also explain the differences in position on the labour market. There is a clear relationship between the time a person has resided in Sweden and the level of unemployment. A longer presence in the country improves one's chances on the labour market.

Formal equal opportunities are a necessary but obviously not sufficient condition for equity as far as employment is concerned. Much stronger corrective measures are required in order to bring about equal opportunities for all residents. Many immigrant women have a low participation in employment. Quite a few are housewives. Others are studying. African and Asian women are least involved on the labour market. To break the negative trend of social exclusion hitting the children of international migrants it is particularly important to take the necessary measures to increase immigrant women's participation in the labour market.

There are differences in the preferences to work in certain sectors of activity among migrant groups. Non-Nordic citizens are over-represented in the service sector (hotels and restaurants or personal service) while Nordic citizens are over-represented in the industrial sector. The weaker position of non-Nordic citizens is also obvious in the higher amount of temporary employments and, especially when women are concerned, more part-time jobs.

Normally compulsory school attendance starts the year that the child is seven, or at the age of six on demand. All children have the right to attend pre-school forms from the age of five. Compulsory school duration is nine years. It is almost inevitable to attend another two to three years of theoretical or vocational studies (75 per cent of all 16-18 year old in 1996). This means that about 25 per cent of this age group actually participates on a regular basis in the labour market. The age of majority in Sweden is 18 years.

Table 14: Total Working Population 1998 by Gender and Age, in Thousands, and for Comparison Unemployment and Participation Indices for 1995

Age	Gender	Employed (1)	Unem- ployed (2)	Non work force (3)	Total po- pulation (4)	Unemploy- ment index (2) by (1)+(2)		Participation index (1) by (4)	
		1998	1998	1998	1998	1995	1998	1995	1998
16-24	M	205	30	248	483	16.7	12.9	41.8	42.4
	F	188	23	251	462	13.9	10.7	43.0	40.7
	M+F	393	53	499	945	15.3	11.9	42.4	41.6
25-54	M	1,571	101	211	1,883	7.2	6.0	84.1	83.4
	F	1,433	86	294	1,813	5.9	5.6	81.1	79.1
	M+F	3,004	187	505	3,696	6.6	5.8	82.6	81.3
55-64	M	303	23	135	461	8.4	7.0	64.4	65.8
	F	279	14	170	463	6.2	4.7	59.3	60.3
	M+F	582	37	305	924	7.4	5.9	61.9	63.0

Sources: AKU 1995 and 1998

The unemployment rate for the 16-24 years old participating in the labour market was 12 per cent for 1998. This compares with 6 per cent for 25-54 year old. For children of international migrants, the overall unemployment rates are considerably higher (over 25 percent, and in the range of 40-50 per cent for some ethnic groups).

The data given in table 14 show that the overall rate of unemployment has decreased since 1995. The principal explanation is a global upturn in the economy which ultimately also affects the Swedish labour market. Secondly, the government has managed to reorganise and restore the public finances to a sounder basis through drastic cuts in public expenses. This has affected work-ing conditions in public health care and schools negatively and the final analysis of the restoration policy is yet to come. Thirdly, the reduction of the unemployment rates is explained to some extent by demographic changes. The number of persons aged 16-24 is lower for 1998 than it was for 1995. Competition for available jobs is less stiff because there are more jobs going as well as fewer competitors. On the other hand, the number of persons aged 55-64 has increased. These demographic trends interact with the upturn of the economy. Fewer people on their way out of the labour market have had to be laid off before retirement because of the better times. Participation in the work force has increased for the 55-64 age bracket but decreased slightly for the 16-24 and 25-54 age brackets.

The issue of discrimination on the labour market in Sweden appears to be more about subjective factors than about legal provisions (discriminatory laws, regulations and rules). A problem that has been discussed is whether and to what extent applicants for certain positions may have been sorted out by prospective employers in the preliminary phase of selecting new staff members, because of their non-Swedish name, or consequent to an interview, showing that the applicant had a 'deviant' skin colour. Discrimination of any kind is prohibited by law. Its occurrence, though, is generally understood to be the main cause for higher unemployment rates among immigrants than for native-born Swedes. In 1990 a commission evaluated the measures against ethnic discrimination, among other things the Law against Ethnic Discrimination adopted in 1986. The office of the Ombudsman against ethnic discrimination was originally set up in 1987, with an explicit function to take action against manifestations of ethnic discrimination on the labour market. On the basis of these experiences a revised law against ethnic discrimination was adopted in 1994. Its impact on discriminatory practices in the labour market has been questioned, as it proved to be rather toothless. Only one single case invoking this law was tried in Court. After evaluation by a second commission the law was replaced with a new law coming in to force in May 1999.

3.5. Social Policy

Once granted a resident status, aliens benefit from the same rights as citizens. This is the basis on which social rights are established. The main principle for granting social rights to a person is the domicile principle. There is no difference whatsoever between social rights of international migrants and their children and Swedish nationals. Consequently, there are no specific provisions regarding children of international migrants, besides special classes in Swedish and their mother tongue.

On the other hand, many immigrants may remain relatively isolated from the core of the Swedish society, not in the least due to language problems, but also due to social and physical barriers with a growing segregation tendency. Initia-

125

tives to counteract these effects are rather undeveloped. A recent programme involving a dozen municipalities all over Sweden, aims at giving elderly immigrants the possibility to meet and receive information from a visiting Swedish team. An initiative from the city council of Gothenburg was to pay for dinner at a local restaurant if a Swede and a person of immigrant origin go out together.

In a survey published in 1989, one fourth of the beneficiaries of social welfare were foreign born. This is a considerable over-representation. The trend is evident for all age groups. Obviously, such a situation is bound to have a negative influence on all members of the family.

A report published in 1997 shows that of the refugees who were resettled in 1991, 74 per cent were dependent upon social welfare as late as 1995. Despite of the upturn of the economy over the last few years, there is still not any substantial decrease of the unemployment rates for persons of foreign origin. They continue to depend upon social welfare to a much larger extent than ethnic Swedish citizens. It may still be premature to establish that the migrant population is on its way to form a new underclass in society. But if things don't radically change in the near future, there is a definite risk that a new class structure based on ethnic and racial criteria is in the making.

3.6. Housing

A large proportion of international migrants of various ethnic backgrounds grow up in segregated neighbourhoods within the major cities, with few job opportunities, relatively high rates of criminality and higher social welfare dependency than for the majority population. These neighbourhoods present a multi-ethnic structure with a striking absence of Swedes in the most segregated areas. Characteristically, these housing areas are situated on the outskirts of the city, not as in many European and American cities, in the inner city areas.

There is no comprehensive housing policy directly applying to immigrants (Lange 1991). In practice, however, discrimination arises. Indirect discrimination based on ethnic and racial criteria leading to segregation on the housing market has been a central concern since the 1960s, reported in a number of studies. The situation for immigrants began to be focussed more intensively during the 1970s, through a number of official investigations. In 1984, Danermark identified thirteen studies on housing segregation, of which five focused on the ethnic dimension of segregation.

The situation in the housing market has been studied as part of the integration discourse. The 1988 government commission on Problems Specific to Large Cities had the task to analyse the apparent increase of housing segregation in major cities. The main causes of segregation were identified as the housing policies of the 1970s-1980s, and the unequal income development among the various population groups.

In 1995, three other commissions analysed these and related issues. A conclusion of these studies was that segregation is increasing. Some analysts maintain that there is a free choice effect as many immigrants prefer to live in housing areas dominated by immigrant groups, thus feeling less exposed to manifest discriminatory attitudes, cultural clashes or at a loss in communicational skills. Molina (1997, 19-22) strongly argues against the 'free-choice' theory as a cause of segregation. The patterns of segregation characteristic for Sweden fail to confirm choice based ethnic patterns. Rather they point to a lack of choice. According to Molina, this rather has to do with power relationships in the society, conferring or not a real choice to those concerned, where ethnicity is but one of the influencing output factors.

By international comparison the most striking element of segregation in the Stockholm case seems to be not so much a situation of ethnically distinct housing areas, although there is a tendency to for some ethnic groups, most notably for the Turkish born, but rather that foreign born persons are lumped together in residential areas with very few Swedish born inhabitants. Andersson (1996) constructed a segregation index on data from fourteen cities (table 15). He found that Turks and some other ethnic groups from the Middle East are residents of the most segregated areas. What is more apparent is that ethnic segregation in housing is increasing.

Table 15: Segregation Index in 14 Cities 1995*

	Immigrated before 1985		Immigrated after 1985	
Country of birth	Segregation index	Number of persons	Segregation index	Number of persons
Turkey	0.69	13,267	0.77	3,091
Lebanon	0.68	2,392	0.73	8,333
Ethiopia	0.62	2,029	0.69	6,715
Iraq	0.65	2,084	0.68	12,400
Chile	0.53	6,073	0.64	7,707
Iran	0.52	4,479	0.58	24,139
Poland	0.37	12,757	0.50	7,100
Finland	0.30	63,572	0.41	8,855
All foreign born	0.25	219,906	0.47	188,276
Total population		2,312,483		210,282

*the higher the numbers, the greater the segregation

Source: Andersson 1996

127

In some ethnically segregated housing areas (parts of *Kista* is an interesting case) education among some dominant groups of foreign born (Iranians) is high, yet unemployment is also high. In the district of *Hammarby*, with a relatively low percentage of foreign born, education is low and unemployment high.

Youth in general have difficulties of finding accommodation of their own. Whether this problem affects children of international migrants more than their Swedish-born peers is hard to tell, as no data on this aspect of the problem is available.

No special legal dispositions have been adopted in order to combat discrimination in the access to housing. The general anti-discriminatory provisions apply to this field and can consequently be invoked. The criteria to attribute housing are general and publicly defined. Special reasons of health may take precedence over almost all others.

Various studies indicate that children of international migrants may have trouble with integrating into society. In a broad survey of reported crimes Ahlberg (1996) established that children of international migrants are over-represented in the criminal justice statistics. The media have written extensively about street fights, gang warfare and vandalism in which children of international migrants at times are involved. Over the years this has reinforced a stereotype of children of international migrants as a problematic group in society.

Delinquency and criminal behaviour start to appear in police reports when the offenders are in the early teens. The number of persons suspected of crime (or using another statistic, brought to justice) increases rapidly from the age of fourteen and peaks at around the age of twenty, then gradually to decrease. After the age of forty the rates are very low. Crime and delinquency is definitely a youth problem. Of the 85,250 persons suspected of some offence in 1997, almost one fourth (18,926) were in the age brackets 15-19 years. The official and published criminal justice data do not provide information on citizenship, country of origin or ethnicity. In his systematic analysis of criminal justice data, Ahlberg found an over-representation of foreign-born. We will not enter into a detailed account of Ahlberg's data and research. A summary and analysis is given in Westin (1998). It should be borne in mind that even though there is a significant over-representation of children of international migrants in the criminal justice statistics, more than ninety per cent of those belonging to this group have not been involved in delinquent or criminal activity that has been reported to the police. It is also important to bear in mind that most of the criminal activity in Sweden is committed by ethnic Swedish citizens.

In a study carried out by Virta and Westin (1999) in segregated housing areas in Stockholm, data consistently show that young Turks, Kurds and Chileans have a greater sense of their own worth, a more positive self-identity, better relationships with their parents and are doing better at school than Swedish and Finnish youth. Social class does not account for this unexpected finding. The sample that was drawn for the survey is not statistically representative for Sweden, not even for Stockholm as a whole, but for lower income, often immigrant dominated housing areas in Stockholm. Since similar results have been found in other countries involved in this study, the results cannot be purely incidental. What it does seem to indicate is that some children of international migrants tend to have higher academic motivation than Swedes and Finns, and that a good training or education in Sweden is seen to be the way for children of international migrants to make it in Sweden.

3.7. Racism and Discrimination

Discrimination is a criminal offence in Sweden. The Swedish Penal Code criminalises racial agitation/persecution since 1989. Specific legal provisions against ethnic discrimination exist. The effect of this law is being evaluated. A possible outcome may be a clearer definition of how the provisions are to be interpreted and applied with more consistency than before. Since the rise of racist and neo-Nazi violence courts regard racial motives of a crime as an aggravating circumstance. The real challenge to the criminal justice system is to prove that an offence has a racial background which is a much more difficult task.

Since adopting the *UN Convention on Eliminating All Forms of Racial Discrimination* in 1966 Sweden considered for many years that its legislation generally met the required international standards. The official policy was one of non-intervention. This was based on two assumptions. First, for many years during the period of labour migration the official understanding was that racial and ethnic discrimination existed elsewhere, not in Sweden. Secondly, the Swedish authorities traditionally observed a policy on non-intervention in labour market negotiations. Discrimination in the labour market or at the workplace were problems that the parties in the labour market (trade unions and employers' organisations) were expected to solve. For these reasons Sweden had virtually no legislation against discrimination in the labour market. When attention was called to problems of this nature in the 1980s parliament was still most reluctant to legislate. Eventually some provisions were implemented in Swedish legislation. Anti-discrimination legislation has been toothless as several independent commissions had pointed out. The most recent law about measures against discrimination on the labour market represents various modifications aimed to counteract discrimination in the labour market. It is too early to determine whether this law is going to be more effective than its predecessors.

4. Conclusions

There is a clear and distinct immigration and integration policy in Sweden, characterised by a tendency to limit the intake of new immigrants while allotting increasing resources to promote the integration of those already accepted. In this context, children of international migrants are a particular group whose integration is favoured. When a return to the country of origin may come into question, the Swedish system offers incentives and certain assistance for immigrants willing to return, irrespective of the category they may belong to. Mostly, this applies to newcomers. In the case of children of international migrants, however, the general policy is of encouraging them to integrate.

Sweden is a highly centralised democratic state characterised by a balance of power between a strong central government on the one hand and highly independent local authorities on the other. Thus, the policy towards migrants is elaborated on a central plan and applied both centrally and locally. The general policy is to create a multicultural society. Multiculturalism is defined in terms of equality, i.e. equal rights in practically all domains of social life. Multiculturalism is moreover defined in terms of integration into the polity (voting rights in local elections for permanent residents with foreign citizenship, relatively reasonable conditions to become a Swedish citizen, acceptance of dual citizenship in some cases, support for minority and migrant organisations), freedom of religious, ethnic and cultural identification, recognition of linguistic rights of some traditional minorities as well as of the Finnish speaking immigrant community. Multiculturalism, however, is not defined in terms of consolidating distinct ethnic groups of immigrant origin. Sweden has not, and will not, recognise ethnic group rights besides the ethno-linguistic exceptions mentioned above (Finnish, Saami, Yiddishi, Romani). Neither positive discrimination nor affirmative action have been practised as yet, but are being considered by the recently established Board of Integration. The Board of Integration is assigned the task of promoting diversity in Swedish society. The Board has only just started its work. There are no results to draw upon yet, neither has a definite agenda been set. For the time being, the Board is seeking to establish information of good practices that may serve as models of inspiration. The Board is also attempting to monitor public opinion through surveys and in-depth studies. Westin is directing two studies for the Board of Integration evaluating the diversity programme as it has been adopted by several companies and organisations.

All persons legally residing in Sweden have access to the social welfare system. Social welfare is provided by the local authorities on application, under equal conditions for everybody residing within the municipal boundaries. It is difficult to assert whether this has any specific role or in any way affects the integration of children of international migrants.

The Swedish integration policies rely heavily on the general welfare policies administered by the public sector. Sweden has probably one of the largest public sectors among the liberal democracies of the West. It is also known for its high taxes on income and employment. It has therefore been seen as natural that the role of the public sector in promoting integration is large in comparison with many other European countries, where non-governmental organisations have a larger role to play. The Swedish integration policies have developed out of the long process in which the modern welfare state was developed. The Scandinavian, or actually more specifically, the Swedish model has its origins in the grand compromise that was achieved between labour unions and the employers' organisations in the 1930s, which lay the foundation for the peaceful transition of a class-based and highly stratified society into the modern welfare state, in which class differences are no longer as glaringly salient as they used to be. We are not suggesting that class differences have been eliminated, far from it, but the welfare system has made them less visible. As long as the Swedish economy was in a state of growth, this was (still) possible.

The welfare state developed as a result of a series of reforms affecting the educational system, health care, social services, pensions, housing, working life, consumer goods, recreation and sports. Interest organisations played a central role in bringing about change, interest organisations that developed from below. Many of them supported the Social Democratic movement. Sweden developed into a corporatist society where the Social Democratic government could negotiate directly with the interest organisations, thus bypassing the normal parliamentary procedure. The most powerful organisation was the Labour organisation, whose leader was at times a member of the government. The Social Democratic party ruled uninterruptedly from 1936 to 1976, – during World War II in coalition with three non-Socialist parties, and in the 1950s in coalition with the small agrarian party. It was also in power 1982 to 1991 and again as from 1994. The model that developed was in effect a model for integrating a society marked by class differences. The instruments that were employed, the interest organisations, gradually became more and more alienated from the grass roots that had started them. These organisations have a democratic structure, but their function today is different from what it used to be. Many of them have turned into top-heavy bureaucratic mechanisms of power. They have lost their revolutionary ideals, if ever there were any, and have turned into rather conservative bastions. Their purpose is to look after the interests of their members, but membership has become a mere formality, there is hardly any commitment involved any more. Many of these interest organisations, though not all of them, are symbiotically linked with the public sector. This is particularly obvious in communities where the local government is Social Democratic. They operate towards the same objectives.

When the question of integrating the immigrant population arose, nothing was more obvious than to make use of the same public sector/ interest organisation model that had proved to be successful earlier. This explains some of the elements of the integration /immigration policies, that otherwise may seem contradictory. The emphasis on equality is obvious; it is accepted and taken for granted. The emphasis on freedom of choice is somewhat more problematic, because in its continuation, it may lead to demands that go against the general trend. This is why the Social Democratic government was strongly opposed to ethnic, religious or cultural schools for minorities. The specific needs for language education were ideally to be handled within the comprehensive school. An important model for the integration of immigrant minorities was support for their organisations. Ethnic or cultural organisations were entitled to seek public support, provided that they met a number of specified criteria. These requirements mirrored closely the structure of the Swedish interest organisations that had developed some sixty to seventy years earlier.

Given the growing proportion of persons with immigrant background in the total population of Sweden, one can expect certain structural changes of approach in the years to come. In the political and public discourse, one may already notice an intensification of the debates around the general problematic related to the role and importance of immigration and integration, in present as in future perspective, even as related to the very future of the Swedish welfare system, e.g. when related to the issue of pension rights in a society when an ever increasing proportion of the population tends to belong to the older age-groups, while a continued low nativity indicates a comparative proportional decrease of the working population. The Canadian model, where an increased immigration is seen as a solution to this dilemma, has recently become an issue of public debate. The integration problems that already settled immigrants are confronted with highlights the opposite aspect of unemployment and social exclusion that hardly places these groups in a position to play the role of "working part of the population".

The Swedish example remains a special case, which may contribute to finding more general solutions to the burning issue of integration in and through diversity.

References

Ahlberg, J. 1996:

Invandrares och invandrares barns brottslighet. En statistisk analys (Criminality amongst Immigrants and Children of Immigrants), Stockholm: Brottsförebyggande rådet (BRÅ), BRÅ-rapport 1996:2

AKU 1995:

Employment Survey 1995, Örebro: Statistics Sweden

AKU 1998:

Employment Survey 1998, Örebro: Statistics Sweden

Ålund, A. / Schierup, C.-U. 1991:

Paradoxes of Multiculturalism – Essays on Swedish Society, Aldershot: Avebury

Andersson, R. 1996:

'Socio-Spatial Dynamics: Ethnic Divisions of Labour and Housing in post-Palme Sweden', *Urban Studies*, 14

Arvemo-Nostrand, K. / Theorin, H. 1996:

'Invandrarungdomars utbildning och arbete', *Välfärdsbulletinen*, 5, pp. 24-25

Danermark, B. 1984:

Boendesegregationens utveckling i Sverige under efterkrigstiden, Redovsning av ett uppdrag från Bostadskommittén [Bo 1982:02] till Berth Danermark vid Högskolan i Örebro, Ds Bo 1984:4, Stockholm: Liber/ Allmänna förlag

Hammar, T. (ed.) 1985:

European Immigration Policy. A Comparative Study, Cambridge: Cambridge University Press

Hansegård, N. E. 1968:

Tvåspråkighet eller halvspråkighet?, Stockholm: Aldus/Bonniers

Hyltenstam, K. (ed.) 1996:

Tvåspråkighet med förhinder? Invandrar- och minoritetsundervisning i Sverige, Lund: Studentlitteratur

133

Hyltenstam, K. / Tuomela, V. 1996:

'Hemspråksundervisningen' in Hyltenstam, K. (ed.), *Tvåspråkighet med förhinder? Invandrar- och minoritetsundervisning i Sverige*, pp. 9-109, Lund: Studentlitteratur

Lange, A. 1991:

Flyktingskap, boende och agen, Stockholm University: Centrum för invandringsforskning

Malmberg, B. 1964:

Språket och människan, Stockholm: Aldus/Bonniers

Molina, I. 1997:

Stadens rasifiering – etnisk boendesegregation i folkhemmet, University of Uppsala: Dept. of Social and Economic Geography [Kulturgeografiska institutionen]

Olkiewicz, E. 1990:

Invandrarfamiljer i förändring, Stockholm: Internationell pedagogik

Virta, E. / Westin, C. 1999:

Psychological Adjustment of Adolescents with Immigrant Background in Sweden, Stockholm: CEIFO

Westin, C. 1996:

'Equality, Freedom of Choice and Partnership. Multicultural Policy in Sweden' in Bauböck, R. et al. (eds.) *The Challenge of Diversity. Integration and Pluralism in Societies of Immigration*, pp. 207-226, Aldershot: Avebury

Westin, C. 1998:

'On Migration and Criminal Offence. Report on a Study from Sweden', *IMIS-Beiträge*, 8, pp. 7-30

Westin, C. / Dingu-Kyrklund, E. 1997:

Reducing Immigration, Reviewing Integration, Stockholm: CEIFO

Hans Mahnig / Andreas Wimmer

Integration without Immigrant Policy: The Case of Switzerland

1. Introduction

In a famous lecture at the University of Zurich in the 1970s, Karl Deutsch portrayed Switzerland as a "paradigmatic case of political integration". According to him, Switzerland, in spite of being a multicultural society divided by religion, language, class and ideology, had become one of the most stable countries in Europe. Deutsch identified two historical factors as the main reasons for this paradox. First, the Swiss peasantry resisted the development of a feudal state between the tenth and the twelfth centuries, thus leading to strong municipal autonomy. Second, the rate of popular participation during the epoch of industrialisation was comparatively high – the percentage of citizens with the right to vote was higher during the eighteenth and nineteenth centuries in Switzerland than in its neighbouring countries (Deutsch 1976). However, other scholars puzzled by Switzerland's stability insisted on different explanations: for example the recognition of the multicultural character of the country by its federal institutions (Schnapper 1997, 146), or the use of proportional representation in political institutions and of compromise to achieve conflict resolution, often called *consociational* or *consensus democracy* (Steiner 1974, Linder 1999, 359-369, Lijphart 1977). Finally, certain observers see an important explanation of the country's stability in the idea of forming a community of destiny – an image nourished by the Swiss citizens' sentiment that as members of a small country they were and are threatened by their larger neighbouring nation-states (Kriesi 1995, 15-17).

Apart from being historically a multicultural society, during the 20th century Switzerland has had one of the highest immigration rates in Europe. According to the last census about one fifth of its population is foreign-born (Haug 1995, 28), a figure twice as high as that of the USA, and considerably higher than that of Canada, two classic countries of immigration. However, contrary to its multicultural character, Switzerland does not recognise the fact that it is an immigration country and has no real immigrant policy on the federal level. Another paradox concerning immigration is the fact that despite the absence of most of the problems with which other European immigration countries are confronted – such as high unemployment rates among immigrants, ethnic segregation and social unrest (see Mahnig 1999) – the immigration issue has almost constantly occupied Switzerland's political agenda since the 1960s.

These paradoxes require an explanation, which this text will try to provide. Its central hypothesis is that the same patterns which can be considered as crucial for the political integration of Switzerland are also to a large extent responsible for the specific way Switzerland treats its immigrants and their children. However, in the latter case these patterns had a much more ambiguous impact than in the former. Today they cannot be relied upon to guarantee the integration of immigrants and to ensure the customary social stability. Thus, in recent years Switzerland's traditional modes of inclusion have increasingly been challenged and new policies, deviating from historical traditions, have emerged.

In the following text we shall first sketch the process of immigration to Switzerland during the 20th century and present some data on immigrants and their children (2). Secondly we shall emphasise four factors explaining to a large extent the integration of migrants in Switzerland: federalism (3.2.), municipal autonomy (3.3.), consociational and direct democracy (3.4.) and the specific character of Swiss national identity (3.5.). However, the integration of immigrants and their children in Switzerland cannot be understood without two additional explanations: first the peculiarity of the Swiss immigration policy (3.1.), and secondly the autonomous organisation of immigrants themselves (3.6.). In the conclusion (4.) we will summarise the increasing contradictions among the traditional modes of integration and discuss recent developments indicating new ways of inclusion.

2. Immigrants and their Children in Switzerland: Some Demographic Data

The transformation of Switzerland into an immigration country took place at the same time as the industrial take-off during the second part of the nineteenth century. The proportion of foreigners in the total population increased from 3% in 1850 to 14.7% in 1910. In 1888 the migration balance reversed: immigration became more important than emigration (Arlettaz 1985). At the eve of World War I about 600,000 foreigners were living in the country, 15.4% of the total population. However, during the two world wars the foreign population in Switzerland significantly decreased. In 1920 their percentage of the total population fell to 10.4%, and in 1941 to 5.2% (see table 1).

Table 1: Foreign Residents in Switzerland According to the Federal Census (1900-1990)

	1900	1910	1920	1930	1941
Total population	3,315,400	3,753,300	3,880,300	4,066,400	4,265,700
Foreign population	383,400	552,000	402,400	355,500	223,600
% foreign population	11.6%	14.7%	10.4%	8.7%	5.2%
	1950	1960	1970	1980	1990
Total population	4,715,000	5,429,100	6,269,800	6,366,000	6,873,700
Foreign population	285,400	584,700	1,080,100	945,000	1,245,400
% foreign population	6.1%	10.8%	17.2%	14.8%	18.1%

Source: BFS 1997, 67

Neither Switzerland's economic system nor its financial structure suffered during the war. After the end of the war in 1945, economic demand by neighbouring countries stimulated a rapid growth in the Swiss economy. By the end of the 1940s a second immigration cycle had begun. Since then a steady and massive flow of foreign workers has come to Switzerland. Their numbers increased from 285,000 in 1950 (6.1% of the total population) to 585,000 (10.8%) in 1960 and to 1,080,000 (17.2%) in 1970. Predominantly Italian during the 1940s and 1950s, their composition became more diverse in the 1960s: while more than half of them were still Italians in 1970, natives of neighbouring Germany, France and Austria represented about 20%, Spaniards 10% and Yugoslavs, Portuguese and Turks together around 4% (see table 2).

The international economic crisis of 1973/74 had an important impact on the number of immigrants living in Switzerland: the total percentage of the foreign population fell from 17.2% in 1970 to 14.8% in 1980 (see also 3.1). After the years of the crisis, the Swiss economy recovered and during the 1980s stimulated a renewed demand for foreign labour which made the number of foreigners rise steadily. Their part of the total population increased from 14.8% (945,000 persons) in 1980 to 18.1% (1,245,400 persons) in 1990 and 19.2% (1,368,000 persons) in 1999. During the 1980s a large part of the increase is due to family reunification.

Table 2: Composition of Foreign Residents in Switzerland by Country of Origin and Percentage of the Total Foreign Population (1900/1930/ 1960/1990/1999)

	1900	1930	1960	1990	1999
Germany	43.9	37.8	16.0	6.9	7.4
France	15.3	10.5	5.4	4.2	4.2
Italy	30.5	35.7	59.2	30.8	24.3
Austria and Liechtenstein	6.4	6.2	6.8	2.6	2.2
Other European countries	3.9	8.2	7.1	39.1	46.5
Other countries	-	1.5	5.6	16.4	15.4
Total foreign population	100	100	100	100	100

Sources: Haug 1995, 31; BFA 1999, 83

During the 1980s the immigration of asylum seekers – as everywhere else in Western Europe – also became increasingly important: their number rose from 9,700 in 1985 to 16,700 in 1988 and 41,600 in 1991. After this peak the numbers fell to around 20,000 a year during the first half of the 1990s. In 1997 there was a renewed increase in the number of asylum-seekers: compared to 1996 their number rose about one third, from 18,001 to 23,982. This increase continued in 1998 and 1999; 41,302 respectively 46,068 persons were registered as asylum-seekers (BFF 2000, 3).

The diversification of the countries of origin of the labour migrants (workers from former Yugoslavia, Portugal and Turkey became increasingly significant during the 1980s) and the asylum seekers (Sri Lanka, former Yugoslavia and Turkey) led in the last few years to an increasing heterogeneity in the cultural background of the immigrant population. However, in 1999 the most important foreign groups were Italians (24.3%), people from the former Republic of Yugoslavia (14%), Portuguese (9.9%), Germans (7.4%) and Spaniards (6.5%). The so-called "traditional recruitment countries" are thus still the most important countries of origin of immigrants in Switzerland (see table 3).

Table 3: Composition of Foreign Residents in Switzerland by Country of Origin and Percentage of the Total Foreign Population (1999)

Nationality	Number	%
Total of Foreigners	1,361,405	100
Italy	330,697	24.3
Republic of Yugoslavia	190,095	14.0
Portugal	135,377	9.9
Germany	100,536	7.4
Spain	88,111	6.5
Turkey	79,837	5.9
France	56,974	4.2
Austria	28,087	2.1

Source: BFA 1999, 83

Most of the countries of origin of immigrants in Switzerland are members of the European Union: in 1999, 59.7% of the foreigners living in Switzerland came from EU member states (BFA 1999, 83). With the exception of Luxembourg, Switzerland is the European country with the highest percentage of foreign residents. This phenomenon is due in part to the comparatively restrictive access to citizenship (see 3.3.). However, the proportion of foreign-born persons in Switzerland – to use an indicator used by classic immigration countries – is, as already mentioned, about one fifth of the overall resident population and mirrors the fact that Switzerland has experienced a proportionally higher immigration rate since 1945 than many traditional immigration countries.

For the children of immigrants the term "second generation" is commonly used in Switzerland. Because of the restrictive access to citizenship the majority of them still have the nationality of their parents and are thus in fact "immigrants of the second generation". Of all the foreigners living in Switzerland in 1996 with a one-year or a permanent residence permit, 22.8% were born in Switzerland. This proportion differs according to their nationality: 37% for Italians, 32% for Turks and 27% for Spaniards.

If one looks only at foreign children under twenty years living in Switzerland in 1996 with a one-year- or a permanent residence permit, one gets the number of 353,900 people; 205,262 of them, that is 58%, were born in Switzerland. From this group 61,300 or 29.8% are Italian, 49,300 or 23.9% come from the former Yugoslavia, 23,400 (11.4%) from Turkey, 22,000 (10.7%) from Portugal and 17,200 (8.3%) from Spain (see also table 4)[1].

---

[1] Data provided by the Federal Office of Statistics.

Table 4: Foreigners Born in Switzerland According to Age and Nationality (1996)

	0-4	5-9	10-14	15-19	20-24	25-29	30-34	35+	Total
EUROPE	77,490	50,835	34,471	30,024	33,062	29,951	19,905	15,325	291,063
EU / EFTA	40,497	30,631	23,605	24,003	29,886	29,056	19,728	15,108	212,514
Germany	2,416	1,444	937	1,016	1,380	1,648	1,550	2,048	12,439
France	1,863	1,245	899	704	733	658	394	1,096	7,592
Italy	15,822	15,038	14,476	15,991	2,118	21,897	14,859	10,298	129,561
Austria	531	390	380	414	579	812	770	829	4,705
Portugal	12,874	6,772	1,878	492	250	81	57	40	22,444
Spain	4,719	4,260	3,875	4,326	4,750	3,053	1,585	174	26,742
Others	2,272	1,482	1,160	1,060	1,014	907	513	623	9,031
NON-EU / EFTA	36,993	20,204	10,866	6,021	3,176	895	177	217	78,549
Eastern Europe	415	376	423	92	44	56	53	112	1,571
Former Yugoslavia	28,637	1,258	5,346	2,713	1,377	377	39	73	51,142
Turkey	7,885	7,240	5,095	3,211	1,754	460	85	26	25,756
Others	56	8	2	5	1	2	0	6	80
AFRICA	1,724	1,090	581	132	64	22	18	16	3,647
AMERICA	964	621	437	203	84	76	45	52	2,482
Northern America	432	209	126	75	55	63	39	40	1,039
Latin America	532	412	311	128	29	13	6	12	1,443
ASIA	3,942	2,032	950	354	88	57	36	21	7,480
SOUTH PACIFIC	51	15	9	12	3	6	4	6	106
STATELESS	14	40	19	4	0	3	3	16	99
TOTAL	84,185	54,633	36,467	30,729	33,301	30,115	20,011	15,436	304,877

Source: Federal Office of Statistics

3. Traditional Integration Patterns and their Effects on Migrants and their Children

In this section we will now turn to the six main factors explaining the integration of immigrants and their children in Switzerland. After describing the impact of the Swiss immigration policy, (3.1.) we will discuss federalism (3.2.), municipal autonomy (3.3.) consociational and direct democracy (3.4.) and the specific character of Swiss national identity (3.5.), and finally the role played by immigrants' organisations (3.6.).

3.1. The Impact of Admission Policy

An important feature for the understanding of the nature of the current integration of migrants and their children is that Switzerland was the European country which succeeded best in using foreign labour as an "economic buffer" during the international crisis of 1973/74. This buffer system was itself made possible by the Swiss immigration policy formulated in the inter-war period. In 1931 the Federal Law of Residence and Settlement of Foreigners *(Bundesgesetz über Aufenthalt und Niederlassung der Ausländer – ANAG)* was enacted. It can be regarded as a "police-law" (Thürer and Kaufmann 1990, 48) aiming at border control and the defence of the national territory, profoundly inspired by the international political context of the time, the economic crisis and widespread xenophobia (Moser 1967, 358). Xenophobia was during this period directed against what was called "overforeignisation" ("*Überfremdung*"), meaning a situation in which society had become "foreign" to its own members because of immigration and establishing a causal link between the number of foreigners and the threat to Swiss identity (Misteli and Gisler 1999, 96) (see also 3.5.).

The ANAG mirrored these fears of identity loss by mentioning the danger of *Überfremdung* as one of the principal issues that authorities should address in the implementation of their policy (ANAG, art. 16a). The law was also based on the assumption that it is not so much the number of foreigners which leads to *Überfremdung* but their wish to stay in Switzerland. In other words, according to the Swiss government there was "no reason to object to an influx of foreigners as long as they do not wish to settle" (Feuille fédérale 1924, 522-523). However, if after World War II the idea of *Überfremdung* remains a point of reference for the federal administration (Tanner 1998), afterwards the authorities have been more preoccupied by the fear that a new economic crisis could lead to widespread unemployment, and that the presence of immigrants could therefore cause social tensions. The idea of granting foreign workers only a precarious legal status, making it easy to send them home, was therefore also promoted by economic interests (Cerutti 1994, 49). Thus the recruitment treaties with Italy (1948) and later with other Mediterranean countries only granted a permanent residence permit to foreigners after they had stayed in Switzerland for ten years.

When the international economic crisis hit Switzerland severely in the mid-1970s, the regulations described above proved to be "efficient". Between 1974 and 1977, the Swiss economy lost 10% of its jobs. Primarily affected were foreign workers: 228,000 out of 340,000 dismissed persons, that is 67%, were foreigners. By estimation about 35% of them went back to their country of origin between 1974 and 1976 (Haug 1980, 7-8). The decrease was, in part, the effect of the Swiss authorities' policy: at this time many foreign workers only had temporary residence permits and could therefore be sent home by simply not extending their permits. Additionally many foreign workers did not have an unemployment insurance – which was not compulsory at the time in Switzerland – and thus preferred to return home (Schmidt 1985, 22).

The regulation of foreign labour through a restrictive admission system as well as the weakness of the Welfare State, or in Manfred G. Schmidt's words a "delayed Welfare State" and a "national-liberal" labour market policy (1985, 111, 123-127), secured a low unemployment rate among foreigners during the 1970s and the 1980s. It is more controversial whether the same factors also explain the country's general low unemployment rate during the same period (see for example Lambelet 1994, 144-159). However, even if during the short recession of 1981-83 the buffer system no longer worked as well (Schwarz 1986), at the end of the 1980s scholars could still claim that in Switzerland "the unemployment of foreigners is rare, his social identity non-existent" (Bolzmann et al. 1987, 62). Wider social problems linked to unemployment – as for example social exclusion, ethnic segregation and social unrest – did therefore not develop in Switzerland. In other words: the specific interplay of exclusion and inclusion through restrictive immigration regulation and market forces is the first characteristic of the Swiss mode of integration of immigrants (see also Hoffmann-Nowotny 1985, 227 and Niederer 1967).

However this system does not work anymore today because its basis has been increasingly eroded. The first important change was the improvement of the residence status of foreigners due to the pressure placed on Switzerland by the countries of origin – primarily Italy – and on the basis of bilateral agreements. Nevertheless, these treaties do not give all immigrants the same rights. If in principle the permanent residence permit *(Niederlassungsbewilligung)* is still given to foreigners only after they have stayed in Switzerland for ten years, most EU nationals now have the right to obtain the residence permit after only five years[2]. Many other nationalities in administrative practice obtain the permanent resident permit even though, theoretically, they do not have the right to the permit[3]. The United States is the only non-European country which is part of this last group (Gutzwiller and Baumgartner 1997, 28-29). At the end of 1997, 73% of the foreigners living in Switzerland had a residence permit, and if one also includes asylum seekers and seasonal workers *(Saisonniers)*, the proportion is 67.5%. The second important change in the immigrant situation can be attributed to the development of the Swiss Welfare State since the middle of the 1970s. In 1975 an unemployment insurance was created by a federal decree, in 1976 the obligation to take out unemployment insurance was voted

---

[2] The countries concerned are Belgium, Germany, Denmark, France, Greece, Italy, Liechtenstein, the Netherlands, Portugal and Spain. Persons with refugee status are treated in the same way.

[3] The countries concerned are Andorra, Finland, Great Britain, Ireland, Iceland, Luxembourg, Monaco, Norway, San Marino, Sweden, and the Vatican.

for by the Swiss population and since then other social welfare provisions have been introduced (see Wimmer 1998).

Therefore, when in the beginning of the 1990s the general increase of unemployment in Switzerland struck immigrants disproportionately, because they were often employed in economic sectors suffering from restructuring, they were not forced to leave the country as in 1973-74. And even if many older migrants nevertheless decided to return to their countries of origin (see Roselli 1998), social exclusion and segregation began to develop. That is why interest in a federal integration policy has multiplied since the beginning of the 1990s. The promoters have been primarily Switzerland's larger cities where the social effects of unemployment are concentrated and thus more visible. However, these claims stand against a strong political tradition in Switzerland: federalism.

3.2. Federalism

As already mentioned, Switzerland is a multicultural society: 75% of the country's Swiss population speak German, 20% French, 4% Italian and 1% Raetho-Romanic[4]. It is primarily through the institutions of federalism that the country succeeded in accommodating its cultural diversity: Switzerland is made up of 23 cantons (three of them are divided in two half-cantons) which have a large autonomy in a variety of policy fields as for example education, police and taxes. According to federalist principles, the Swiss parliament is divided into two chambers, the *Nationalrat* (the representatives of the people) and the *Ständerat* (the representatives of the cantons). New laws must be passed by a majority vote in each chamber.

Besides federalism, the system of consociational democracy (see 3.4.) protects native cultural minorities from detrimental majority decisions. Additionally the Federal Constitution guarantees the defence of all four national languages. However, this does not imply that there are general group rights for cultural minorities: the languages are only protected as principal languages of certain territorial units and each canton is free to choose its official language (in linguistically heterogeneous cantons, however, specific provisions for indigenous cultural minorities exist). Therefore, only territorialised linguistic minorities are recognised. Furthermore, the learning of a second national language is an obligation in school and all linguistic groups – except the Raetho-Romanic – have a complete television and radio programme (Linder 1999, 40-45).

---

[4] The Raetho-Romanic are a cultural minority speaking a Romance language. Consisting of about 50,000 persons, they live in the canton of Graubünden.

Concerning the inclusion of immigrants, federalism has its most important impact in two domains: education and religion. Public primary schools can be regarded as the most important agent of the integration of young immigrants because they have always been conceived as a school for all children *(Volksschule)*, regardless of their social or ethnic background. Nevertheless the educational system is organised by the cantons, which means that immigrants and Swiss citizens from other linguistic regions within the country are required to adopt the dominant cantonal language. During the 1970s, when because of the family reunification process a lot of immigrant children entered school, cantonal educational systems had difficulties in respecting the cultural differences of their new students and in guaranteeing them equal educational opportunities at the same time. Many immigrant pupils with language difficulties were sent – on the grounds of linguistically-based intelligence tests (Schuh 1977) – to special classes for pupils with general learning difficulties, a treatment which was considered as discrimination by their parents. Such problems still persist. However, since 1972 the federal education authorities *(Schweizerische Konferenz der kantonalen Erziehungsdirektoren – EDK)*, partly because they were urged to do so by the Italian government during the bilateral negotiations on immigration, regularly publish recommendations for the better integration of immigrant children in public schools. These recommendations stress the need of special support for immigrant children and the necessity to beware of discrimination. Since 1991 they also insist on intercultural education (Allemann-Ghionda 1997, 330-333). However, the implementation of these recommendations is left to the cantonal authorities who favour other solutions.

Contrasting cantonal responses correspond roughly to linguistic cleavages. In German-speaking cantons one can observe the education system's tendency to set up specific and separate institutions for immigrant children, whereas in French and Italian-speaking cantons the response has been to integrate them into mainstream institutions. However, the outcome of these different cantonal responses to the integration of migrant children has so far not been analysed (Allemann-Ghionda 1997, 354). The same difference between linguistic regions can also be noticed with regard to the treatment of non-Christian religions by school systems, especially Islam. Compared to other European countries, Islam in Switzerland has so far not become a politicised issue (Haenni 1994)[5]. Nevertheless the question of whether Muslim girls should have the right to wear a headscarf in class has become a topic of discussion. Whereas German speaking

---

[5] An estimated 200,000 Muslims currently live in Switzerland. Their immigration has been a recent phenomenon, and their national and social composition is regionally heterogeneous: whereas in the French-speaking part of Switzerland a lot of Muslims come from Arab countries and belong to the middle-class, in the German-speaking part the majority of Muslims are workers with a low level of education coming from Turkey, Bosnia and Kosovo (Fähndrich 1998, 249-252).

cantons, for example Zurich, have taken a pragmatic approach to respond to this question, tolerating the scarf in most cases, in French-speaking cantons, for example Geneva and Neuchâtel, the idea that government should protect public space from cultural and religious markers, in the French republican tradition, is much stronger.

This leads to the question of religion in general, the second important domain in which federalism plays a crucial role for the inclusion of immigrants. The Swiss Constitution guarantees religious freedom, which obliges local communities to respect religious neutrality and to treat the different religious groups on equal terms, but the concrete relationship between State and Church is determined by the cantons. This means that there are twenty-six ways of defining the place of religion in public life, extending from a relatively close relationship between State and Church (mostly in German-speaking cantons) to a complete separation (as in Geneva and Neuchâtel) (Friederich 1995, 25-28). The Muslim community has, because of its national and political heterogeneity, the same difficulties to establish a common organisation on the national level in Switzerland as the Muslim community in Germany (Heine 1997, 112-133) and France (Cesari 1997, 177-190), but these difficulties are accentuated by the fact that religious matters are not organised on the national level. In 1989 the *Gesellschaft der islamischen Organisationen in der Schweiz* (Society of the Islamic Organisations in Switzerland), which includes twenty-five separate organisations, has been founded but a union of all Muslim communities on the national level does not yet exist.

The federalist structure of the country therefore requires Muslims to address their claims, for example for the construction of mosques or the setting up of Muslim cemeteries, to the cantonal authorities. One of the most important claims of Muslim communities is to be recognised as a corporation under public law *(öffentlich-rechtliche Körperschaft)*, a status which would give them the right to receive public subsidies and which has been granted in several cantons to Christian minorities (in the protestant canton of Zurich for example to the Catholics) or to Jewish communities (the latter only being recognised as such in a small number of cantons). So far, there are no cantons which have recognised Islam in this form (see Fischli-Giesser 1995).

Federalism has furthermore an impact on the political rights of immigrants in Switzerland, even if its influence in this domain is more anecdotal. In spite of the failure to set up local voting rights for foreigners during the 1980s and the 1990s (Cueni and Fleury 1994, 15-17), there are, nevertheless, two exceptions. In the canton of Neuchâtel, ever since the cantonal Republic was founded in 1848, all foreigners with a permanent residence permit and who have lived there for one year can vote. In the canton of Jura, the youngest canton of Switzerland, local voting rights were given to all foreigners in 1978 who had lived for at least ten years in the canton (Marquis and Grossi 1990, 24-25). For the understanding of the immigrant's access to political rights through naturalisation, however, the crucial factor is not federalism but municipal autonomy (see 3.3.).

Finally, the claims for an immigrant policy on the national level have always been rejected with the argument that the integration of migrants is the cantons' duty. There has been only one exception: in 1970, in answer to widespread xenophobia (see 3.4), the Swiss government created the "Federal commission for foreigners" *(Eidgenössische Ausländerkommission – EKA)* which is currently the most important institution for the integration of immigrants on the national level. The resources of this institution are, however, quite limited. Considered to be a place where problems concerning immigration can be discussed, its function is purely consultative[6]. The EKA, whose members come from trade unions, employers' organisations, school authorities, churches, NGOs, immigrant associations and from federal and local administrations, has favoured a federalist approach to immigration by claiming that the responsibility for the integration of migrants should be on the cantonal and the local level (EKA 1989).

In all of the three above-mentioned domains, i.e. school, religion and local voting rights, the federalist mode of integration has never been really challenged, even if in the field of education the EDK tries to use its influence, and even if in religious matters the Federal Court has several times ruled against the decisions of cantonal authorities, forcing them to respect the rights of Muslims (see Kälin 1998). However, the federalist approach has been questioned in a wider sense because of the increasing integration problems since the beginning of the 1990s; even the EKA itself asked for a stronger commitment of the federal government (EKA 1996). The inclusion of an article on integration in the Federal Law of Residence and Settlement of Foreigners (ANAG), passed by parliament in June 1998, can be considered as a first deviation from traditional paths. Nevertheless this article, which allows the federal government to subsidise integration measures, is not far-reaching and the difficulties its supporters had to face in the parliament in order to enact it showed once more the strength of federalist traditions.

---

[6] The official self-definition of the EKA is the following: "Wichtigster Auftrag der EKA ist es, Möglichkeiten für ein besseres Zusammenleben von Schweizern und Ausländern aufzuzeigen sowie entsprechende Initiativen anzuregen und zu unterstützen. Bei dieser Aufgabenstellung ergeben sich zwei Hauptadressaten. Einerseits hilft die EKA mit, dem Schweizer die Andersartigkeit des Ausländers und dessen Probleme verständlicher zu machen. Mangelnde Information und vor allem Desinformation schüren die Angst und Sorge um den möglichen Verlust der Existenzgrundlagen, der schweizerischen Kultur und Identität. Neben Bemühungen um eine bessere Information des Ausländers, unterstützt die EKA anderseits Anstrengungen, die dem Ausländer gezielte Gelegenheiten bieten, in die schweizerische Umgebung hineinzuwachsen, die ortsüblichen Denk- und Verhaltensweisen kennenzulernen und Kontakte zum Schweizer zu pflegen." (EKA 1989, 101)

3.3. Municipal Autonomy

As Stein Rokkan (1973, 81) showed in his conceptual map of Europe, Switzerland developed in the middle of the "dominant city network of the politically fragmented trade belt from the Mediterranean to the North". Political fragmentation and strong trade are the historical reasons for the prevailing autonomy of its municipalities and for the fact that Switzerland is composed of a network of relatively small cities. Some scholars believe that this urban structure explains why, in comparison to other European countries, segregation indices of Swiss cities are low and why the spatial distribution of migrants has never been an issue of politics until a few years ago (Arend 1991): the possibility that segregated and homogeneous areas can form is quite limited in small cities. A comparative analysis of ethnic segregation in Switzerland and Germany has pointed out, however, two additional factors for the low indices in Swiss cities: the relatively tight control of the housing sector in Switzerland, which reduces the opportunities for landlords to let apartments of bad quality at expensive prices to immigrants, and the fact that Swiss inhabitants do not move even if the percentage of foreigners increases (Arend 1982, 361-372). Even if, as already stated (see 3.1.), segregation has increasingly become an issue of politics in the last years, it seems that this is not necessarily the expression of an objective tendency towards higher segregation; as recent scientific analysis shows, indices have stayed quite stable (Huissoud et al. 1999, 137-141).

The domains in which municipal autonomy has to be considered as the key factor for the inclusion (and exclusion) of migrants, are citizenship and naturalisation. The naturalisation process in Switzerland consists of three stages. The federal Constitution stipulates that in order to get the Swiss nationality one must first become the citizen of a municipality and then of a canton. The candidate for naturalisation must first apply for a federal authorisation for naturalisation from the federal Department of Police. Once in possession of this document, he or she must apply for the right of citizenship *(droit de cité)* in a municipality. The federal authorities intervene only at the first and the last stages when they are informed about the decision of the municipality (Cent-livres 1990). Whereas the federal constitution only prescribes that, in order to apply for Swiss citizenship, a foreigner must prove that he has lived legally in Switzerland for 12 years[7], the municipalities have the right to establish additional criteria, which are frequently grounded on an ethno-cultural "logic". Additionally, the naturalisation procedure is often very costly.

Local communities implement these principles in different ways. In large municipalities a commission elected by the Municipal Council (the municipal parliament) is responsible for considering the naturalisation demands, whereas

---

[7] The years spent in Switzerland between the 10th and 20th birthday are counted twice.

147

in small municipalities all the citizens decide on the requests. However, an important difference exists between two groups of cantons: in some cantons only the citizens who originally are from the municipality[8] are entitled to decide on the naturalisation of foreigners, whereas in others all the inhabitants have this right (see EKA 1998). The canton of Zurich, for example, the most populated canton of Switzerland, belongs to the first group. Therefore, the naturalisation commissions in Zurich are composed only of municipal council who are citizens of the municipality. In small municipalities only the inhabitants who are citizens of the town or city "through origin or naturalisation"[9] have the right to vote.

There is once more a dividing line between the French-speaking cantons, which have more formalised naturalisation procedures, and many German-speaking cantons which continue to adhere to the principle of citizen participation. In this latter case the naturalisation procedure can of course easily be influenced by prejudice. Recent cases indicate that citizens are much less likely to grant Swiss citizenship to people of certain nationalities (for example persons from former Yugoslavia and Turkey) than others. However, no precise analyses of this situation exist at present. Furthermore, in municipalities with less formalised naturalisation procedures the candidates are often required to prove that they have adopted the "values and traditions of the local community". This means that in Switzerland naturalisation is to a large extent based on an ethno-cultural "logic", even if the country is built on the idea of a political contract (Centlivres and Schnapper 1991) (see 3.5.).

The idea that the integration of immigrants in Switzerland has to be based on their previous inclusion in and adaptation to local communities, is not only an essential element of the naturalisation process, but also has repercussions in other policy sectors. The Federal commission for foreigners (EKA) writes in *"Foreigners in the Municipality"*, one of its most important publications, that "the integration of foreigners has after all to be encouraged where autochthonous and foreigners live together. Therefore, integration has to be promoted by the municipality. Neither the Confederation nor the cantons can take over this task." (EKA 1989, 1). Alluding to Swiss political traditions, the EKA insists that "in conformity with our democratic customs, solutions adapted to local conditions should be looked for. Each municipality has to find its own way" (EKA 1989, 7). The resulting heterogeneity of more than 3000 approaches – for that is the number of municipalities in Switzerland – has led some scholars to speak of the Swiss "integrationist federalism" (Cattacin 1996); it would be more appropriate to speak of "integrationist municipalism".

---

[8] It is also possible to acquire the *droit de cité* of a municipality after having lived there for a certain time. The municipality becomes then the municipality of origin.

[9] See footnote 8.

Thus two facets are characteristic peculiarities of the Swiss naturalisation process: the responsibility for decision making at local levels and the broad dimension of citizen participation in Swiss democracy.

3.4. Consociational and Direct Democracy

Consociational and direct democracy, two characteristics of the Swiss political system, are more important for the understanding of immigrant *politics* than immigrant *policies*. However, we would like to show that by shaping politics, consociational and direct democracy are responsible, on the one hand, for the high politicisation of immigration in Switzerland and, on the other, for the exclusion of immigrants from political rights (see also Ireland 1994).

Consociational democracy is based on two essential characteristics: the proportional representation of different minorities (political, religious, linguistic) in the federal institutions and the search for compromise between political forces, which goes beyond the search for simple majorities (Linder 1999, 359). Therefore the seven ministers of the Swiss government as well as the members of the higher administration are chosen in proportion to their party affiliation and their linguistic and regional origins. All the major political forces and all the linguistic groups (except the Raetho-Romanic) are represented, and Swiss politics is characterised by a permanent process of compromise-building between these groups.

Direct democracy gives social groups more opportunities to participate in the political process than political systems of the representative type (Linder 1999, 236). The instruments which guarantee this direct participation in Switzerland are the popular initiative[10] and the referendum[11]. They exist on the national as well as on the local level. According to certain observers it is direct democracy which made the consociational system emerge, because each law voted in parliament can be submitted in a referendum to a vote of the whole population and needs therefore the support of the widest alliance possible within the political elite (Neidhart 1970).

In the domain of immigrant policy these two main characteristics of the Swiss political system can be considered as responsible to a large extent for the high politicisation of immigration and the exclusion of immigrants from poli-

---

[10] The popular initiative permits launching a political idea in the form of a constitutional amendment, which is then submitted to the Swiss people. In order to succeed, a popular initiative must gather the signatures of at least 100,000 voters in a period of eighteen months. It is then followed by a popular vote (*Volksabstimmung*).

[11] The referendum permits each law adopted in parliament to be submitted to a popular vote if 50,000 signatures are collected in the three months following its adoption.

tical rights. First, consociational democracy often makes the decision-making process very lengthy because the different forces must negotiate a compromise. Concerning immigration this system led to long periods of "non-decision" because the interests concerning immigration were often so divergent that a compromise could not be found (Mahnig 1997, 4-5). Second, the instruments of direct democracy make it possible to force the political elite to deal with a question to which it had not previously given enough attention (Kriesi 1995, 90). Thus immigration became one of the central issues of Swiss politics during the 1960s and the first half of the 1970s. During this period small political parties gained large public support for their claim that Switzerland was *über-fremdet* by the high number of immigrants. Using one of the instruments of direct democracy, these xenophobic movements succeeded in putting the government under pressure by launching several popular initiatives asking for a radical diminution of the number of foreigners living in Switzerland. Even though all these initiatives were rejected in popular votes, they nevertheless urged the Swiss government in 1970 to adopt a more restrictive admission policy (Mahnig 1998, 178-179).

If direct democracy is therefore responsible for the strong influence of xeno-phobia on the political agenda, certain observers also believe that due to the "very institutionalised and politicised nature of conflict (...) there have been few instances of overt hostilities at the work place or in the streets" (Schmitter 1980, 191). Others see direct democracy as an important factor behind the absence of strong extreme-right parties in Switzerland. Allowing the expression of xenophobic claims, direct democracy acts as a safety valve (Armingeon 1995, 55-57).

Direct democracy also had a strong impact in the field of political rights. First because the right to referendum makes it difficult to contain controversial questions in the parliamentary arena: politicians can neither limit the debate nor, often, the decision on granting rights to immigrants to the parliamentary arena. A strategy of consistently making policy "behind closed doors" is there-fore next to impossible in Switzerland. According to several authors, such a strategy is, however, the crucial factor explaining why new rights have been gained by immigrants in Europe (Guiraudon 1998, 293), the most prominent example probably being the granting of local voting rights to immigrants in the Netherlands (Rath 1988, 29). Secondly, in a direct democracy, the decision on the political inclusion of denizens can be considered as a zero-sum game, as Linder (1999, 60-62) argues in the case of voting rights for women (which were granted only in 1971 in Switzerland). In a political system of the representative type there are, on the contrary, inherent incentives for the political elite to promote voting rights for all residents because parties can reasonably expect that the new citizens will vote for the political organisations which defended their interests. Furthermore, parties can present the issue in their programmes together with other aims, which attract the votes of people not necessarily in favour of voting rights for a new group. In a direct democracy, on the contrary, "package deals" are not possible because important issues are voted upon separately.

Of course, the argument that granting political rights to immigrants is a zero-sum game could be questioned on the grounds that inclusion of all members benefits all the citizens of a society. Obviously this view is not shared by a majority of the Swiss population, which leads us to an explanation for the exclusion of immigrants in liberal democracies, which was proposed by Rogers Brubaker. According to him, a society's attitude towards migrants is not so much the effect of institutions and political processes, but of cognitive structures and historical representations (Brubaker 1995). Let us therefore turn to the question of Swiss national identity.

3.5. National Identity

In presenting this factor and its link to the attitude towards migrants we do not argue that Switzerland's national identity has a more important impact on the exclusion of immigrants than national identity has in other countries. (This argument would be, in any case, difficult to prove.) Here we only want to describe its particular form and the implication national identity has on the *perception* of immigrants. Of course, the hostile attitude of larger segments of the Swiss population towards immigrants has been explained, as for other countries, by sundry variables: for example, structural tensions caused through immigration (Hoffmann-Nowotny 1973), or "white backlash" and appeals to the national solidarity pact by underprivileged Swiss (Braun 1970, 332-426; Wimmer 1997). However, an important number of scholars also tried to link the fear of *Überfremdung* to the peculiarities of Swiss national identity (see Windisch 1978).

Defining what Swiss national identity means is difficult. The Swiss Federation was founded in 1848. It was clear that neither culture and language, nor religion and ethnicity could be the basis of the new political community, but only the recognition of the same liberal and democratic principles. For this reason Switzerland is often called a *Willensnation*, a nation built on the will of its members (Linder 1999, 30). However these liberal and non-ethnic foundations came under heavy pressure at the beginning of the twentieth century when the industrial revolution led to social eruptions and intensified class-struggle and when Switzerland's neighbouring countries became consumed by ethnic nationalism. Around 1910 *Überfremdung* became the key-concept for the discussion of the "foreigners' question" *(Ausländerfrage)*. At this time, however, the presence of immigrants was considered as a problem of political loyalty which might be resolved by a broad naturalisation policy (Romano 1996). Only in the 1930s *Überfremdung* received another meaning: it now meant a threat to

151

Swiss identity and was chosen because a positive racial or ethno-cultural definition was not available because of the multicultural structure of the country (Tanner 1998).

Therefore, Swiss national identity is, on the one hand, dominated by the projection of local particularities on the national level. In other words the idea that cultural pluralism is one of the basic characteristics of Switzerland "allows every local and every particular manifestation, to understand itself as an element of national identity" (Kreis 1992, 788-789). On the other hand, Swiss national identity has been reinforced by the use of *Überfremdung* as a concept which defines the boundaries of this identity. Recent sociological studies of Swiss media show, that the fear of *Überfremdung* increased every time discontinuities in social change led to a crisis of collective identity; immigrants became then identified as the reason for the widespread social malaise (Imhof 1993, Misteli and Gisler 1999).

Other authors, however, link Swiss xenophobia more precisely to the interwar-period. The so-called "intellectual defence of the country" *(geistige Landesverteidigung)*, which was developed as an answer to fascism and Nazism and changed into anti-communism during the 1950s and 1960s, has been considered as a pattern of collective consciousness responsible for xenophobia (Braun 1970, 379-385).

The impact of popular xenophobia on the integration of immigrants, however, is difficult to evaluate. In the 1960s and 1970s people directed their animosity against Italians (Hoffmann-Nowotny 1973), primarily those coming from the rural South (Niederer 1967). A recent inquiry shows that this has clearly changed. Italians are not negatively perceived anymore, whereas other groups, for example Turks, Tamils, Africans and persons from former Yugoslavia have become the object of prejudice (Hoffmann-Nowotny et al. 1997, 72-77).

Having presented five traditional patterns influencing the inclusion and exclusion of immigrants in Switzerland, we now have to add a final factor without which the situation of immigrants in Switzerland cannot fully be understood: their autonomous organisation.

3.6. The Autonomous Organisation of Immigrants

Because the Swiss State can be regarded as comparatively weak (Kriesi 1995, 348-349), it has never succeeded in controlling the private associations of its citizens: regulations on organisations have always been very liberal and immigrants have never been submitted to restrictions in this field as in France for example, where they gained the right to set up associations only in 1981. Swiss associations and organisations of civil society, however, did not favour the integration of migrants: on the contrary, observers found in early 1970s that there was little interaction between them and Swiss organisations (Hoffmann-Nowotny 1973) and that Swiss associations even were important agents of their exclusion (Braun 1970, 341-355). The same has been observed concerning churches and welfare organisations: "unlike their German counterparts, the Swiss welfare organisations and churches remained aloof from any formal involvement with the predominantly Italian migrants. They did not, by and large, provide any special services or train foreigners to take positions within their organisational structures" (Schmitter 1980, 187). This observation can be extended to the trade unions, at least in regard to their policy until the end of the 1960s (see Riedo 1976).

In a different way, however, the possibility to organise freely had an important impact on the integration of migrants in Swiss society: migrants used the opportunity for self-organisation, especially Italians who were the most important immigrant group before World War I and became so once more after 1945. As scholars have observed, the *associazionismo italiano* is particularly well developed in Switzerland: although only 10% of all Italian emigrants world-wide lived in Switzerland during the 1970s, about one third of all their associations were established here (Leuenberger 1984, 5). The strong associative structure of Italians can be explained by the fact that, on the one hand, the Italian immigration at the end of the 19th century had already laid the groundwork for their various organisations which developed after World War II (see Morach 1979) and that, on the other hand, the Italian State as well as Italian political parties and trade unions actively tried to organise "their" emigrants.

One of he most important institutions for supporting Italian immigrants became the *Missione Cattolica Italiana*, which had already been founded in 1898 (Ciapparella, Gatani 1997). Led by Salesians, the *Missione Cattolica* continued its religious and social support of Italian immigrants after World War II; a network of about ninety *Missioni* exists in Switzerland today (Von Ah 1999, 62). The most important association, the *Colonie Libere Italiane in Svizzera*, has its roots in the 1930s, when Italian antifascists of different political orientations tried to escape the ideological control of the Italian State by setting up their own organisations. In 1943 they founded a federation of ten associations, the *Federazione delle Colonie Libere Italiane in Svizzera* (FCLIS). Their aim was to pursue the antifascist struggle for a new democratic Italy and to defend the interests of Italian migrants (Leuenberger 1984, 136-137).

Because of its class-struggle orientation and because of the membership of many of its leaders in the Italian Communist Party, the FCLIS became the object of official control during the 1950s and 1960s. During this period the Swiss authorities considered the association to be a menace to social freedom. Nevertheless the FCLIS adopted a civil rights perspective during the 1960s and increasingly tried to work together with representatives of other immigrant communities, trade unions, Christian groups and left-wing organisations and launched several petitions for the social and political rights of immigrants. Beginning in the 1970s the FCLIS committed itself to the question of education. As in other countries, the education of their children became one of the issues which brought the immigrants into closer relations through the negotiation process with the authorities of their country of residence (see Layton-Henry 1990, 100-102).

Thus, one could argue that the autonomous organisation of Italian immigrants played to a large extent the same role in Switzerland as that of immigrant organisations observed by the Chicago school in the USA: they are intermediary institutions between country of origin and country of residence which allow the individual immigrant to pass from one society to the other without being uprooted (see Park et al. 1925). The struggle of immigrants for their civil, social and political rights in the new society is part of this integration process, the best example being that some of the leaders of the FCLIS became representatives in Swiss trade unions.

However, organisations of civil society also underwent important changes: in the last decades churches and welfare organisations have become increasingly committed to the integration of migrants; so have trade unions, mostly for the simple reason that a large numbers of their members are immigrants. On the other hand it seems that the strong autonomous organisation of the Italians was a historical exception; most of the new migrant communities do not seem to have the resources to assist their fellow nationals in the same way. As the EKA put it in regard to these groups: "In contrast to what happened previously with the Italians, Switzerland will have to bear in the future the costs for the integration of migrants alone" (EKA 1996, 14).

4. Conclusion

The traditional Swiss way to include immigrants consisted for a long time of a liberal labour-market policy, which made it possible to use foreign workers as an "economic buffer", but which guaranteed immigrants who stayed a solid integration into the labour market. Public schools, in spite of many difficulties concerning to linguistic and cultural differences, have been the main agent of the integration of immigrant children. Because education is organised by the cantons, there is however no national integration strategy in this field. In most other domains of society immigrants were initially excluded. Some groups, especially Italians, could compensate this situation by a strong network of institutions linked to their country of origin and autonomous ethnic organisations, which assisted newcomers in the foreign society.

Because of Italy's and other emigration countries' pressure and on account of constitutional politics, resident status and social rights of migrants have improved with time, including the attitude of civil society and its institutions:

trade unions, churches, associations, became more open towards immigrants (at least towards those who had lived in Switzerland for a long time). Nevertheless, with the exception of the EKA, no national institution in charge of immigrant policy has developed and up to very recently the integration of migrants has been considered a local matter. The peculiar mixture of federalism, municipal autonomy and direct democracy, which are all tightly connected to national identity, explains why Switzerland can be considered one of the most exclusionist countries in Europe in the field of political rights.

This does not mean that no attempts have been made to change these integration patterns. During the 1970s two initiatives tried to promote a more liberal immigrant policy: the committee *"Mitenand"* ("Together"), consisting of representatives of trade unions, Christian groups and left-wing organisations (of migrants as well as Swiss citizens), launched in 1974 a popular initiative with the aim to give more extensive rights to immigrants in Switzerland (Haug 1980, 90). In the same period, the Swiss government proposed a reform of the Aliens law improving the legal status of foreigners, though in a less ambitious way than the initiative *"Mitenand"*. The two projects, however, failed in two popular votes in 1981 and 1982.

In regard to naturalisation, municipal autonomy has already been challenged twice and projects for a more liberal naturalisation procedure have been presented by the government: whereas in 1983 the project of increasing the weight of the Confederation in the naturalisation procedure of the second generation has been rejected by 54.3% of the voters, it has been adopted in 1994 by 52.8% and was only rejected because a majority of cantons voted against it. Double nationality, however, has been admitted in Switzerland since 1992.

As one of the main elements of the Swiss mode of integration has become eroded, because most of the immigrants have settled and cannot be used as an "economic buffer" anymore, the other traditional patterns have come under attack, particularly in a period of economic restructuring and increasing unemployment. As already mentioned (see 3.1.), this new problem is felt most dramatically in urban centres. Therefore many cities, as for example Bern (in 1996), Zurich (in 1998) and Basel (in 1999), have published "integration models" *(Integrationsleitbilder)* which aim at a comprehensive immigrant policy concerning the integration in the labour market, the support of immigrant organisations, the struggle against urban segregation and the political inclusion of immigrants. At the same time the cities lobby for a stronger commitment of the federal government in matters of immigrant policy. The inclusion of an article on integration in the Federal Law of Residence and Settlement of Foreigners (ANAG) in 1998 can be regarded as a reaction to these claims and as a first step in the direction of a national immigrant policy and a deviation from traditional federalist principles. Additionally in September 1994 a law against racism was adopted in a popular vote which led to setting up of the Federal Commission Against Racism. The law allows prosecuting racist publications and public statements.

The traditional Swiss mode of integration is thus changing. While municipal autonomy, federalism and national identity will certainly continue to be challenged in the future changes will take time, due to consociational and direct democracy.

References

Allemann-Ghionda, C. 1997:

'Schule und Migration in der Schweiz. Zwischen dem Ideal der Integration und der Versuchung der Separation', *Schweizerische Zeitschrift für Soziologie*, 23, 3, pp. 329-357

Arend, M. 1982:

'Sozialökonomische Analyse der kleinräumigen Ausländerverteilung in Zürich', in Hoffmann-Nowotny, H.J. and Hondrich, K.O. (eds.), *Ausländer in der Bundesrepublik Deutschland und in der Schweiz – Segregation und Integration: eine vergleichende Untersuchung*, pp. 294-374, Frankfurt a. M.: Campus Verlag

Arend, M. 1991:

'Housing Segregation in Switzerland', in Huttman, E. D. (ed.), *Urban Housing Segregation of Minorities in Western Europe and the United States*, pp. 155-167, Durham and London: Duke University Press

Arlettaz, G. 1985:

'Démographie et identité nationale (1850-1914). La Suisse et la "question des étrangers"', *Etudes et Sources*, 11, pp. 83-180

Armingeon, K. 1995:

'Der Schweizerische Rechtsextremismus im internationalen Vergleich', *Schweizerische Zeitschrift für Politische Wissenschaft*, 1, 4, pp. 41-64

BFA 1999:

Die Ausländer in der Schweiz – Retrospektive Bestandesergebnisse, Bern: Bundesamt für Ausländerfragen

BFF 2000:

Asylstatistik 1999, Bern: Bundesamt für Flüchtlinge

BFS 1997:

Statistisches Jahrbuch der Schweiz 1998, Bundesamt für Statistik, Zürich: Verlag Neue Zürcher Zeitung

Bolzmann, C. et al. 1987:

'La deuxième génération des immigrés en Suisse: catégorie ou acteur social?', *Revue Européenne des Migrations Internationales*, 3, 1/2, pp. 55-72

Braun, R. 1970:

Sozio-kulturelle Probleme der Eingliederung italienischer Arbeitskräfte in der Schweiz, Zürich: Eugen Rentsch Verlag

Brubaker, R. 1995:

'Comments on "Models of Immigration Politics in Liberal Democratic States"', *International Migration Review*, Vol. XXIX, 4, pp. 903-908

Cattacin, S. 1996:

'"Il federalismo integrativo" - Qualche considerazione sulle modalità di integrazione degli immigrati in Svizzera', in Cesari Lusso, V. et al. (eds.), *I come identità, integrazione, interculturalità*, pp. 67-82, Zurich/Messina: Federazione Colonie Libere Italiane in Svizzera

Centlivres, P. (ed.) 1990:

Devenir Suisse, Genève: Georg Editeur

Centlivres, P. / Schnapper, D. 1991:

'Nation et droit de la nationalité suisse', *Pouvoirs*, 56, pp. 149-161

Cerutti, M. 1994:

'Un secolo di emigrazione italiana in Svizzera (1870-1970), attraverso le fonti dell'Archivio federale', *Studie e Fonti*, 20, pp. 11-95

Cesari, J. 1997:

Être musulman en France aujourd'hui, Paris: Hachette

Ciaparella, A. / Gatani, T. 1997:

Missione Cattolica Italiana Zurigo. I Salesiani di Don Bosco al servizio delle fede e dell'immigrazione, Zurigo: Missione Cattolica Italiana Don Bosco

Cueni, A. / Fleury, St. 1994:

Stimmberechtigte Ausländer. Die Erfahrungen der Kantone Neuenburg und Jura, Bern: Nationale Schweizerische UNESCO-Kommission

Deutsch, K. W. 1976:

Die Schweiz als ein paradigmatischer Fall politischer Integration, Bern: Haupt Verlag

EKA 1989:

Die Ausländer in der Gemeinde, Bern: Eidgenössische Kommission für Ausländerprobleme

EKA 1996:

Umrisse zu einem Integrationskonzept, Bern: Eidgenössische Ausländer-kommission

EKA 1998:

Die Einbürgerung der Ausländer in der Schweiz, Schönbühl: Eidgenössische Ausländerkommission

Fähndrich, H. 1998:

'Unverträgliche Mentalitäten? – Muslime in der Schweiz', in Prodolliet, S. (ed.), *Blickwechsel – Die multikulturelle Schweiz an der Schwelle zum 21. Jahrhundert*, pp. 249-25, Luzern: Caritas-Verlag

Feuille fédérale 1924:

Message du Conseil fédéral à l'Assemblée fédérale concernant la réglementation du séjour et de l'établissement des étrangers par le droit fédéral du 2 juin, II, pp. 511-536

Fischli-Giesser, L. 1995:

'Die öffentlich-rechtliche Stellung "anderer" Religionsgemeinschaften' in Loretan, A. (ed.), *Kirche - Staat im Umbruch*, pp. 160-168, Zürich: NZN-Buchverlag

Friederich, U. 1995:

'Einführung in das schweizerische Staatskirchenrecht', in Loretan, A. (ed.), *Kirche - Staat im Umbruch*, pp. 19-32, Zürich: NZN-Buchverlag

Guiraudon, V. 1998:

'Citizenship Rights for Non-Citizens: France, Germany and the Netherlands' in Joppke, C. (ed.), *Challenge to the Nation-State – Immigration in Western Europe and the United States*, pp. 272-318, Oxford: Oxford University Press

Gutzwiller, P. M. / Baumgartner, U. L. 1997:

Schweizerisches Ausländerrecht, 2. Auflage, Basel: Helbing & Lichtenhahn

Haenni, P. 1994:

'Dynamiques sociales et rapport à l'Etat. L'institutionalisation de l'Islam en Suisse', *Revue Européenne des Migrations Internationales*, Vol. 10, 1, pp. 183-198

Haug, W. 1980:

... und es kamen Menschen. Ausländerpolitik und Fremdarbeit in der Schweiz 1914 bis 1980, Basel: Z-Verlag

Haug, W. 1995:

Vom Einwanderungsland zur multikulturellen Gesellschaft, Bern: Bundes-amt für Statistik

Heine, P. 1997:

Halbmond über deutschen Dächern. Muslimisches Leben in unserem Land, München: List-Verlag

Hoffmann-Nowotny, H.-J. 1973:

Soziologie des Fremdarbeiterproblems, Stuttgart: Ferdinand Enke Verlag

Hoffmann-Nowotny, H.-J. 1985:

'Switzerland', in Hammar, T. (ed.), *European Immigration Policy. A Comparative Study*, pp. 306-336, Cambridge: Cambridge University Press

Hoffmann-Nowotny, H.-J. et al. 1997:

Das 'Fremde' in der Schweiz – 1969 und 1995, Zürich: Soziologisches Institut der Universität Zürich

Huissoud, T. et al. 1999:

'Structures et tendances de la différenciation dans les espaces urbains en Suisse', Rapport de recherche Nr. 145 du Programme National de Recherche 39 "Migrations et relations interculturelles"

Imhof, K. 1993:

'Nationalismus, Nationalstaat und Minderheiten. Zu einer Soziologie der Minoritäten', *Soziale Welt*, 44, 3, pp. 327-357

Ireland, P. 1994:

The Policy Challenge of Ethnic Diversity. Immigration Politics in France and Switzerland, Cambridge (Mass.): Harvard University Press

Kälin, W. 1998:

'Grundrechte in der Einwanderungsgesellschaft', in Prodolliet, S. (ed.), *Blickwechsel – Die multikulturelle Schweiz an der Schwelle zum 21. Jahrhundert*, pp. 37-49, Luzern: Caritas-Verlag

Kreis, G. 1992:

'Die Frage der nationalen Identität', in Hugger, P. (ed.), *Handbuch der schweizerischen Volkskultur*, Vol. 2, pp. 781-799, Zürich: Offizin-Verlag

Kriesi, H.-P. 1995:

Le système politique suisse, Paris: Economica

Lambelet, J. C. 1994:

L'Economie suisse, Paris: Economica

Layton-Henry, Z. 1990:

'Immigrant Associations', in Layton-Henry, Z. (ed.), *The Political Rights of Migrant Workers in Western Europe*, pp. 94-112, London: SAGE

Leuenberger, G. 1984:

Der Antifaschismus in der italienischen Emigration in der Schweiz 1943-1945. Die Entstehung und die Gründung der Federazione delle Colonie Libere Italiane in Svizzera, Universität Zürich

Lijphart, A. 1977:

Democracy in Plural Societies. A Comparative Exploration, New Haven/London: Yale University Press

Linder, W. 1999:

Schweizerische Demokratie – Institutionen, Prozesse, Perspektiven, Bern: Haupt Verlag

Mahnig, H. 1997:

Konturen eines Kompromisses? Die migrationspolitischen Positionen schweizerischer Parteien und Verbände im Wandel, Neuchâtel: Schweizerisches Forum für Migrationsstudien

Mahnig, H. 1998:

'Between Economic Demands and Popular Xenophobia: the Swiss System of Immigration Regulation' in Böcker, A. et al. (eds.), *Regulation of Migration: International Experiences*, pp. 174-19, Amsterdam: Het Spinhuis

Mahnig, H. 1999:

'La question de l'intégration ou comment les immigrés deviennent un enjeu politique. Une comparaison entre la France, l'Allemagne, les Pays-Bas et la Suisse', *Sociétés Contemporaines*, 33/34, pp. 15-38

Marquis, J.-F. / Grossi, G. 1990:

Einwanderer – Minderheit ohne politische Rechte?, Schweizerischer Gewerkschaftsbund.

Misteli, R. / Gisler, A. 1999:

'Überfremdung – Karriere und Diffusion eines fremdenfeindlichen Deutungsmusters', in Imhof, K. et al. (eds.), *Vom Kalten Krieg zur Kulturrevolution*, pp. 95-120, Zürich: Seismo

Morach, M. 1979:

Pietro Bianchi. Maurer und organisiert, Zürich: Limmat Verlag Genossenschaft

Moser, H.-P. 1967:

'Die Rechtsstellung des Ausländers in der Schweiz', *Zeitschrift für schweizerisches Recht*, 86, pp. 325-488

Neidhart, L. 1970:

Plebiszit und pluralitäre Demokratie: eine Analyse der Funktion des schweizerischen Gesetzesreferendums, Bern: Francke

Niederer, A. 1967:

'Unsere Fremdarbeiter volkskundlich betrachtet', *Wirtschaftspolitische Mitteilungen*, 23, 5, pp. 1-19

Park, R. et al. 1925:

The City. Suggestions for Investigation of Human Behavior in the Urban Environment, Chicago: University of Chicago Press

Rath, J. 1988:

'La participation des immigrés aux élections locales aux Pays-Bas', *Revue Européenne des Migrations Internationales*, 4, 3, pp. 23-35

Riedo, R. 1976:

Das Problem der ausländischen Arbeitskräfte in der schweizerischen Gewerkschaftspolitik von 1945-1970, Bern: Lang

Rokkan, S. 1973:

'Cities, States and Nations: a Dimensional Model for the Study of Contrasts in Development', in Eisenstadt, S. N. and Rokkan, S. (eds.), *Building States and Nations*, Vol. 1, pp. 562-638, Beverly Hills and London: SAGE

Romano, G. 1996:

'Zeit der Krise – Krise der Zeit. Identität, Überfremdung und verschlüsselte Zeitstrukturen', in Ernst, A. and Wigger, E. (eds.), *Die neue Schweiz? Eine Gesellschaft zwischen Integration und Polarisierung (1910-1930)*, pp. 41-77, Zürich: Chronos-Verlag

Roselli, M. 1998:

'Vom Kofferpacken und Fussfassen', in Prodolliet, S. (ed.), *Blickwechsel – Die multikulturelle Schweiz an der Schwelle zum 21. Jahrhundert*, pp. 229-236, Luzern: Caritas-Verlag

Schmidt, M. G. 1985:

Der Schweizerische Weg zur Vollbeschäftigung, WZB, Frankfurt a. M.: Campus-Verlag

Schmitter, B. 1980:

'Immigrants and Associations: Their Role in the Socio-Political Process of Immigrant Worker Integration in West Germany and Switzerland', *International Migration Review,* 14, 2, pp. 179-192

Schnapper, D. 1997:

'Citoyenneté et reconaissance des hommes et des cultures', in Hainard, E. and Kaehr, R. (eds.), *Dire les autres – Reflexions et pratiques ethnologiques, Textes offerts à Pierre Centlivres,* pp. 139-148, Lausanne: Payot

Schuh, S. 1977:

'Was ist Aufgabe der Polizei? – Intelligenztests und Ausländerkinder in der Schweiz', *Tages-Anzeiger Magazin,* 24th of September

Steiner, J. 1974:

Amicable Agreement versus Majority Rule: Conflict Resolution in Switzerland, Chapel Hill (N.C.): The University of North Carolina Press

Schwarz, H. 1986:

'Arbeitnehmerschutz im Rahmen der schweizerischen Fremdarbeiterpolitik', in Blatter N. et al. (eds.), *Mikroökonomik des Arbeitsmarktes: Theorien, Methoden und empirische Daten für die Schweiz,* pp. 155-184, Bern: Haupt-Verlag

Tanner, J. 1998:

'Nationalmythos, Überfremdungsängste und Minderheitenpolitik in der Schweiz', in Prodolliet, S. (ed.) *Blickwechsel – Die multikulturelle Schweiz an der Schwelle zum 21. Jahrhundert,* pp. 83-94, Luzern: Caritas-Verlag

Thürer, D. / Kaufmann, C. 1990:

'Ausländerrecht', in Schindler, D. et al. (eds.), *Die Europaverträglichkeit des schweizerischen Rechts,* pp. 45-73, Zürich: Schulthess

Von Ah, M. 1999:

Binnenorientierung vs. Aussenorientierung? Die Integrationsausrichtung von MigrantInnenorganisationen in der Stadt Zürich, Ethnologisches Seminar der Universität Zürich

Wimmer, A. 1997:

'Explaining Xenophobia and Racism: a Critical Review of Current Research Approaches', *Ethnic and Racial Studies*, Vol. 20, 1, January, pp. 17-41

Wimmer, A. 1998:

'Binnenintegration und Aussenabschliessung. Zur Beziehung zwischen Wohlfahrtsstaat und Migrationssteuerung in der Schweiz des 20. Jahrhunderts', in Bommes, M. and Halfmann, J. (eds.), *Migration in nationalen Wohlfahrtsstaaten. Theoretische und vergleichende Untersuchungen*, pp. 199-221, Osnabrück: Universitätsverlag Rasch

Windisch, U. 1978:

Xénophobie? – Logique de la pensée populaire, Lausanne: L'Age d'homme

Jeroen Doomernik

Integration Policies towards Immigrants and their Descendants in the Netherlands

1. Introduction

In the past, for example during the 17th century, immigration into the Netherlands was probably larger in relative terms than it is today (Lucassen/ Penninx 1994). And even during the second half of the 19th century the country witnessed considerable labour immigration, albeit often seasonal (Lucassen 1984). In spite of this tradition, last century the Netherlands started off being a country of emigration. Even during the 1960s and 1970s, when considerable numbers of guest workers arrived, the government tried to stimulate its citizens to move abroad to countries like Canada, the US, Australia and New Zealand. Population forecasts made many fear that the country would not be able to accommodate all, in terms of geographical space, housing, and in terms of labour market needs. The paradoxical nature of having policies for both importing and exporting labour, at the time appears not to have been noted or publicly discussed.

The ban on recruitment in 1974, in contrast to some other countries, did not coincide with any extensive measures to stimulate return migration among guest worker populations, in the Dutch case mainly of Moroccan and Turkish origin. Indeed, unlike in Germany there were few attempts to seriously curb the ensuing process of family reunification, although the official policy was not to encourage this immigration (Lucassen/Penninx 1994, 147). The numbers of Turkish and Moroccan immigrants thus increased considerably. Because their integration, on the labour market and otherwise, did not pass without problems, their presence gradually created policy challenges for the government. The same applied to the increasing numbers of immigrants from Surinam, a former colony and part of the Kingdom of the Netherlands[1]. Because of this status Surinamese were by definition Dutch citizens and free to settle in the Netherlands. In retrospect, it has become clear that Surinamese independence in 1975 was at least as much an attempt from the Dutch side to curtail further immigration as a genuine wish

---

[1] The Charter for the Kingdom of The Netherlands of 1954 included Surinam and the Dutch Antillean Islands as parts of the Kingdom and its citizens hence were given full citizenship rights.

from the Surinamese people to free itself of colonial rule[2]. Today the Kingdom still encompasses parts of the Caribbean: the Dutch Antilles and Aruba. People originating there are free to migrate to the Netherlands which, in some instances, causes problems surrounding their integration.

In 1981 the government published its policy document on minority policies (*Ontwerp – Minderhedennota*). It formulated two basic ideas: those immigrants who preferred to stay and settle should be allowed to do so and their integration would need to be stimulated, those immigrants who preferred to return should be assisted. As to the integration of those who settled, categories of target groups were pinpointed: besides former guest workers, (post) colonial immigrants from Surinam, the Caribbean, Dutch East Indies/Indonesia[3], and, somewhat idiosyncratically, caravan dwellers and gypsies (Penninx 1988). At a later stage refugees also became a category for explicit government attention. Mindful of the ethnic minority position of many Blacks in the United States at that time, the aim was to avoid the same outcome in the integration process of immigrants in the Netherlands. Long term marginalisation coinciding with ethnic difference would, in the government's view, over subsequent generations lead to the formation of ethnic minority groups. Nevertheless, policies were never aimed at assimilating newcomers. Indeed, their cultural autonomy (e.g. in the field of religion) was explicitly safe-guarded as group formation as such was not contrary to Dutch tradition. Indeed, the Netherlands has since its inception as a modern democratic state in the second half of the 19th century known explicit respect for cultural and religious groups within the native population.

This minority policy has remained fundamentally unaltered since then, even though subsequent governments have set different accents and have moved into the direction of policies that should ensure self-sufficiency among immigrants and their descendants instead of what came to be known in the media as 'cuddling-them-to-death'. Behind this rhetorical change we mainly find that policies, in the fields of welfare and labour, with a few exceptions are no longer targeted at ethnic minority groups but take all disadvantaged categories into consideration. In other words: *direct* immigrant policies have made way to *indirect* immigrant policies (cf. Hammar 1985, 9). Indirect immigrant policies are those that affect the position of immigrant groups to any major extent without

---

[2] As Van Amersfoort (1987) points out, declaring Surinamese independence, was extremely counterproductive in terms of immigration control: it created a considerable movement of Surinamese people to the Netherlands. Many Surinamese preferred an economically more or less secure life in the Netherlands above an unsettled future in their country of origin.

[3] These mainly were people of mixed descent (i.e. Dutch and Indonesian) who decided to migrate to the Netherlands upon Indonesia's independence in 1949. Sociologically speaking these immigrants and their descendants have meanwhile 'disappeared' into mainstream society. We therefore do not pay further attention to them in this discussion.

singling them out because they are *immigrants* but because they are marginalised, or are at risk of becoming so. Such policies can also be labelled *general* integration policies which, arguably, is a more suitable term, especially in societies where the differences in legal rights between natives and immigrants and – especially – their descendants to all intents and purposes do not differ.

The broad Dutch policy goal of arriving at a multi-cultural society where groups from different ethnic and/or cultural backgrounds live side by side peacefully and enjoy equal opportunities to participate in society's core fields, calls for a close monitoring of the integration of immigrants and members of, what in the Netherlands has become known as, ethnic minorities (basically precluding the question of whether those minorities have already come into being – in the sense as defined above – or are likely to be a reality in the foreseeable future). This then means that it is of importance to know what their position on the relevant societal fields looks like. This is reflected in the data that are collected for statistical purposes. Population and other statistics do not only include nationality and country of birth but also enumerate the country of birth of a subject's parents.

Table 1: Largest Categories of Ethnic Minorities in the Netherlands, 1990 and 1998, in Thousands

Ethnicity*	1990**	1998
Turkish	206	279
Turkish National	(191)****	(83)
Born in Turkey	NA	172
Netherlands born with two foreign born parents***	NA	107
Moroccan	168	234
Moroccan National	(148)	(136)
Born in Morocco	NA	146
Netherlands born with two foreign born parents***	NA	88
Surinamese	237	257
Surinamese National	(15)	(11)
Born in Surinam	NA	180
Netherlands born with two foreign born parents	NA	77

Source: 1990: CBS 1997a; 1998: calculations based on CBS 1999b

* calculated according to the official definition; i.e. born abroad or having at least one foreign born parent
** figures are rounded off
*** of which the mother is for certain born in the respective country
**** these are persons who have retained their original nationality and have not naturalised, see also footnote 4.

Table 1 provides an illustration of the Dutch government's desire to keep track of the size of its immigrant population and its offspring. It, furthermore, shows that the naturalisation rates among, especially Turkish, immigrants have been considerable. Of the 279,000 ethnic Turks in the Netherlands only 83,000 do not have Dutch citizenship (many will still also retain their Turkish passport but for Dutch statistics this is deemed irrelevant)[4]. Table 1 also indicates that the considerable increase in size of ethnic minorities between 1990 and 1998 (about a third for the Turkish and Moroccan populations and 18 per cent for the Surinamese) to a large extent can be accounted for by a growing presence of a second generation. Among those young people, both parents of whom in most instances will have been foreign born, many and probably most are Dutch nationals. Among Surinamese hardly any members of the second generation are foreign nationals but this is almost entirely to be explained out of the fact that Surinamese immigrants were Dutch nationals in the first place.

In addition to table 1, figure 1 clearly shows, exemplified by the Turks, the increasing significance of persons born in the Netherlands within the ethnic Turkish population at large. The criterion used here to establish the size of the second generation is having two parents born in Turkey. A definition also commonly used is that at least one parent should be foreign born. It is another way of establishing the size of populations comprised of immigrants and their descendants, at least for the time being. Rates of mixed marriages are still relatively low. If, however, this were to change – and such a phenomenon could arguably be considered to be the indicator for social integration *par excellence* – the strange result would be that the size of ethnic minorities would rapidly *increase* whereas their sociological relevance would *decrease* at a similar rate[5]. This is especially true if we want to measure their sizes once a third generation has reached marriageable age. When these children are Dutch nationals, and Dutch law provides for this to be the rule rather than the exception (Fleuren 1996, 53), place of birth of one or two grand parents is the only suitable statistical variable left. Even though the absolute numbers are still small, increases in

---

[4] By law, anyone permanently residing in the Netherlands who has two nationalities is from a Dutch point of view *only* considered to be a foreign national when in that particular other country. In any other country, this person is *only* a Dutch national. If, for instance, a person with the Dutch and the Turkish nationality and who is a permanent resident in the Netherlands travels to Germany or another third country, he is considered to be a Dutch national. Only if he were to move to Turkey and take up his habitual address there, would he or she under the same circumstances be a Turkish national. Dual citizenship, in effect, does not truly exist because, in legal terms at any point in time there is always just one nationality "active".

[5] This points at the problematic nature of enumerating whether *either* parent is foreign born. If, for example, one parent is born in Turkey and the other in Surinam, their children will be labelled as belonging to both the Turkish and the Surinamese ethnic communities, thus inflating the size of either category.

mixed marriages are already observable and appear to be gaining importance rapidly during the past few years as the children of the original migrants are reaching marital age (Hooghiemstra 2000).

Figure 1: Age Structure of the Turkish Population in the Netherlands (Immigrants and their Descendants) Compared with Entire Population

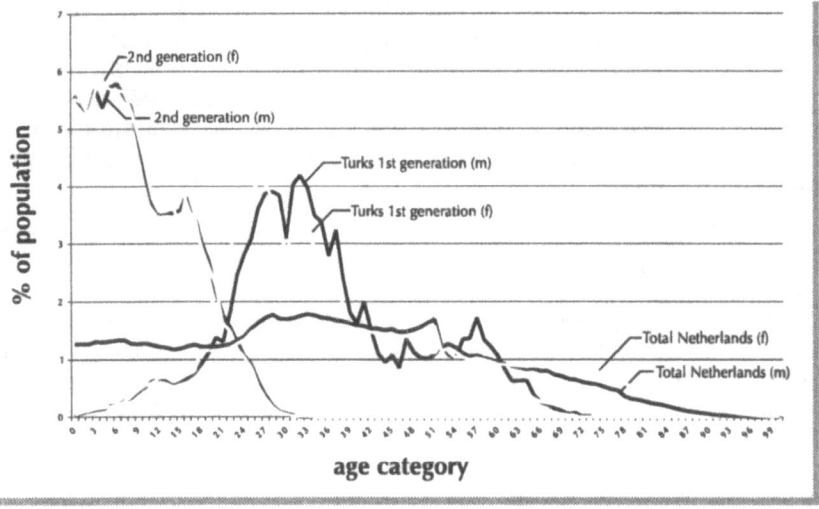

Source: unpublished CBS data (for 1 January 1998)

Note: 1st generation covers all foreign born persons with at least one foreign born parent. 2nd generation denotes all Netherlands born persons with two foreign born parents.

Another effect of the Dutch government's concern with the societal position of the country's immigrants and their descendants is the institutionalisation of an annual report on these matters published by the Social-Cultural Planning Bureau (*Sociaal Cultureel Planbureau*, SCP). Its analyses are predominantly based on national statistics and recent academic research findings. National statistics provided by the Central Bureau for Statistics (*Centraal Bureau voor de Statistiek*, CBS) include those from the population registers and the Labour Force Survey (*Enquete Beroepsbevolking*, EBB), a continuous survey yielding data on more than 100,000 persons aged 15 and over, aggregated and published annually. In addition, systems have been devised by which to monitor the performance of children from ethnic minority groups during their school career. Since the 1988/89 school year 12,000 primary school pupils are bi-annually tested in their language proficiency and their ability to do sums (*Landelijke evaluatie onderwijsvoor-*

rang, LEO). Secondary education is covered by the CBS which maintains a cohort survey of pupils who entered in 1989 (*Voortgezet-onderwijscohort leerlingen 1989*, VOCL '89). A major source on the position of young people is the survey on the social position of the allochthonous and their use of services (*Survey sociale positie en voorzieningengebruik van allochtonen*, SPVA) enumerated by the Instituut voor Sociologisch en Economisch Onderzoek (ISEO) of the University of Rotterdam. Data collection for the SPVA has taken place since 1989 and focuses (most recently in 1998) on young people aged 15-24 of Turkish, Moroccan, Surinamese, and Antillean/Aruban origin, and contains a control group of native peers (Tesser/Veenman 1997). The annual SCP reports offer unsparing accounts of the major problems currently facing people of Turkish and Moroccan origin and most other categories of immigrants from the non-industrialised world; in finding employment, in their educational attainment, on the housing market, and on their disproportionate presence in correctional institutions.

2. Policies of Integration

The fact that the Netherlands knows a long standing tradition as a consociational democracy (Lijphart 1977), a system whereby the inclusion of minority groups – in the Dutch case Catholics, Protestants, Liberals and Socialists – is made possible by making them institutionally independent from each other. In fact, the term 'minority group' is not completely apt as it implies the presence of a majority which did not exist in the Netherlands. The situation was to a certain extent comparable with those still found in Belgium or Switzerland where distinct groups, or perhaps even nations, find themselves sharing the same state. And they hence need to find ways to mutually manage national politics. In these two countries those groups as a rule are geographically separated. This was not the case in the Dutch situation even though, for instance, Roman Catholics were predominantly found in the Southern provinces.

Only at the level where policies were made, these separate 'pillars' met, most clearly in Parliament and Government – where political parties each clearly represented one of the groups – but also in other formal and informal settings. Even though this 'pillarisation' of Dutch society was most significant from the early part of this century until the 1950s or 1960s, it did much to set the tone in political and public debate until today. The main characteristic of a consociational democracy is that political disagreements are settled not so much by confrontation but by pacification and compromise, leading to equal access to society's resources for all parties involved. This has resulted in a legal framework guaranteeing minority groups the possibility to create their own institutions, fully funded by the State. This included separate education (from kindergarten up to the university level), medical care (e.g. separate hospitals) and radio and television broadcasting organisations[6]. These rights extend to new-comers. The Netherlands, as a result, for example know a considerable number of Islamic and some Hindu primary schools and Islamic and Hindu national broadcasting corporations (Doomernik 1995). In other words: Dutch society is founded on the principle of 'differences' perhaps just as much as on the idea of 'commonness', which helps to explain the present stance towards recent newcomers, and has been conducive to formulating the idea of a Dutch multi-cultural society. This stands in marked contrast to the tenets underlying neigh-bouring nations like France and Germany, respectively being representatives of the Republican model and the ethnic model (Castles/Miller 1993, 39). The first type stresses equality before the law but refuses to encourage cultural difference, whereas the second model links political rights to cultural or ethnic common-ness[7].

2.1. General Policies

As briefly mentioned in the introduction to this paper, many policies that were put in place in the 1980s that specifically aimed at the integration of immigrants, were substituted during the mid-1990s by general integration policies for all disadvantaged persons, natives and immigrants alike: minority policies thus changed into integration policies. During the formation of the new government upon the 1998 parliamentary elections it was furthermore decided to appoint a minister for these integration policies (*Minister voor Grote Steden – en Integratiebeleid*). His department is part of the Ministry of the Inte-rior. Shortly after his appointment, this minister, Roger van Boxtel, made pub-lic that he considered the Netherlands to have become a country of immigra-tion; perhaps not in the classical sense but at the very least de facto. This implies that society should be geared to welcome a permanent influx of new-comers and suitable policies be put in place. And henceforth *all* persons legally residing in the Netherlands, meaning regardless of their nationality, should be considered to be citizens[8] of that country.

---

[6] Also without state funding, institutions were highly segregated: e.g. trade unions and em-ployers organisations.

[7] In all fairness it should be pointed out that the German SPD-Green government that came into power in 1998 has significantly changed policies pertaining to naturalisation, thus enabling children of immigrants to obtain German citizenship without great obstacles. See also the article on Germany in this volume.

[8] Citizen is here used as a translation of the Dutch term *burger*, meaning a person who is allowed to fully participate in society and shall in no way be discriminated against. It is not synony-mous with having been granted Dutch nationality.

Already earlier governments had started to make large sums available to combat social exclusion in the four main cities (Amsterdam, Rotterdam, The Hague and Utrecht), or at least to eradicate its most depressing symptoms. The most visible result of this has been the urban renewal of run-down neighbourhoods were ethnic minority groups are particularly present. This presence is on the one hand the result of general policies in the allocation of low-rent housing based upon objective criteria like income, household size and urgency, and on the other of the fact that many middle class families leave the larger cities and move to the suburbs with semi-detached houses. Spatial segregation therefore should be understood as the outcome of socio-economic differences within the population at large. To ensure a better mix of different ethnic and socio-economic groups, which is generally considered to be beneficial to society, currently schemes are being implemented whereby more expensive rented and owner-occupied housing is built as part of the renewal programmes for those deprived areas. Policies whereby segregation is prevented by the establishment of quota for certain ethnic groups have been discussed at earlier stages, predominantly on the local government level, but were never put in place in the Netherlands. These would have been contrary to the non-discrimination principles laid down in the first article of the Dutch constitution.

As to labour market integration, comprehensive efforts have been, and are still being, made. The main general policy instrument is the creation of additional jobs; i.e. employment beyond the needs dictated by the free market. The oldest of those schemes (1992) is aimed at the young and is called Youth Employment Guarantee Law (*Jeugdwerkgarantiewet*, JWG) which makes available work for every person under 21 years of age (until age 23 for school leavers) who has been unemployed for six months. Not accepting this offer means losing social security benefits for three months. As long as subjects have not found regular employment they may remain in this scheme until they reach their 27th birthday.

In 1995 policies came into force that target all long-term unemployed. Many of those jobs are created in the public sector and are usually referred to as *Melkert* jobs, after the then Dutch minister for Employment and Social Affairs. The basic funding of these additional jobs is mainly provided for by the reallocation of social security benefits participants would otherwise be entitled to. The minimum duration of unemployment required in order to qualify depends on the precise modalities of the job-creation scheme, of which there are several, and ranges between one to three years. *Melkert 1* jobs are planned to be a permanent addition to the labour market and 40,000 long term unemployed should be reintegrated as a result. The *Melkert 2* scheme (1995-1998) is intended to create jobs for which employers receive a substantial subsidy (Fl. 18,000 annually) if they take on long-term unemployed workers for a minimum duration of six months and a maximum of two years. *Melkert 3* jobs are created by allowing jobless persons who depend on social security to retain their benefits while pursuing job-training or accumulating working experience. The *Melkert 4* programme, lastly, resembles *Melkert 2* in that it subsidises the labour costs (again Fl. 18,000 per annum) for employers but this time solely for cleaning services. The goal of all these schemes is on the one hand to increase the quality of public life (reducing crime rates and vandalism by employing people as *stadswacht* (literally city guard) or as ticket collector in the public transport sector to reduce fair dodging, in nursing and the like, and to stimulate people to seek for or retain employment in the private sector. It is hoped that people who were no longer used to a regular work life and without recent working experience, after some period in an employment scheme will be better qualified and more attractive to employers. In 1996 around 73,000 people were employed through such job schemes (accounting for 13 per cent of total employment growth between 1990 and 1996) (CBS 1997b, 77).

We have not been able to establish in detail the relative or absolute numbers of long-term unemployed from ethnic minorities employed through the several *Melkert* schemes. We do have, however, some data for Amsterdam from which it becomes evident that long-term unemployed natives are twice as likely to be employed in a *Melkert*-job than would be expected from their relative share among such unemployed workers. The reverse is true for Turks and Moroccans who are only half to one fourth as likely to find such employment (Sandburg 1998). The reasons for this phenomenon could not be established. Other sources indicate that young people with a Turkish, Moroccan, Surinamese or Antillean/Aruban background seem to benefit to a considerable extent from the existence of the Youth Employment Guarantee Law (JWG) (Tesser/Veenman 1997, 203). Given their relatively poor performance in the educational system (see below) this, in itself, is not surprising. For the Youth Employment Guarantee Law the net-effectivity rate for those young people (i.e. the proportion of those who would probably not have been able to enter the regular labour market without it) is estimated to lie at 25 per cent against an overall figure of 18 per cent (op.cit., 204).

2.2. Targeted Policies

Since the early 1980s, the Dutch government has pursued a policy that should extend a maximum of legal and social rights to foreign residents, in the hope that such rights would enhance their overall integration. The current emphasis on "citizenship", as pointed out above, is basically a reinforcement of this policy. Basically, after five years of legal residence the rights of non-nationals only differ from those of nationals where provincial and national elections are concerned and in access to certain government positions and the right to serve in the armed forces[9]. After the same amount of time foreigners can also apply for naturalisation (after three years when having a Dutch national as spouse). In addition, naturalisation and citizenship laws have been further relaxed over time and between 1991 and 1996 dual nationality, e.g. Turkish and Dutch, was possible[10]. For those persons who cannot surrender their old nationality because the law of their country of origin does not permit them to, and for those from whom it cannot be expected to contact the authorities of their state of origin (e.g. refugees), double nationality remains possible. Naturalisation rates are considerably higher in the Netherlands than they are in France or Germany: 8.7 per cent of all foreign residents in 1997 and as high as 17.5 for Turkish nationals[11] (CBS 1999a, 73). Currently more Turkish born immigrants are registered as Dutch nationals then as Turkish nationals (88,000 as compared to 83,000 in 1998). Among Moroccans the desire to become Dutch nationals appears to be smaller (52,000 and 93,000 respectively).

The past decades have seen several policies specifically targeted at increasing the employment levels of immigrant groups. Probably the oldest example stems from the 1980s when a quota of public sector jobs became reserved for Moluccan immigrants[12]. Since 1987 the government attempts to increase the relative size of employees from immigrant origin in the public sector: a policy named Ethnic Minorities in the Public Sector (*Etnische Minderheden bij de Overheid*, EMO). Its instruments were targeted recruitment, the setting of target figures, monitoring and publicising the ethnic composition of the public sector labour force, evaluation of selection procedures, information, and, when equally qualified, preferential hiring (Tesser et al. 1996, 127). Although this policy has not had the overall desired effect, it did help to double the number of Moroccan and Turkish young people in the civil service between 1987-1989 and 1993-1995 (Tesser/Veenman 1997, 134). On the local level, similar initiatives have

---

[9] Conscription has been suspended in the mid 1990s.

[10] In 1991 the Second Chamber of Parliament had agreed on this and anticipating it becoming part of Dutch nationality law the administration started implementing dual nationality. However, in June 1996 legislation formalising the practice did not pass the First Chamber of parliament.

[11] It should be born in mind that the rate increases when the number of non-naturalised persons decreases. Among Turks meanwhile at least half the population holds a Dutch passport.

[12] Predominantly former soldiers in the Dutch-Indian colonial army and their families who were brought to the Netherlands upon Indonesian independence and who had long hoped to be able to return soon to their own independent state on the Molucca Islands.

been developed, mainly in the form of preferential hiring practices[13]. These policies, however, are neither prescribed nor enforced by the national government.

Employers in the private sector, meanwhile, did not want to commit themselves to a similar effort. In 1990, under government threats to enforce quota for the recruitment of workers from ethnic minorities, an agreement (*Stichting van de Arbeid*[14], STAR) was reached to increase the number of employees from ethnic minorities by 60,000 in the period between 1990 and 1995. To assist in this, the labour exchanges were to appoint officials whose task it would be to balance the needs of employers with those of job-seeking members of ethnic minority groups (Tesser et al. 1996, 129-30). As it turned out the readiness among employers to implement the STAR agreement has not been as large as originally anticipated. This again fuelled discussions on the possible advantages of installing legal quota or devising policies similar to those known as contract compliance in Northern America. Judging this to be a step too far, the government in 1993 proposed a law on the promotion of equal employment participation of the allochthonous (*Wet bevordering evenredige arbeidsdeelname allochtonen*, WBEAA). This law required all private and public enterprises with 35 employees or more to register their employees' ethnic background and to strive for a work force which is representative of the overall population. Moreover, the WBEAA included the obligation to publish plans detailing how the employer intended to increase (where applicable) the number of non-natives in his workforce. Both employers and employees organisations initially showed considerable reluctance to implement this law but after a large PR offensive most of them agreed to comply (op.cit, 140-2). With time it became increasingly evident that employers were unwilling to implement this law. As it did not contain provisions on sanctions against unwillingness the government decided to amend the WBEAA, removing the obligation to publish ambitions and policies towards them, and it these days goes by the name Law on Stimulating Employment among Minorities (*Wet Stimulering Arbeid Minderheden*, Wet

---

[13] The Amsterdam municipality, for example, commits itself to the preferential hiring of women, and of members of ethnic minorities if such a candidate has the same qualifications as a native applicant. Currently 15,1% of its employees belong to ethnic minority groups, which is considerably less than the 26% of their proportion in the city's labour force. Nevertheless, the city council considers its effort successful because the municipality's employees are, by nature, disproportionately skilled, whereas members of ethnic minorities relatively often lack those skills.

[14] The Dutch Social Economic Council, a platform for dialogue between employer organisations, trade unions and the government.

SAMEN[15]). Whether this new law will indeed have the desired effect for the time being remains an open question.

In education, special facilities exist for primary schools with disproportionate numbers of immigrants' children. These high numbers can be attributed to two factors; the unequal geographical distribution of immigrant families, and the selective preference among native parents for schools that are predominantly frequented by ethnic Dutch children. In the media the former schools are frequently labelled 'black schools', a depiction that in the light of the pupils' diverse ethnic backgrounds has little bearing on social reality. Notably the fact that 'black schools' receive additional staffing funds, and are thereby able to decrease class-sizes and hence increase the amount of attention spend per child, is an important policy tool.

The targeted policies mentioned above are mainly relevant for those immigrants who have been in the Netherlands for some length of time, and for their descendants. From January 1, 1996 there are in addition policies specifically aimed at the integration (*Inburgering*[16]) of newcomers. This *Inburgerings-beleid* is principally aimed at refugees and those arriving as asylum seekers who have been granted a leave to stay, immigrants who arrive in the course of family formation and reunification (usually with a partner who is considered to belong to one of the ethnic minorities), and Antilleans and Arubans (who are Dutch nationals) older than 18 years of age in case they run the risk of becoming marginalised. To assess this risk all newcomers mentioned are invited for an intake session where, if necessary, a tailor-made integration programme is agreed upon. The immigrant subsequently is under legal obligation to complete this programme. If he fails to do so, sanctions can be imposed[17]. The policy has a three stage goal: social, educational and professional self-reliance. The first foregoing the second stage and that again the last one, whereby social self-reliance is seen as the absolute minimum for an immigrant to be able to function in Dutch society. The first stage is achieved when the immigrant has a basic knowledge of the Dutch language and has absolved a course in Dutch culture and society (600 hours). The second stage prepares the immigrant for entrance in the educational system, and the last stage enables him to take up employment (Brink et al. 1997). The years 1996 and 1997 were considered to

---

[15] This acronym in Dutch means 'together'.

[16] A term stressing that this policy aims to equip newcomers to become full *burgers* who are able to enjoy all rights and comply to all duties.

[17] These sanctions are imposed by the municipal authorities and take the shape of a relatively small cut of the immigrant's social security benefits. In case the immigrant does not comply because he has meanwhile found employment, he is expected to pay a fine as if still receiving benefits. The effects of this sanction can thus only be marginal.

be a trial period[18]. From then on the necessary educational capacities should be in place and the programme no longer is merely on a voluntary basis. Even though the policy is primarily geared towards the integration of newcomers who depend on benefits, this does not mean that those who are not dependant on financial assistance or those who have been in the country for a longer time cannot participate. The 1996-97 trial period has meanwhile been evaluated (ibid.) but the relative small numbers of participants and the limited amount of time that has elapsed since the implementation started, do not allow for any firm conclusions as to the effectiveness of this policy. Nevertheless, early in 2000 Parliament was of the opinion that the policies appeared not to be sufficiently effective and demanded a more active implementation. It appears there are considerable differences between municipalities in this respect[19]. This was reflected by the fact that of a nationally available budget of around 300 million distributed over the municipalities, one sixth had remained unused (Tweede Kamer der Staten Generaal 1999-2000, doc. nr. 27083).

Immigrants who come to the Netherlands in order to work, are exempted from the integration programme. The idea behind this exemption has been a) that these immigrants do not settle permanently (work permits as a rule are granted for a limited period of time), and b) that by virtue of the fact that they are needed on the labour market, their integration is assured as far as necessary. One exception to this rule has been formulated some years after the law came into force. In a number of instances, that often sparked headlines in the Dutch newspapers, some imams (who usually hold a three year working permit and are subsequently replaced by another newcomer from the country of origin) were found to hold discriminatory opinions on homosexuality, and/or made derogatory remarks about Dutch (secular) society in their Friday sermons. It is assumed that this is the result of ignorance about the finer points of Dutch society, for instance the first article of the Constitution, which prohibits all forms of discrimination. To remedy this, imams recently have been included in the integration programme.

---

[18] This policy is underpinned by the Law on the Integration of Newcomers (*Wet Inburgering Niewkomers*) which came into effect on 1 October 1998. Under this law, municipalities are obliged to investigate the need for *Inburgering* among all newcomers and to apply all relevant policies in those cases where such need is established.

[19] There appears to be, for instance, considerable reluctance among municipal authorities to impose sanctions in the first place.

3. The Position of Immigrants and their Descendants

If we want to look at the integration of newcomers in a society one should first of all concentrate on two dimensions: structural integration and social integration. For the original immigrants who form the largest categories of the target groups of Dutch integration policies, i.e. former guest worker populations, their relatives and those arriving more recently as asylum seekers and refugees, the general picture does not merit much joy. In structural terms, their position on the labour market is problematic. In spite of a healthy economy and historically low unemployment rates for the population in general, unemployment rates among Turks and Moroccans remain relatively high – even though they do show a downward trend – and in 1998 lie four to five times higher for Turks and Moroccans and approximately two times higher for Surinamese and Antilleans/Arubans (Martens/Weijers 2000). Net participation rates, moreover, are much lower than average for the total population: less then half of Turks and Moroccans is active on the labour market (which includes those who are registered as unemployed) whereas this pertains to two-thirds of the native population aged between 16 and 65. Surinamese and Antilleans/Arubans, however, have a net participation rate which comes close to that of the native population (ibid.).

Integration in social terms is also lagging behind, for instance in terms of inter-ethnic contacts/friendships. Turks and Moroccans of the first generation have fewer such contacts than Surinamese and Antilleans/Arubans, but for all groups a huge increase is visible when we look at their children (ibid.). This should not surprise us as these immigrants in most cases have long lived with the expectation to return to their country of origin and therefore saw little need to integrate into society beyond the structural dimension. Their children, however, being socialised in their parent's host country do generally speaking not share this ambivalent outlook on life.

If we further concentrate our attention on the children of those migrants who were born and bred in the Netherlands the picture becomes much more diverse. Research has shown that the children of Surinamese immigrants in Amsterdam show a very high rate of exogamy once they reach adulthood (Van Heelsum 1997)[20]. In the educational system their participation rate is higher than average compared to their native peers and this also pertains to the levels achieved (ibid.). Gramberg (2000) studied the effects of school segregation on educational attainments and could not find significant disadvantages. Crul (2000a and b), who did of a study of educational careers of children of Turkish and Moroccan immigrants, found that they do much better than is often con-

---

[20] It should be pointed out, though, that these were children who often have one Surinamese and one native Dutch parent which may have distorted the picture to some, unknown, extent.

cluded from the surveys mentioned in section 1. These surveys do not differentiate between children born abroad and entering the educational system at a later age and those children who were born in the Netherlands or arrived at pre-school age. If the former are excluded, Moroccan and Turkish children seen as a category may still not reach educational attainment equal to that of their Dutch peers, but on the individual level Crul finds many examples of children who do well in school and have a good perspective on attaining university degrees. Given the fact that their parents as a rule are poorly educated, and especially among Moroccans often illiterate, this development merits the expectation of a gradual emancipation from working class to middle class for these groups as a whole within a few generations. This then would closely resemble the emancipation of the native working classes which also took more than a single generation to pass.

4. Conclusion

The dominant mode of integration pursued in the Netherlands during the past decades – after it became evident that immigrants with diverse ethnic backgrounds would become part of Dutch society – has been one of extending rights. Those rights are seen as a necessary tool towards further integration in all other spheres of life: all legally resident persons, regardless of their nationality, are perceived and treated as citizens (a term frequently leading to misunderstanding abroad where the term is usually synonymous to having the nationality of a state). In this respect, Dutch policies lean closely to those common to the Republican model. In contrast to that model, cultural and religious diversity is actively promoted by the government: the explicit right to be different and develop one's own identity.

This principle is matched with policies that should reinforce the social fabric or, put differently, constantly recreate society. In this view, not any given state society may have should be taken as a standard in to which 'the others' could or should assimilate.

The Dutch government meanwhile officially regards the Netherlands as a multi-cultural society. This obviously has a rhetorical dimension as the fundamental values of Dutch society do not stand open for discussion (these, after all, are laid down in the country's constitution) and a number of practices some would consider essential elements of newly arrived cultures like female circumcision, polygamy or inequality between men and women, are clearly not allowed. Yet, rhetoric matters considerably (Doomernik 2001). It helps to remind citizens of the need for tolerance and may help immigrants feel welcome and their children to belong. Although this can be deemed to be an important policy element, it is backed by investments in the labour and housing markets and in education.

The effect of these policies is the creation of an environment in which the "normal process of emancipation" (i.e. the same process the native population went through during the past few generations) is given free rein. As we have seen in section 3, there are sufficient indications to suggest this policy to be successful by and large.

References

Amersfoort, H. van 1987:

'Van William Kegge tot Ruud Gullit; de Surinaamse migratie naar Nederland: realiteit, beeldvorming en beleid', *Tijdschrift voor Geschiedenis*, 100, pp. 475-490

Brink, M. et al. 1997:

Evaluatie inburgeringsbeleid voor nieuwkomers, Amsterdam: Regioplan

Castles, S. / Miller, M.J. 1993.

The Age of Migration. International Population Movements in the Modern World, Houndmills and London: Macmillan

Centraal Bureau voor de Statistiek (CBS) 1997a:

Allochtonen in Nederland, Voorburg/Heerlen: CBS

Centraal Bureau voor de Statistiek (CBS) 1997b:

Werken en leren 1997, Voorburg/Heerlen: CBS

Centraal Bureau voor de Statistiek (CBS) 1999a:

Maandstatistiek bevolking, April, p. 73

Centraal Bureau voor de Statistiek (CBS) 1999b:

Statistisch Jaarboek 1999, Voorburg/Heerlen: CBS

Crul, M. 2000a:

De Sleutel tot Succes: Over Hulp, Keuzes en Kansen in de Schoolloopbanen van Turkse en Marokkaanse Jongeren van de Tweede Generatie, Amsterdam: Het Spinhuis

Crul, M. 2000b:

'Breaking the Circle of Disadvantage. Social Mobility of Second-Generation Moroccans and Turks in the Netherlands', in Vermeulen, H. and Perlmann, J. (eds.) *Immigrants, Schooling and Social Mobility. Does Culture Make a Difference?*, pp. 223-244, Houndmills: Macmillan

Doomernik, J. 1995:

'The Institutionalization of Turkish Islam in Germany and The Netherlands. A Comparison', *Ethnic and Racial Studies*, Vol. 18, 1, pp.46-63

Doomernik, J. 1998:

The Effectiveness of Integration Policies towards Immigrants and their Descendants in France, Germany and The Netherlands, Geneva: International Labour Office (International Migration Papers 27)

Doomernik, J. 2001:

Immigration, Multi-Culturalism and the Nation State in Western Europe, Paper for the UNRISD conference *"Racism and Public Policy"*, Durban (South Africa), September 3-5

Fleuren, W. 1996:

Oriëntatie in de vreemdelingenwetgeving, Utrecht: Nederlands Centrum Buitenlanders

Gramberg, P. 2000.

De school als spiegel van de omgeving. Een geografische kijk op onderwijs, Amsterdam: University of Amsterdam

Hammar, T. (ed.) 1985:

European Immigration Policy. A Comparative Study, Cambridge: Cambridge University Press

Heelsum, A. J. van 1997:

De etnisch-culturele positie van de tweede generatie Surinamers, Amsterdam: Het Spinhuis

Hooghiemstra, E. 2000:

'Gemengd huwen en transnationaal huwen in Nederland: enkele feiten', *Migrantenstudies*, Vol. 16, pp. 198-208

Lijphart, A. 1977:

Democracy in Plural Societies. A Comparative Exploration, New Haven/London: Yale University Press

Lucassen, J. 1984:

Naar de kusten van de Noordzee. Trekarbeid in Europees perspectief, 1600-1900, Gouda: J. Lucassen

Lucassen, J. / Penninx, R. 1994:

Nieuwkomers, Nakomelingen, Nederlanders. Immigranten in Nederland 1550-1993, Amsterdam: Het Spinhuis

Martens, E.P. / Weijers, Y.M.R. 2000:

Integratiemonitor 2000, Rotterdam: ISEO/Erasmus Universiteit Rotterdam

Muus, P. 1994:

Migration, Immigrants and Policy in The Netherlands (report for SOPEMI/ OECD), University of Amsterdam: Department of Human Geography

Penninx, R. 1988:

Minderheidsvorming en emancipatie. Balans van kennisverwerving ten aanzien van immigranten en woonwagenbewoners, Alphen a/d Rijn/Brussels: Samsom

Sandburg, C. 1998:

Werkt 't of werkt 't niet? Melkert- en andere additionele banen voor allochtonen, M.A. thesis, University of Amsterdam: Department of Human Geography

Tesser, P. et al. 1996:

Rapportage minderheden 1996. Bevolking, arbeid, onderwijs, huisvesting, Rijswijk: Sociaal en Cultureel Planbureau

Tesser, P. / Veenman, J. 1997:

Rapportage minderheden 1997. Van school naar werk; de arbeidskansen van jongeren uit de minderheden in verband met het door hen gevolgde onderwijs, Rijswijk: Sociaal en Cultureel Planbureau

Eve Kyntäjä

Towards the Development of an Integration Policy in Finland

1. Historical and Socio-Cultural Background

It is difficult to understand the situation of ethnic minorities and immigration issues in Finland without knowing the larger socio-historical background of the country. The Finnish social and cultural environment has always developed in an intermediary position between the East and the West. Finland belonged to the Swedish empire until 1809, and between 1809-1917, Finland was an autonomous Grand Duchy under the Russian Empire. The Swedish language subsequently remained dominant in the country throughout the Russian annexation. When Finland gained its independence from Russia in 1917, Finland became a bilingual country. According to the 1919 Constitution Act of Finland, Finnish and Swedish are the national languages of the Finnish Republic. In 1920, the Swedish-speaking minority in Finland amounted to some 11 per cent of the population, but now it has decreased to six per cent (Hannikainen 1996).

Because of the specific role of Swedishness in the history of Finland, the Swedish-speaking Finns today are in an ambivalent position. From the time of the Swedish colonisation to the last decades of the 19th century, the ruling class of Finland was Swedish-speaking. The great majority of the Swedish-speaking Finns such as farmers, fishermen and others living in rural areas had, however, little or no contact with the political and economic elite. It is also noteworthy that the Finnish national movement, which started during the first half of the 19th century, was created and led mostly by Swedish-speaking members of the upper classes. The emergence and maintenance of the stereotype of the Swedish-speaking Finns as an upper class population has influenced the Finnish-speaking people's group consciousness and even today these questions are a matter of public discourse (Liebkind 1995).

Compared to the Swedish-speaking minority, the other "old" minorities in Finland are small, the Sami number some 7,000, the Roma some 6,000 – 8,000, and Jews and Tatars approximately 1,000 each. The Finnish Sami do not enjoy such a privileged status as the Sami have in Sweden and Norway, as the political weight of Finnish Samis is quite small. In 1991 the Sami language was granted a certain semi-official status in the Sami territory in northern Finland. Another major improvement in 1991 was a new provision for the Samis in one of the constitutional laws in the Finnish Parliament Act. According to Section

52a of the Act, the Finnish Parliament shall hear representatives of the Sami (at least the Sami Parliament) before making decisions in matters which affect Sami interests. Another year that has been good for Finnish indigenous minorities was 1995. At this time the Finnish Constitution Act was amended by a provision that allowed the Sami, the Roma, the Jews and the Tatars to have the right to maintain and develop their own language and culture. At the same time the Finnish Parliament enacted laws which specify the content of the cultural autonomy, reorganise the Sami Parliament and improve the role of the Sami in the decision-making process (Hannikainen 1996).

Nowadays the old Russian-speaking minority consists of some 2,500 – 3,000 persons. During the period of autonomy under the Russian Empire, tens of thousands of Russians, mainly soldiers, merchants, civil servants and tourists, lived in Finland as permanent or temporary residents. In particular, the Russian troops stationed in Finland increased the number of Russians in Finland considerably. In peace time they amounted to roughly 10,000; in times of war or civil unrest, their number was naturally higher. Some Russian soldiers and sailors decided upon retirement to remain in Finland (Nylund-Oja et al. 1995). When Finland established its independence in 1917, about 6,000 Russians resided in Finland. After World War I and the Russian Revolution, the number of refugees from Eastern Europe in Finland was more than 33,000, half of these were Russian emigrants. From 1922 onwards, the number of immigrants decreased, as many of the former Russian soldiers moved to the émigré Russian colonies in Paris, Brussels and Berlin. In the late 1930s, the Russian community in Finland consisted of about 15,000 persons (Nylund-Oja et al. 1995).

Finland's long history under foreign powers seems to have influenced the national consciousness and attitudes towards newcomers, and has definitely left an impact on national strategies towards immigration. As a result, Finland has been an ethnically quite homogeneous country after gaining its independence. Furthermore, Finland remained a rural society for a long time, the process of urbanisation beginning there much later than in other Nordic countries. A crucial period in the development of Finnish society has been rapid industrialisation and urbanisation since World War II. Finland has actually been a rather closed society since World War II, mostly because of the Iron Curtain. In comparison with the other Nordic countries and the rest of Europe, Finland's immigration policy has been remarkably restrictive.

2. General Nation State Integration

2.1. Concept of Nationhood in Finland

Many social scientists have claimed that immigration and citizenship policies are linked to the concept of nationhood prevailing in country. According to Brubaker (1994) the restrictiveness of German citizenship towards immigrants reflects an ethnocultural definition of nation-state membership, in contrast to the state-national definition typical of France. In his view, this is an outcome of the political history of Germany, which did not exist as a state before the late 19th century when an ethnocultural understanding of a German 'Volk' had already been developed. This concept of 'Volk' determined the understanding of nation, whereas in France the understanding of the nation developed in the content of an already existing state. With regard to Finland there has been a specific situation. At the advent of Finnish nationalist movement, Fennomania, Finland was not an independent state but a part of the Russian Empire. Still, it already existed as a political unit, the autonomous Grand Duchy of Finland. Finnish nationalism came to be a mixture of culturally marked autonomist nationalism and state nationalism including elements from both an ethnic-genealogical and civic-territorial concept of nation (Laari 1998). According to Dominique Schnapper, it is artificial to reduce definitions of nation states either to the ethnic or civic dimension – in today's world nation state refers to both dimensions (Schnapper 1998).

2.2. Acquisition of Finnish Citizenship

The Finnish citizenship law is based on the *jus sanguinis* tradition. It is not possible to acquire Finnish citizenship automatically by residing in the country for a number of years. Finnish citizenship can be acquired on the basis of birth, by application or by notification.

Children receive Finnish citizenship *at birth* if, among others, the child's mother is a Finnish citizen, if the child's father is a Finnish citizen and the mother foreign and the parents are married to each other, or when the child was born in Finland and did not acquire the citizenship of any other country at birth. Foreigners may *apply* for Finnish citizenship if they have reached the age of 18, have lived in Finland long enough before submitting an application (5 years as a rule), have lived a "respectable" life, have a secure income and are proficient in Finnish or Swedish. The acquisition of citizenship via *notification* is easier than via the application procedure. Notification is possible, for example, for children whose father is a Finnish citizen and whose mother is a foreigner, but who are not married to each other, for adopted children of Finnish citizens and for former citizens of Finland (native born).

Even if an immigrant manages to become a Finnish citizen relatively easily, it is extremely difficult to be considered and accepted as a "Finn" by the host population. There seems to be no proper category for an immigrant who has received a Finnish passport and has become a Finnish citizen. It seems that immigrants living in Finland are still regarded as foreigners even after residing in the country for many years and having been naturalised.

2.3. The Role of the Nordic Universalistic Welfare State

The Nordic countries are unique in a number of areas in comparison to Western European countries, universalistic social welfare systems being one of them. The idea of the Nordic system is that social benefits are allocated according to universal criteria to all residents, regardless of whether one has been employed or not. In this way Nordic social policy is different from German corporative and British liberalistic welfare systems, where social security is based on factors such as working experience, insurance, family, non-governmental organisations and church affiliation.

According to the Finnish legislation on social welfare, everyone in Finland is entitled to social security and welfare services on the basis of permanent residence. The social security system in Finland, like in other Northern countries, is based on residence instead of work. The freedom to choose one's place of residence in Finland is guaranteed by the Finnish constitution. According to Article 7, all people residing legally in Finland, no matter whether they are Finnish or foreign citizens, are entitled to move freely within the country and choose their place of residence. The right to receive municipal services is granted to all residents of a municipality. The responsibility of municipalities for welfare services is much more extensive in the Nordic universalist system than in Central and Southern Europe, where municipalities are often the last resort in providing social support, and support provided by them is mainly financial and not in the form of services (Kosonen 1998).

In Finland, immigrants are often accused of living on welfare. On the other hand, in public discussions immigrants are at the same time criticized for "taking our jobs". The high level of unemployment in Finland makes it very hard for an immigrant to find a job, and a majority of foreign citizens is unemployed. Certain immigrant communities are in danger of becoming marginalised and forming a kind of sub-culture.

3. From Emigration to Immigration Country – Main Migratory Flows in Finland After World War II

Historically, Finland has mainly been a country of emigration. The turning point came in the 1980s when emigration reached its lowest post-war level, whereas immigration was high. Until the end of this decade, however, most of the immigrants were Finnish returnees. In comparison with the rest of Scandinavia, Finland has until quite recently been a rather isolated spot, virtually untouched by either global or European migrations. Figure 1 provides the statistics of Finnish emigration and immigration between 1945-2000.

Figure 1: Migration Flows in Finland 1945-2000

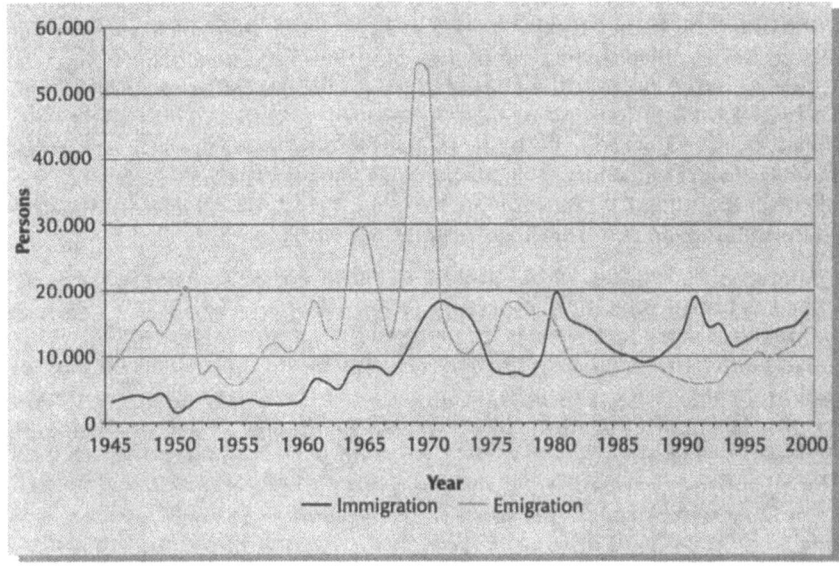

Source: Statistics Finland

As the process of integration in Europe advances the opportunities for studying and working abroad improve, interest in leaving Finland for Europe increases. However present estimates indicate that mass emigration along past lines is unlikely. The opposite is more likely. Finland appears to be changing into a receiving immigration country.

3.1. Emigration

During the last one hundred years, more than one million Finns have moved abroad, nearly 500,000 of them before World War II and about 700,000 after the war. Before the war, the majority of the emigrants moved to North America and, after the war, about 75 per cent went to Sweden. Approximately half of these emigrants have returned to Finland. Emigration has generally followed economic development in target countries to the extent that during booms it has increased, and during recessions it has decreased correspondingly (Korkiasaari 1992 and 1993).

In the Nordic countries – Denmark, Finland, Iceland, Norway and Sweden – a common labour market, a passport union and the agreement on non-discrimination and far-reaching social rights for people migrating from one Nordic country to another have been in place for four decades. Since the establishment of the Common Nordic Labour Market in 1954, more than one million Nordic citizens have availed themselves of the opportunity to move freely within the Nordic region. A noteworthy feature of most of the inter-Nordic movements has been a high proportion of migrants returning to their country of origin. Moreover, since the early 1980s, the migratory flows between the Nordic countries have been comparatively small and have tended to balance each other out. Likewise, the migratory movements between the Nordic countries and other Western European countries have been rather small.

Migration to Sweden – and formerly to North America – can clearly be described as labour migration, especially in the 1960s and 1970s, since most of the migrants were seeking jobs to earn their livelihood. Unemployment in Finland and better salaries in Sweden were the dominant motives for this migration. In the 1980s, this migration decreased noticeably due to economic reasons. The main reasons for this were depression and structural changes in the Swedish economy, as well as the narrowing of the differences between the Finnish and Swedish economies and standards of living. Thus current motives for moving to Sweden are primarily non-economic or personal, as they have long been in emigration to other European countries (Korkiasaari/Söderling 1998).

Only about 25 per cent of Finnish post-war emigrants have moved to countries other than Sweden. The majority of these emigrants have been women, especially as far as migration to Western and Southern Europe is concerned. These migrants have tended to be older and to have higher educational qualifications than migrants to Sweden. In addition, the motives for migration have been quite different. In the 1980s, marriage was the most important individual motive for migration to countries outside Scandinavia.

3.2. Immigration

3.2.1. General Picture

Until quite recently, Finland has not been exposed to the consequences of massive migration. The number of foreigners had remained fairly constant at around 10,000 for a long time, the exact figure in 1950 was 11,423 (0.3 % of the whole population) and it was still 12,000 in 1976. About one hundred refugees from Chile were admitted in 1973 and the first Vietnamese 'boat people' arrived in 1979. Also some small voluntary immigrant groups arrived (e.g. Turks). A slow increase then began to take place during the 1980's, and this was followed by a wave of immigration beginning in 1990. The steepest annual rise was recorded in 1991 with over 11,000 persons entering the country. The largest groups were from the former Soviet Union and asylum seekers from Somalia (Statistics Finland 1997b, 1998b).

Until the end of the 1980s, approximately 85 % of the immigrants coming to Finland were returning migrants from Sweden and their families. So the majority of these immigrants were actually former Finnish citizens who had received Swedish citizenship during their residence in Sweden. In the 1990s, however, more than half of the immigrants were persons of foreign origin. In 1980, the number of foreign citizens residing in Finland was about 13,000, but it exceeded 80,000 in 1997. During the same period, the number of foreign-born persons increased from 39,000 to about 117,000. The total number of foreign citizens in Finland is still very small: approximately 1.7 per cent out of five million inhabitants, a lower percentage than in most countries in Europe (Statistics Finland 1997b, 1998a, 1998b, Finnish Population Register Centre 2000).

The reasons for increased immigration were partly international and partly domestic in origin: the collapse of the Soviet Union and the civil war in former Yugoslavia as well as developments in Asia and Africa. A shortage of domestic labour at the end of the 1980s also affected immigration, but because of the economic recession in 1990s this impact was short-lived.

During recent years, the number of immigrants from the former Soviet Union has increased quite rapidly in Finland. Almost 40 % of all immigrants (33,000) are from the former Soviet Union. There are approximately 20,000 Russian and 11,000 Estonian citizens, and 2,000 persons still hold the Soviet passport (Finnish Population Register Centre 2000). Many of the people in these groups are of Finnish origin.

3.2.2. Ethnic Finns (Ingrian Finns) as Return Migrants From the Former Soviet Union

A special characteristic of the Finnish migration situation is the phenomenon of ethnic migration from the former Soviet Union. The majority (70 %) of the immigrants from the former Soviet Union (22,000) have the status of a so-called *Ingrian, i.e. return migrant*, because of their Finnish ethnic background (Ministry of Labour 1998). Ethnic migration, or "return migration" refers to citizens of the former Soviet Union with a Finnish ethnic background. Finnish origin is, however, defined on the basis of quite distant relationships. The return migration of Soviet (Ingrian) Finns started in 1990 when the former Finnish President Mauno Koivisto raised the issue of ethnic Finns living in the Soviet Union, declaring that the same criteria of return migration should be applied to Soviet Finns as to ethnic Finns returning from Sweden (or other Western countries). President Koivisto's statement started a large movement that brought over 10,000 Ingrian Finns to Finland within a couple of years. Currently, there are approximately 22,000 Ingrian Finnish returnees – including their family members – living in Finland. A similar process of return migration from the former Soviet Union – migration that is based on ethnicity – is also common in Germany, Greece and Israel (Kyntäjä 1997).

Ethnic Finns from the former Soviet Union can be defined as descendants of Finns who settled in these countries in the 17th century in the vicinity of present-day St. Petersburg when the district became a part of the Swedish Kingdom. The 1926 Soviet census indicated that there were about 135,000 Ingrians living in the Soviet Union. As a result of Stalin's repressions in the 1930s, all Ingrian Finnish parishes were abolished, Finnish language teaching was forbidden, and about 50,000 Ingrian Finns were deported or exiled to Siberia and Central Asia. During the Second World War, a part of Ingria was left to Germany in the siege of Leningrad. According to the agreement between Germany and Finland (1942), about 63,000 Ingrians were transferred to Finland. Later, however, the interim peace treaty between the Soviet Union and Finland contained a clause which decreed that all Soviet citizens, including Ingrians, had to be returned to the Soviet Union. About 55,000 Ingrians decided to leave Finland, and although they were promised that they could go back to their homes, the majority of them were deported directly to Siberia or Central Asia. After the death of Stalin most of the deported people, including the Ingrians, were allowed to return back home. Nevertheless, the Ingrians were not allowed to settle in their former homes villages in Ingria (near St. Petersburg). Most of them settled in Soviet Carelia, but about 1/3 started a new life in Soviet Estonia because the living standard was better there. The majority of the Ingrian Finns' descendants speak Russian, but there is also a small group that speak Estonian (Kyntäjä 1997).

3.2.3. Refugees and Asylum Seekers

The arrival of refugees in Finland from remote countries dates back to the 1970s when the country accepted the first 100 refugees from Chile in 1973. Between 1973 and 1977 a total of 182 refugees came to Finland from Latin America, the majority of whom have since returned home or moved to another country. In 1979, Finland accepted the first Vietnamese boat people. The Vietnamese were all placed within the vicinity of Helsinki. The next group of over 100 arrived in 1983. Since 1986 Finland has regularly accepted a specific number of refugees according to an annual quota – about 500-1,000 people depending on the refugee situation in Europe. There are, however, far fewer refugees (17,000) in Finland today than there were directly after the Russian Revolution in 1917 when Finland gained its independence (Nylund-Oja et al. 1995, Ministry of Social Affairs and Health 1995, Statistics Finland 1998b, Finnish Population Register Centre 2000).

Since the mid-1980s, the number of asylum-seekers has soared in Nordic countries. Most of these went to Sweden, amounting to about 233,000 persons in 1989-95. In Denmark the number of asylum-seekers was around 55,000, in Norway 36,000 and in Finland 12,500. The first asylum-seekers arrived in Finland in 1990 from Somalia. After this, the amount of asylum seekers increased rapidly, but during 1995 it dropped considerably – the reason being stricter control at the Eastern border and by the redefinition of Russia and Estonia as safe countries of origin (Söderling 1993, Sopemi 1995).

4. The Composition of the Immigrant Population in Finland

Statistics in Finland still use the word "alien" in relation to foreign-born and foreign citizens. Civil servants and policy-makers have started to use "immigrant" instead of "alien" or "foreigner" when dealing with people of foreign origin who have permanent residence in Finland. According to the small number of foreign citizens residing in Finland, the Centre of Statistics began to provide special statistics on aliens living in Finland in the early 1980s. It is now possible to find data about persons who are living permanently in Finland: their nationality, country of birth, native language, gender and age. There are also statistics on immigrants' naturalisation, unemployment, divorces and mixed marriages. Statistics on foreigners' educational background and occupational qualification are insufficient at present, because there have been problems in classifying immigrants' jobs and education standards. Unfortunately there are no official statistics on immigrants' socio-economic position, income, and housing. Some sociological research has been done on this, but the results only describe the period when the research was carried out. Finnish statistics on aliens and international migration is developing fast and soon more specific statistics will be available.

193

Questions of second generation immigrants, or children of international migrants, have not been on the agenda in Finnish society yet, and so far there are no statistics on this group. Public discussion is more interested in those immigrant teenagers who have moved with their parents to Finland some years ago, and who have great difficulties in adaptation.

The foreign population living in Finland can be divided into four main groups that partly overlap:

1. Spouses of Finnish citizens;

2. Ethnic return migrants from the former Soviet Union (Ingrian Finns);

3. Return migrants from Sweden (former Finnish citizens who have returned to Finland, i.e. former emigrants and their children);

4. Refugees and asylum seekers (with residence permit).

Marriage has been one of the principal reasons for migrating to Finland for a long time. Approximately 2,000 aliens marry a Finn every year. In 1997 over 23,000 aliens who were married to a Finn resided in the country (part of them are of Finnish origin, however; e.g. returnees from Sweden and Ingrian Finns). Common-law marriages increase the number to over 30,000. As for labour migration the number of actual labour migrants in Finland is extremely small.

4.1. National and Gender Composition

The largest groups of foreigners have come to Finland from Russia, Estonia, Sweden and Somalia. Table 1 provides the statistics for the foreign resident population in Finland.

It is remarkable that almost 40 % of all immigrants have come from the former Soviet Union. Men make up 51 % of the foreign population. The largest refugee groups have all a male majority except for the Vietnamese. Foreigners in Finland speak about 150 different languages. Women account for roughly half of the total, but the ratio varies ethnically: the majority of Africans and Southern and Western Europeans are men, whereas the majority of Russians, Estonians, people still with Soviet passport, Filipinos and Thais are women. Regionally, the majority of all immigrants have concentrated in big cities. In fact, half of the alien population in Finland resides in Uusimaa (a district near Helsinki), mostly in the metropolitan area (Statistics Finland 1997a, 1998a, 1998b).

Table 1: Largest Groups of Foreign Citizens According to Nationality and Gender (Oct. 31, 2000)

Nationality	Total	Males	Females	Females percent %
Russia + Soviet Union	22,738	8,873	13,865	61.0
Estonia	10,738	4,266	6,472	60.3
Sweden	7,891	4,401	3,490	44.2
Somalia	4,220	2,107	2,113	50.1
Federal Republic of Yugoslavia	3,562	1,951	1,611	45.2
Iraq	3,110	1,723	1,387	44.6
United Kingdom	2,220	1,679	541	24.4
Germany	2,160	1,410	750	34.7
USA	2,064	1,184	880	43.6
Iran	1,961	1,105	856	43.7
Vietnam	1,813	874	939	51.8
Turkey	1,766	1,334	432	24.5
China	1,687	813	874	51.8
Bosnia-Herzegovina	1,614	814	800	49.6
Thailand	1,276	213	1,063	83.3
Others	21,241	10,597	9,119	42.9
Total	90,504	43,345	45,1594	49.9

Source: Finnish Population Register Centre, Monthly Statistics

4.2. Employment and Labour Market

As has been said earlier, Finland is not a country of labour migration, and no systematic recruitment of foreign labour has been conducted. The majority of the immigrant population is of working age but faces great problems finding work. Since the sharpest increase in the alien population coincided with the years of recession, unemployment has emerged as a major barrier to integration into Finnish society. Given a national unemployment rate of 12.2 % in 1991, the percentage among immigrants was double this figure. According to the Ministry of Labour, about half of the immigrant population is unemployed. Currently the real number of unemployment rate is estimated to be much higher. The unemployment problem does not seem to be disappearing and so the majority of immigrants will probably continue to face exclusion and marginalisation in the future (Similä 1996, Statistics Finland 1998b, Ministry of Labour 2000).

Table 2: Unemployment Rate Among Foreign Residents in 1994-30.4.2000

Nationality	Unemployment rate in regional labour statistics			Estimate of Ministry of Labour		
	1994	1997	1998	1997	1998	30.4.2000
Iraq	91	79	81	76	93	79
Iran	78	69	66	72	77	75
Somalia	92	74	64	75	66	69
Bosnia-Herzegovina	-	80	67	78	92	60
Vietnam	63	60	59	70	80	58
Federal Republic of Yugoslavia	88	74	67	73	64	51
Morocco	70	57	58	66	66	51
Russia+USSR	-	56	53	57	56	47
Russia	79	64	58	-	-	-
USSR	49	38	34	-	-	-
Turkey	54	42	37	43	37	37
Thailand	58	43	39	43	37	34
Estonia	63	40	32	43	33	30
Norway	24	23	14	16	15	14
Italy	-	33	19	22	19	13
Poland	28	24	18	24	14	13
China	20	17	13	14	12	13
United Kingdom	25	17	15	17	13	12
Sweden	32	25	21	16	11	11
Germany	19	17	12	16	10	11
France	-	15	15	16	13	10
USA	-	14	11	15	10	8
All foreign residents	53	44	39	43	38	34

Source: Statistics Finland, Ministry of Labour

The worst hit by unemployment refugees were from Bosnia-Herzegovina, Iraq and Somalia. A clear distinction also emerges between immigrants from the "East" and immigrants from the "West". Citizens of the Western Europe countries are much better employed than are migrants from the former Eastern block.

4.3. The Ethnic Hierarchy of Foreigners

According to Jaakkola's sociological research (1991), British, North American, Japanese, ex-Soviet, Western and Eastern Europeans had the highest socio-economic status in the 1980s. These nationalities were most likely to be found on the primary labour market where salary, promotion, influence and tenure are better. On the other hand, Southern Europeans, South Asians and Africans were more often to be found on the secondary labour market where salary and socio-economic status are low.

The most common occupations among foreigners at the time of research were language teaching and music. Although they only account for a low percentage of the employed foreigners, the figure is quite high among certain nationalities. Language teachers are often British or French, whereas musicians are often Eastern Europeans. Germans and Swiss were most likely to be found in managerial posts in business and commerce, while Southern Europeans, Africans and South Asians, notably the Vietnamese, were more often working in industry or in low-paid service occupations (Jaakkola 1991, Nylund-Oja et al. 1995, Statistics Finland 1994, 1996).

5. Public Attitudes towards Immigrants in Finland

Magdalena Jaakkola's (1995, 1999) studies describe the changing trends in Finns' attitudes to refugees and other immigrants in 1987, 1988, 1993, 1998 and 1999. The main reason for the negative attitudes in 1993 was that Finns felt a socioeconomic threat and particularly a fear of unemployment. A marked increase had arisen in negative attitudes towards Russian, Polish, Turkish, Vietnamese, Chilean, Kurdish, Somalian and the former Yugoslavian immigrants. Estonians were still quite accepted (among the five most preferred immigrant groups), but, relatively, negative attitudes towards them had developed, too (Jaakkola 1995). After the improved economic situation in 1998, Finns' attitudes towards immigrants became more positive. The attitudes towards Scandinavians, Ingrian Finns (or Soviet Finns) and Anglo-Saxons were still the most positive, while the attitudes towards Russians, Arabs and Somalis were the most negative (Jaakkola 1999). The attitudes in 1999 were not, however, as positive as before the recession in 1987 when there were few immigrants in Finland.

Despite official efforts to foster integration, immigrants are not always easily accepted in Finnish communities (Liebkind 1996). The high unemployment rate on one hand, and negative attitudes of Finns towards immigrants, on the other hand, could create a situation where all immigrants (except immigrants from the Western countries) are under the threat of becoming stigmatised. According to the research conducted by Jasinskaja-Lahti and Liebkind (Liebkind/Jasinskaja-Lahti 1997, 2000; Jasinskaja-Lahti 2000), the majority of young immigrants (especially Russians, Somalis, Arabs, Turks) had experienced racism and discrimination to a certain extent.

6. Refugee Resettlement Policies

Finland has similar refugee resettlement and reception policies as other Nordic countries. The Finnish policy focuses on integration of refugees into society. Integration is encouraged through an extensive programme of language training and orientation courses. The emphasis in these programmes is often on finding employment for the refugees. The introductory courses for immigrants include practice at different jobs and extensive guidance about different career opportunities. In Finland, as elsewhere, employment is seen as a key factor in the integration of refugees.

There is a kind of multi-cultural ethos embedded in the official resettlement policies in Finland. However, as Matinheikki-Kokko (1997) has pointed out, Finnish policies are contradictory. The government papers about refugee re-settlement are based on liberal pluralist ideas, but the policy recommendations are still universalistic. Of course, discrepancies between theory and practice also exist in the immigration policies of other Nordic countries.

In practice, Finnish resettlement policy is often based on rather unrealistic expectations of a fast integration or even assimilation of refugees. At the same time, refugees are often seen as persons who have lost everything, in terms of material, social and cultural capital. Consequently, refugees are sometimes treated in the same way as small children, or as persons who must undergo a kind of re-socialisation into Finnish society.

One policy which has been criticised by many authors is the policy of dispersal according to which refugees are resettled in small groups throughout the country (Liebkind 1995, Matinheikki-Kokko 1997, Walhbeck 1997, Valto-nen 1997). This practice does not support the establishment of cultural com-munities among refugees, nor does it try to take into account the resources which exist within the refugees' own social networks. Furthermore, Liebkind (1996) has argued that lack of cultural communities is a detrimental factor affecting the psychological well-being of refugees in Finland. Walhbeck has conducted a study on the Kurdish diaspora in Great Britain and Finland, and finds that Finnish resettlement system has not taken into account the trans-national networks and the diasporic nature of the Kurdish refugees' experi-ences. Instead, the resettlement system has been dominated by the Finnish authorities' preoccupation with "integration issues" (Walhbeck 1997).

Nevertheless, it is important to remember that the resettlement policies actually do work very well in some respects. For example, one sympathetic feature of the Finnish resettlement policies is that the refugees' stay in the country easily becomes permanent, therefore temporary status and special arrangements have largely been avoided.

7. From ad-hoc Responses towards the Development of an Integration Policy – Policy Programmes 1980-1994

Immigration and integration policies are not only questions of ideas and concepts but also of budgets, administrative practices, and finally, border control. Three refugee policy programmes were published during 1980-1994. When the first refugee groups arrived from Chile in 1973, and from Vietnam in 1979 the Refugee Committee was a central channel of collaboration for the government. This committee prepared and coordinated settlement programmes under the administration of Ministry of Labour. In 1980, the Committee published the Report of the Refugee Committee and this was the first time official guidelines for refugee care were laid down. According to the Committee settlement had been of an ad hoc nature between 1973-1980, and often involved uncoordinated reactions to particularly pressing problems as they arose. A coherent, overall strategy did not exist.

In 1981, an act of Parliament shifted the responsibility for refugee care to the Ministry of Social Affairs and Health. As a result, the Department of Refugee Affairs took over the role of the Refugee Committee. In 1989, the Department published its programme for Finnish Refugee Policy.

In 1992, the Advisory Board for Refugee and Migration Affairs, as part of the Ministry of Labour, became the central inter-administrative body for policy-making. This board was appointed by the Council of State for a period of three years. The Advisory Board began to coordinate, develop, plan and evaluate both refugee and migration policy. In 1994, the Board defined new goals and guidelines for refugee and migration policy entitled *"Principles of Finnish Refugee and Migration Policy"*.

8. The 1997 Government Programme on Immigration, Integration and Refugee Policy

In 1995, the Finnish Government set up the Committee on Immigration and Asylum Policy in order to prepare a policy programme for the government. This committee consisted of different political party members, NGOs, and leading civil servants. In the beginning of 1997, the committee completed its work and submitted its proposals to the Minister of Interior.

According to the committee's chairman, a consensus had been reached among representatives from the various political parties, authorities and NGOs that Finland's first programme on immigration and refugee policy should be implemented within the next 3 to 5 years. Dissenting opinions were added to the report by the representatives of three ministries. The committee's general conclusion was that immigration should be promoted, taking into consideration the current economic and social situation. The report included almost 300 concrete recommendations for action. The report of the Commission for Immigration and Refugee Policy was entitled *"Controlled Immigration and Efficient Integration. The Proposal for Immigration and Refugee Policy"*.

Finland did not have an officially defined immigration and integration policy before this report. Practice has, to a great extent, been based on legislation, instructions of different ministries and decisions made by authorities. Finnish authorities declared in their new report that the "objective of Finland's immigration policy is the flexible and efficient integration of all immigrants, i.e. migrants, returning migrants and refugees, into society and working life". Integration of immigrants was defined as "the immigrants' participation in the economic, political and social life in society". This report also declared that "the adoption of the language and the rules of the game in society are the precondition for success in Finland. The advantage to Finnish society and the immigrants living here is the fact that they can maintain their language and cherish their culture".

8.1. A Three-Level Policy as a New Approach

The Government agreed on the *Programme on Immigration and Refugee Policy* in principle on October 16, 1997. The defined objective of this policy is to support the integration of immigrants whose residence in Finland is considered to be legal and permanent, and who have been entered in the population register. According to the programme, integration means that the immigrants participate in the economic, political and social life of society as equal members. Simultaneously immigrants have the possibility of maintaining and developing their own culture and religion in harmony with the legislation in Finland.

A three-level policy is pursued when implementing the integration of immigrants:

▶ National integration policy: the Government will include a section dealing with immigration policy in its annual report to Parliament.

▶ A municipal immigration policy programme and an integration plan: In their immigration policy and integration plans, individual municipalities, or neighbouring municipalities together, define the aims and measures, resources and cooperation activities relating to the integration of immigrants.

▶ Integration plans for individuals and families: these include measures (e.g. language instruction, daily routines, drawing up of a plan for studies or employment, practical training, vocational training and social contacts) that contribute to the integration of the immigrant.

8.2. The Guidelines of the New Policy Programme

The programme is supposed to be implemented gradually within the limits of the state's economic resources. The programme can be described as follows:

8.2.1. Compensation System

The compensations municipalities receive for offering integration services aim at stimulating municipalities to implement policies that promote integration, prevent marginalisation, stimulate immigrants' own initiative and compensate for costs that the home municipality has incurred at the initial stage of immigration.

An agreement drawn up by the municipality and the State is required before a municipality can receive compensation for the costs incurred by the reception of refugees and measures taken to promote integration. A municipal integration plan or a commitment to draw up one has to be included in the agreement.

The compensation system will also cover the returnees from the former Soviet Union. The compensation system will be revised within 2-4 years. At the same time a need for a compensation system concerning all immigrants will be examined.

8.2.2. Measures Promoting Structural Integration

Settlement: Immigrants are in the same position as the rest of the population when choosing the place and form of residence. At the initial stage of immigration, however, refugees are placed in municipalities that have made an agreement with the state concerning provision of services to promote integration and compensation of costs. It is also required that the municipality or neighbouring municipalities together have drawn up a local or regional integration plan for immigrants. When distributing apartments, attention is paid to the creation of adequately large ethnic groups so that the social and ethnic composition of the total population in the area remains heterogeneous.

Young People and Children: Within child welfare, a programme will be developed that includes facilities to help children and young people coming from areas of war and crisis. Municipalities must arrange the daycare of immigrant children as required by their special needs, taking especially into account support for the child's own language and culture. Municipalities and non-governmental organisations will hire immigrants to work with children and young people. The immigrants' native language teaching will be increased in comprehensive school from the present two hours a week per group to 3-4 hours a week as an additional course. Immigrants will also be taught their native languages in the upper secondary school and basic vocational training.

Preparatory training is also arranged in comprehensive schools, upper secondary schools and basic vocational training. Young persons over 16 years of age whose comprehensive school education has been interrupted are given complementary comprehensive school education through special arrangements.

Adult Education: The general aim is to give all adult immigrants a chance, when necessary, to participate in adult immigrant education fostering integration into society and working life. If necessary, adult immigrants are given basic and further vocational training. Adult immigrant education will be financed and arranged as employment training. There is no special programme for immigrant adult education like, for instance, in the Netherlands.

The scope and length of adult immigrant education is determined on the basis of the individual's needs. Young and adult immigrants who are illiterate and/or lack basic education are provided with expanded immigrant education in which basic education is included. Education and labour administration consider the needs of adult immigrants in employment training, vocational adult education, university studies, apprenticeship and liberal education.

Employment: Unemployment is a factor that hampers immigrants' integration to a great extent. Immigrants are entitled to all existing labour services. The aim is to support employment of immigrants, especially in sectors where they can utilise their knowledge of language and culture (export, tourism, service sectors, immigrant services, and public administration).

The employment of immigrants will be supported by providing immigrants with a sufficient amount of language teaching and training that supplements their vocational skills, by setting up networks of self-employed persons that offer immigrants posts as trainees or apprentices or subsidised work, which all lead to employment, and by promoting immigrants' corporate and cooperative entrepreneurship. According to the guidelines of the programme it is of utmost importance that immigrants are hired to duties in public administration. This statement, like many others, is just a general recommendation as there is no concrete action plan for this.

Social Welfare and Health Care Services: Those multicultural working methods that can be used to support the immigrants' own initiative and participation will be included in basic and further training in social welfare. Courses in "multicultural health care" will be incorporated in basic and further health care training. Health care services will be developed so that immigrants coming from areas of war and crises (e.g. children that have been tortured and suffer from mental disorder) can be provided with treatment and rehabilitation. The special needs of immigrant women and elderly persons will be taken into consideration when planning the contents of integration plans at local level.

Protection of Family Life and Implementation of Children's Rights: It has been proposed that the Aliens' Act and the Convention on the Rights of the Child will be coordinated by amending acts, decrees and instructions in order to protect children's interests materialise under all circumstances.

Immigrants' Participation and Right of Initiative: Employees with an immigrant background will be trained and hired to tasks in public administration, and their expertise will be utilised when planning and implementing services for immigrants. The Decree on the Advisory Board for Refugee and Migration Affairs will be amended to the effect that the Advisory Board will work in two compositions: one will be equal to the present composition, and in the other composition, half of the members will represent traditional and new groups of immigrants. The Advisory Board will be consulted as an expert when legislation that concerns immigrants and ethnic minorities is under preparation, and when ministries issue norms.

8.2.3. Measures Promoting Cultural and Social Integration

Supporting Immigrants' Native Language and their Own Culture: The aim is to help immigrants maintain and develop their own language and culture and practise their religion. A sum in the state budget will be allocated annually for the activities of immigrants' own associations, for instruction in their native language and culture, for the production of newspapers/magazines and radio programmes in their own language and for presentation of their own culture to the majority population. The Finnish Broadcasting Corporation will develop programme activities in the immigrants' own languages, making use of international cooperation.

Interpretation and Translation Services, Information to Immigrants: The aim is to provide immigrants with interpretation and translation services to guarantee all with permanent residence in Finland equal access to public services. The authorities are responsible for the availability of interpretation and translation services and for resources. Different authorities, coordinated by the Ministry of Labour, shall produce information material for immigrants in their native language.

Fostering Tolerance: Human rights, foreigners' legal status, interaction between different cultures and tolerance shall be discussed in basic and further training of different occupational groups, especially if the groups come into contact with immigrants in their work. The work of non-governmental organisations and other local activities will be supported so that the fostering of

203

tolerance and cooperation with immigrants becomes a natural part of these activities. The field of activity of the Ombudsman for Aliens will be extended to also cover ethnic discrimination. The Ministry of Labour, in cooperation with the other responsible ministries, will establish a system for monitoring racial discrimination and violence aimed at ethnic groups. The need for legislative amendments for the implementation of the UN Convention against racial discrimination will be checked.

8.2.4. Actors and Political Responsibility in Immigration and Integration Policy

The Government sets the general objectives for immigration and refugee policy pursued in Finland. Parliament can regularly influence the policy pursued by means of a report procedure, when the Government submits its annual report or whenever the need arises.

A new provision will be incorporated in the Aliens' Act and in the future law concerning reception of refugees and measures promoting immigrants' integration. According to this provision, the Government sets the general objectives of immigration and refugee policy pursued in Finland.

A ministerial working group on immigration and refugee policy will be appointed consisting of the Minister for Foreign Affairs, Minister of the Interior, Minister of Labour, Minister of Social Affairs and Welfare, Minister of Education and Science and Minister of Justice.

The central actors in immigration and refugee affairs are the Ministry for Foreign Affairs, the Ministry of the Interior and the Ministry of Labour. According to the so-called two-pillar model there is a clear division of duties concerning permit administration and surveillance (Ministry of the Interior) on the one hand and questions related to reception and integration of refugees (Ministry of Labour) on the other hand.

9. Towards Realisation of the New Integration Policy Programme

9.1. Immigrants as New Actors in the Integration Policy – Towards Social Integration and Partnership?

The proposal for the Finnish Immigration and Refugee Policy included a suggestion by the Commission that the Advisory Board on Refugees and Migration Affairs (PAKSI) should be developed into a panel which would provide immigrants with the opportunity to participate in preparing reforms concerning their own affairs. On May 15, 1998 the Finnish Government appointed the Advisory Board for Ethnic Relations (ETNO) for a period of three years. ETNO assists the ministries in coordinating refugee and migration affairs in state administration and in developing, planning and monitoring refugee and migration policy. ETNO also promotes interaction between authorities, civic organisations operating in the field, migrants and ethnic minorities. This advisory board has developed and supported measures to promote migrants' integration into society as well as to promote tolerance and good ethnic relations in society, especially at the place of work. Fourteen representatives have been appointed by different ethnic minorities and language groups. This is the first time immigrants can participate in the decision-making process and affect decisions that concern themselves.

9.2. New Integration Law – Combining Duties and Rights – Towards Communitarism?

The government agreed on the *Programme on Immigration and Refugee Policy* in principle in 1997. The next step was taken in the spring of 1998, when the Finnish government submitted the new bill for the integration of immigrants. The Act on Integration of Immigrants came into force on May 1, 1999. The act prescribed that general development, planning, control, coordination and supervision of immigrants integration are attended to by the Ministry of Labour. At the regional level, the Employment and Economic Development Centres are responsible for the integration into the society and working life. At the local level, the municipality prepares an integration programme together with the employment and other appropriate authorities. These programmes include clear aims, procedures and resources for integrating the immigrants into the municipality.

The new policy has also an individual level, which means that immigrants have to draw up a personal integration plan together with a representative from an employment office. Individual integration plans concern only these immigrant newcomers who are registered as unemployed job-seekers and who receive public assistance. Integration plans for individuals include measures (e.g. language instruction, daily routines, drawing up of a plan for studies or employment, practical training, vocational training and social contacts) that should contribute to the integration of the immigrant into Finnish society. Commitment to an integration plan gives immigrants a right to receive public assistance, the so called "integration support", instead of "ordinary" unemployment benefits like before. In case of refusing to follow the plan, immigrants will lose a part of their public assistance.

In short, the new law means that rights are given to immigrants while at the same time duties are assigned to them. Implementing the Integration of Immigrants Act will be a challenge, but it also addresses possible problems regarding use of power by municipal authorities who are dealing with these integration plans. On the other hand, the new act could also bring new tools and opportunities for immigrants themselves to integrate into Finnish society and working life, to maintain their native language and to cherish their culture. The new integration policy is trying to unite the rights and duties in the spirit of communitarism, a new development in the Finnish universalistic welfare state.

10. Conclusions

Finland has traditionally been a country of emigration. Until the 1990s, most foreign citizens who settled in Finland were returning Finnish emigrants. The proportion of immigrants constitutes about 1.7 % of the total Finnish population, which is one of the lowest percentages in Europe. The number of refugees is extremely small in Finland. Until 1994, settlement policies were developed only for people with refugee status, and actually, even refugee policy implementation was mostly of an ad hoc nature until 1980. There was no official national immigration and integration policy programme until 1995 in Finland. Since becoming a member of the European Union, Finland was obliged to start harmonising its immigration policy in respect to other member countries. In 1995, the government set up the Committee on Immigration and Asylum policy. In 1998 a bill for the integration of immigrants was adopted that was enacted in 1999.

Living on social welfare is an accusation directed against many immigrants in Finland. The social security system in Finland, like in other Nordic states, is based on residence instead of employment. In other words, all residents, no matter whether they are Finnish or foreign citizens, are entitled to social security and welfare services. Instead of integration, the system of social welfare may, in some cases, contribute to a negative development. The new integration policy is trying to link rights and duties of immigrants in the spirit of communitarism, which is new for the Nordic universalistic welfare state. The new law of integration has also a function of social control.

A special characteristic of the current situation is the phenomenon of ethnic migration from the former Soviet Union, which is similar to Germany (Aussiedler). Ethnic migration or "return migration" as it has been defined, refers to the citizens of the former Soviet Union with a Finnish ethnic background. The process of ethnic migration started in 1990 as an *ad hoc* policy, but fairly soon it became obvious that nearly all returnees needed Finnish language teaching and other preparatory training, just as refugees do. It is still not clear what the political motivation was when descendants of Soviet Finns' were defined as return migrants, which automatically meant that they were given all rights to a permanent residence permit and to social welfare. Many social scientists in Finland suggest that the criteria to get a residence and work permit should be more equal for all applicants and should not be based to any imaginary "blood-tie" ideology.

Finnish immigration and integration policy has focussed primarily on the immigration status. Integration training, Finnish language teaching and other preparatory training programmes, have been available mainly to refugees and the ethnic return migrants from the former Soviet Union. According to official ideology, the aim of this policy is to develop and support measures to promote migrants' integration into society, as well as to promote tolerance and good ethnic relations in society, especially in working life. Integration is defined as an option, while immigrants can maintain their own culture, language and ethnic identity but at the same time adjust to the host society. The Advisory Board (ETNO) has been creating an image of a multicultural Finland and national framework for multicultural policy.

To conclude, the current situation can be interpreted as taking basic steps towards a national integration policy towards immigrants. Discrepancies between theory and practise still exist – despite the new policy programme being based on the general ideas of multiculturalism, the policy recommendations in that programme are still quite universalistic and play on the rules of the host population. During the 1990s multiculturalism became a buzzword in policy regarding foreign residents. In practise, however, multiculturalism has been considered an issue directly related to immigrants: firstly as being a consequence of their presence, and secondly as giving them the responsibility to learn Finnish customs and the Finnish language while preserving their own culture. But the crucial question is: *does the term FINN actually refer to any Finnish citizen, or to someone who can be ethnically or culturally defined as Finnish?* The conceptual boundary between a Finnish-born Finn and a foreigner with a Finnish passport appears to be virtually insurmountable (Lepola 2000). Immigrants are left outside the concept of Finnish identity and Finnishness. Whether immigrants in Finland can ever actually become Finns will depend on whether Finnish identity stresses ethnic origin or Finnish citizenship, residence in Finland and integration in Finnish society.

References

Brubaker, R. 1994:

Citizenship and Nationhood in France and Germany, Cambridge (Mass.): Harvard University Press

Finnish Population Register Centre 2000:

Monthly Statistics (unpublished)

Hannikainen, L. 1996:

'The Status of Minorities, Indigenous Peoples and Immigrant and Refugee Groups in Four Nordic States', *Nordic Journal of International Law*, 65, pp. 1-71

Jaakkola, M. 1991:

Ulkomaalaiset Suomessa. Perhe, työ ja tunteet, Helsinki: Työministeriö

Jaakkola, M. 1995:

Suomalaisten kiristyvät ulkomaalaisasenteet, Työpoliittinen tutkimus 101, Helsinki: Työministeriö

Jaakkola, M. 1999:

Maahanmuutto ja etniset asenteet, Työpoliittinen tutkimus 213, Helsinki: Edita

Jasinskaja-Lahti, I. 2000:

Psychological Acculturation and Adaptation among Russian-Speaking Immigrant Adolescent in Finland, University of Helsinki: Department of Social Psychology (Research Reports)

Korkiasaari, J. 1992:

Siirtolaisia ja ulkosuomalaisia. Suomen siirtolaisuus ja ulkosuomalaiset 1980-luvulla, Työpoliittisia tutkimuksia 33, Helsinki: Työministeriö

Korkiasaari, J. 1993:

'Siirtolaisuus – ja ulkomaalaistilastot' (Migration Statistics of Finland), *Population 1993: 8*, Helsinki: Statistics Finland

Korkiasaari, J. / Söderling, I. 1998:

'Finland: From a Country of Emigration to a Country of Immigration', in Söderling, I. (ed.), *A Changing Pattern of Migration in Finland and Its Surroundings*, pp. 7-28, Helsinki: The Population Research Institute

Kosonen, P. 1998:

Pohjoismaiset mallit murroksessa, Tampere: Vastapaino

Kyntäjä, E. 1997:

'Ethnic Remigration from the Former Soviet Union to Finland – Patterns of Ethnic Identity and Acculturation among the Ingrian Finns', *Yearbook of Population Research*, 34, pp. 102-114

Laari, O. 1998:

'Immigrants in Finland: Finnish-to-be or Foreigners forever – Conceptions of Nation State in Debate on Immigration Policy', in Söderling, I. (ed.), *A Changing Pattern of Migration in Finland and Its Surroundings*, pp. 29-48, Helsinki: The Population Research Institute

Liebkind, K. 1995:

'Some Problems in the Theory and Application of Cultural Pluralism: The Complexity of Ethnic Identity', in Pentikäinen, J. and Hiltunen, M. (eds.), *Cultural Minorities in Finland. An Overview towards Cultural Policy*, pp. 28-43, Helsinki: Publications of the Finnish National Commission for UNESCO No 66

Liebkind, K. 1996:

'Acculturation and Stress. Vietnamese Refugees in Finland', *Journal of Cross Cultural Psychology*, 27, 2, pp. 161-180

Liebkind, K. / Jasinskaja-Lahti, I. 1997:

'Maahanmuuttajien onnistuneen integroitumisen esteitä (Obstacles to Successful Integration of Immigrants)', in Schulman, H. and Kanninen, V. (eds.), *Sovussa vai syrjässä? Ulkomaalaisten integroituminen Helsinkiin (Together or Separate? The Integration of Foreigners in Helsinki)*, pp. 93-104, Helsingin kaupungin tietokeskuksen tutkimuksia/City of Helsinki Urban Facts, 1997:12

Liebkind, K. / Jasinskaja-Lahti, I. 2000:

'The Influence of Experiences of Discrimination on Psychological Stress among Immigrants: A Comparison of Seven Immigrant Groups', *Journal of Community and Applied Social Psychology*, 10, 1, pp. 1-16

Lepola, O. 2000:

Ulkomaalaisesta suomenmaalaiseksi. Monikulttuurisuus, kansalaisuus ja suomalaisuus 1990-luvun maahanmuuttopoliittisessa keskustelussa (From Foreigner to Finlander. Multiculturalism, Nationality and the Finnish Identity in the Political Debate on Immigration during the 1990s), Helsinki: SKS

Matinheikki-Kokko, K. 1997:

Challenges in Working in a Cross-Cultural Environment. Principle and Practice of Refugees Settlement in Finland, Jyväskylä: University of Jyväskylä

Ministry of Labour 1998:

Inkerinsuomalaisten maahanmuutto Suomeen (Immigration of Ingrian Finns to Finland). Työhallinnon julkaisu (the Reports of the Labour Department)

Ministry of Labour 2000:

Unemployment Rate among Aliens (unpublished)

Ministry of Social Affairs and Health (Office for Refugee Affairs) 1995:

Basic Facts about Refugees and Asylum Seekers in 1995, Helsinki

Nylund-Oja, M. / Pentikäinen, J. / Jaakkola, M. / Yli-Vakkuri, L. 1995:

'Finnish Emigration and Immigration', in Pentikäinen, J. and Hiltunen, M. (eds.), *Cultural Minorities in Finland. An Overview towards Cultural Policy*, pp. 173-228, Helsinki: Publications of the Finnish National Commission for UNESCO No. 66

Schnapper, D. 1998:

Community of Citizens. On the Modern Idea of Nationality, New Brunswick and London: Transaction Publishers

Similä, M. 1996:

Finland and Immigration in 1995, Report to the European Commission, Dated 31.1.1996

Söderling, I. 1993:

'Social Work with Refugees in a Nordic Welfare State', *A European Journal of International Migration and Ethnic Relations*, Special Issue from Scandinavia (ed. Jan Hjarnö), 18, pp. 171-188

Sopemi 1995:

Trends in International Migration. Continuous Reporting System on Migration, Annual Report 1994, Paris: OECD

Statistics Finland 1994:

'Ulkomaalaiset Suomessa. The Foreign Population in Finland', *Population 1994:3*, Helsinki

Statistics Finland 1996:

'Ulkomaalaiset ja siirtolaisuus. Aliens and International Migration', *Population 1996:6*, Helsinki

Statistics Finland 1997a:

'Perheet. Families 1996', *Population 1997:11*, Helsinki

Statistics Finland 1997b:

'Ulkomaalaiset ja siirtolaisuus. Aliens and International Migration', *Population 1997:14*, Helsinki

Statistics Finland 1998a:

'Väestörakenne. Population Structure 1997', *Population 1998:5*, Helsinki

Statistics Finland 1998b:

'Ulkomaalaiset ja siirtolaisuus. Aliens and International Migration 1997', *Population 1998:8*, Helsinki

Valtonen, K. 1997:

The Societal Participation of Refugees and Immigrants. Case Studies in Finland, Canada and Trinidad, Turku: Institute of Migration

Walhbeck, Ö. 1997:

Kurdish Refugee Communities. The Diaspora in Finland and England, Dissertation, Submitted to the University of Warwick

Rosa Aparicio / Andrés Tornos

Towards an Analysis of Spanish Integration Policy

1. The Scenario of Immigration to Spain

1.1. Demographics of Migration

It has become a topic to say that Spain has only recently turned from a country of emigration to one of immigration. The fact is that it is only in the 1990's that the net migratory balance for the Spanish population begins to show negative signs (i.e. there are more returnees than emigrants)[1]. The decade of the 1960's experienced the largest outward flows when 2.5% of the Spanish population emigrated to foreign lands. The rate decreased to 1.3% in the 70's, reaching a low of 0.5% in the 80's[2]. The end in the early seventies of the economic boom in industrialised countries which resulted in more restrictive measures for foreign labour in Western and Northern Europe, and the later rise of the Spanish economy which from 1975 onwards began to grow offering more opportunities in the labour market as well as better living conditions, accounted for this turn. But even now that emigration has become stabilised with larger return flows than outward flows, Spain still counts with a significant number of Spanish people (almost 2,000,000) in the nations to which they emigrated, more than double the amount of foreign immigrants in the country.

The number of legal foreign residents in Spain begins to rise in the decade of the seventies coinciding with the decrease of emigration, but it is not until the end of the 1980's and beginning of the 1990's when figures become really significant and start to cause alarm. If we look into these figures we see that, according to official sources, the number of legal foreign residents in Spain rises from 148.400 in 1970 to 1,109,060 in 2001. We find a moderate rate of increase until the end of the 1980's, which then accelerates between 1990 and 1994. Then it begins to slow and is reaching stability until 2000, when figures rise again, as can be seen in table 1 below[3].

---

[1] The net migratory balance for the year 1998 was -25.726 (this figure only takes into account the movements by Spanish nationals; it does not consider international migrants).

[2] Source: Ministry of Labour and Social Affairs, *Anuario de Migraciones 1996*, p. 34.

[3] This rise coincides with two extraordinary regularisation processes as a consequence of the approval of Law 4/2000 of January 11th 2000 . It was nonetheless seen by many not only as an effect of bringing to light the concealed pouches of irregular migrants but as a "calling effect"

Table 1: Foreign Population in Spain (1953-2001)

Year	Total Foreign Population	Percentage Increase
1953	59,483	-
1960	64,660	1.2
1970*	148,400	12.9
1980**	182,045	2.3
1990**	276,796	5.2
1992**	402,350	22.6
1994**	461,364	7.3
1995**	499,773	8.3
1996**	538,984	7.8
1997**	609,813	13.1
1998**	719,647	18.0
1999**	801,332	11.3
2000**	895,720	11.8
2001***	1,109,060	23.8

Sources: Own elaboration from:
* Ministry of the Interior (quoted by Izquierdo 1992, 55)
** *Anuario Estadístico de Extranjería*, Ministry of the Interior (Home Office)
*** Provisional figures provided by the OPI, Ministry of the Interior

In spite of its significant increase during the recent decade, the population of foreign residents on Spanish territory only represents a small percentage of the total population. That is 2.7% (1.9% if we leave out EU citizens), a percentage far below that of many other countries in the European Union.

It is true that official figures are on the low side because they do not take into account several categories of migrants, some legally in the country, others not. The holders of asylum permits, those with a student visa and EU citizens with conditional or temporary residence permits would be in the first category. Irregular migrants as well as persons from other European countries who reside in Spain for most part of the year but do not hold a residence permit would be in the second category (the latter would be the case of many British, German and Dutch pensioners, amongst others). Finally, naturalised migrants are also

---

(*efecto llamada*) put in motion by the same law which favoured irregular migrants with almost the same rights as regular immigrants. Law 8/2000 modified the previous law, hardening conditions for these migrants. It remains to be seen whether this will have an effect on the flow of irregular migrants. Recent signs are nonetheless not very encouraging.

not included in the number of regular migrants yet their acquired legal status as Spanish citizens does not automatically make them such culturally and otherwise.

Looking into the available figures for the excluded categories we find that the number of asylum seekers has never been high in Spain and has been steadily going down since 1995, partly as a result of the more restrictive law and regulations passed relatively recently. Thus numbers have gone down from 12,615 in 1993, the year for which there were the most applicants, to 6,764 in 1999[4], which means almost a 46.4% reduction in that period[5]. On the other hand, slightly over 1.5% of the foreign population are given Spanish citizenship each year since 1989, the largest percentage being Latin-Americans (59.5% in 2000) who only need to prove 2 years of legal residence to acquire it.

Leaving out foreigners whose stay is supposedly temporary, there can be no registers for the two remaining groups: foreigners from other European countries without a residence permit and irregular migrants. Concerning irregular immigrants, estimates vary widely from around 25% to around 50% percent of the foreign population from third countries[6].

---

[4] Source: Ministry of the Interior, General Police Directorate.

[5] This figure has risen to 7,926 in 2000. Most of this increase can be attributed to the worsening of the armed conflict in Colombia which has lead many to seek refuge in Spain.

[6] The most conservative calculations (for instance those in the report on irregular immigration in Spain presented by Antonio Izquierdo at a seminary organised by the OCDE and the Dutch Authorities in April 1999 in the Hague) are those based on:

1. The number that apply to be included in the yearly quotas for foreign immigrants (it is well known that these are covered mostly by irregular immigrants already in the country and not by new entries as was meant originally thus the quota system is in fact a masked regularisation process);

2. The numbers rejected at the borders or that are returned to their country of origin for different reasons;

3. The regularisation processes of which there have been five (in 1985, 1991, 1996, 2000 and 2001). 246,089 applied for work and residence permits in the regularisation process which ended in July 2000. This figure would represent 27.5% of all regular immigrants.

4. On the other hand, results of a recent transnational study commissioned by Eurostat and carried out in Spain by the CIS under the direction of Joaquin Arango show that as many as 50% of Moroccan and Senegalese immigrants have been irregulars at some time and around 33% are now on Spanish territory without a permit of any kind. This figure is probably below the real one because it is possible that many immigrants were not willing to declare their true legal status, nevertheless it is more reliable than those of other researches which give higher percentages.

In sum, Spain has greatly increased its foreign population since the 1970's and has done so at a particularly fast rate from 1985 onwards. But even if one considered adding the suppressed categories of immigrants to the official statistics on foreign legal residents, the total numbers would still be relatively low, both in absolute and in relative terms, compared to those of other countries of the EU.

In spite of this, Spain has been living for the past ten or so years under the impression, kept up by the media and certain NGO's, of an imminent and unstoppable "invasion" by foreign immigrants. Four factors have contributed to it. On the one hand, the rapid growth in a short span of time of the foreign population partly accounts for this fear. Another is the part induced by EU officials, afraid that Spain might only be a stop over for immigrants who want to reach other destinations in Northern and Western European countries. But an important component of the alarm felt has also been the growing awareness that a new type of immigration from non-industrialised countries had suddenly appeared on the scene and was threatening to outgrow that coming from the industrialised nations. The visibility of the phenomenon due to the concentration of immigrants in only a few of the 17 Autonomous Communities, mainly in the large urban areas and in certain agricultural regions helped to enhance this awareness.

Spain has been since many decades one of the main points of destination for nationals from several Northern and Western European countries – in particular pensioners from the United Kingdom, Germany, France, Belgium and the Netherlands – yet these residents were never considered "immigrants" in the present sense of the word and were more a cause for pride than anything else. There were also a number of foreigners from Latin-American countries, but these were for the most part political exiles or people from relatively well off backgrounds. The shock came when the number of immigrants coming from Africa, Morocco in particular, Latin-America, and now Asia began to grow steadily. Table 2 below illustrates the evolution in the origin of the foreign population in Spain from 1975 to 2001.

Table 2: Foreign Residents in Spain by Country of Origin. Evolution 1975-2001

Country of Origin	1975	1980	1985	1990	1992	1996	1998	2000	2001 **
E.U*	92,917	106,738	142,346	122,333	173,356	252,034	277,468	306,203	325,534
Rest Europe	9,785	11,634	15,780	17,380	24,166	21,257	52,488	55,234	78,444
Portugal	-	24,367	23,342	33,268	26,321	38,316	42,310	41,997	42,634
Poland	-	-	297	613	2,167	3,172	6,651	8,143	11,342
Central and South America	35,781	34,338	38,671	50,592	72,667	100,052	130,203	179,981	275,601
Peru	-	-	1,739	3,872	7,437	18,023	24,879	27,888	33,758
Dominican Rep.	-	-	1,249	2,224	6,766	17,845	24,256	26,481	29,314
Colombia	-	-	-	1,219	2,873	3,621	10,412	24,702	48,710
Ecuador	-	-	-	234	585	2,280	7,046	30,878	84,699
Argentina	-	8,506	9,706	17,679	21,571	18,246	17,007	16,610	20,412
North America	12,361	12,363	15,406	13,686	16,633	21,211	16,997	19,983	20,168
Asia	9,393	11,419	19,541	24,718	33,878	43,466	61,021	71,015	97,967
China	-	729	1,598	4,090	6,783	10,816	20,690	28,693	36,143
Philippines	-	2,865	6,168	7,416	8,004	11,770	13,553	13,160	14,716
Africa	3,232	4,067	8,529	48,742	71,292	98,813	179,487	261,385	309,304
Morocco	-	3,095	5,187	16,665	54,115	77,189	140,896	199,782	234,937
Guinea	-	185	256	839	1,567	2,096	3,158	4,507	4,863
Gambia	-	62	519	1,474	2,952	4,402	6,969	8,840	9,318
Senegal	-	47	-	1,752	3,190	3,575	6,567	11,051	11,553
Cape Verde	-	68	-	1,474	1,939	2,166	2,765	2,052	2,021
Oceania	440	518	748	599	736	929	1,023	902	947
Stateless and unknown	1,380	968	1,040	745	910	1,219	960	1,017	-
TOTAL	165,289	182,045	241,971	276,796	402,350	538,984	719,647	895,720	1,109,060

Sources: Own elaboration from *Anuarios de Migraciones* (Ministry of Labour and Social Affairs). Only the countries with the most number of immigrants have been considered separately for each continent.

* The successive enlargement of the E.U. must be taken into account: Portugal and Spain in 1986, Austria, Finland and Sweden in 1995.

** Provisional figures 2001, Ministry of the Interior 2002

As the previous table shows, nationals from the EU countries continue to be by far the largest group of legal foreign residents in Spain. Nevertheless their relative weight has fallen from 58.6% in 1980 to 29.3% in 2001. The relative weight of foreigners from all the industrialised countries summed up together (EU, USA, Canada and Japan) has followed the same direction: this has gone down from almost 60% of the total foreign population in 1980 to 31% in 2000.

Before 1985, the figures for nationals from non European countries were insignificant. It is around this period that they start to appear in noticeable numbers. In the year 1985, apart from EU citizens, it is the nationals from countries in Central and South America who prevail over those from Asia and Africa, representing 15% of the total foreign population as against 3.5% and 8% respectively for Asians and Africans. But this picture has been gradually changing since then. In 1998, Africans have become for the first time the predominant group, representing almost a quarter of the foreign legal residents in Spain (40.5% if the residents from EU countries are left out), followed by Latin-Americans and Asians[7].

A look into the nationalities of the immigrants originating from Latin-America, Asia and Africa shows that historic and cultural links with former colonies and protectorates have played an important role in the choice of Spain as a country of destination[8]. Amongst other factors would be the more restrictive conditions for entry imposed by former countries of destination (for instance, the USA for Latin-Americans, France, Germany and other European countries for Moroccans) and the growing image of Spain as a country which has acquired a strong economy and a high standard of living.

Thus we find that in the 1980's the main nationalities represented were the Argentineans, the Philippinos and the Moroccans (originating mainly from the regions which were part of the former Spanish Protectorate: Alhucemas, Nador, Tetuán, Larache and Tangier)[9]. In 1985 immigrants from other Latin-American countries also started to appear on the scene in significant numbers, growing steadily throughout the 1990's. The first to come were the nationals from the Dominican Republic, followed by the Peruvians. Both nationalities have finally outnumbered the Argentineans who had kept their position as the most numerous group until 1997. More recently it is the Ecuadorians, Colombians and

---

[7] Contrary to what is commonly believed Africans may soon be outnumbered again by immigrants from Latin American countries if flows from this continent continue as now. In the provisional figures for 2001, the relative weight of Africans has gone down to 39.5% of immigrants from non EU countries, whilst the weight of Latin Americans has gone up from 29% in 1998 to 37.3%.

[8] Legislation on residence and work permits as well as acquisition of nationality privileges nationals from Latin-American countries, Andorra, the Philippines and the former Spanish Guinea. Nationals from these countries are also given preference in the quotas for work and residence permits which are decided each year.

[9] See López García (1996), p. 90.

Brazilians[10] who are immigrating in large numbers. On the other hand whilst the amount of immigrants from the Philippines grew at a lower pace after 1985, the number of immigrants from Morocco continued to increase rapidly, becoming by 1992 the largest group in Spain from one single nationality and representing now almost a third (30%) of the immigrants proceeding from non EU countries.

As a consequence of the globalisation of international migrations, immigrants from countries with no previous special links to Spain are now beginning to appear for the first time or to quickly rise in number. One such case would be that of the Chinese who showed a 48% increase in the figures of foreign legal residents between 1997 and 1998 and are now the fourth largest group of non EU immigrants (that is even without counting with irregular immigration which is probably rather high amongst the Chinese).

The foreign population coming from these countries is unevenly distributed throughout the Spanish geography which greatly contributes to their visibility. Taking as a source the Statistical Yearbook on Foreigners for the year 2000 one finds that only five of the 17 Autonomous Communities concentrate almost 75% of those considered as economic immigrants[11] to Spain. These are: Catalonia with 24% and Madrid with 18.2% which between them already absorb almost half of these immigrants (42.2%); to these must be added Andalusia with 14.7%, Valencia with 9.7% and the Canary Islands with 8.7%[12].

The offer of unqualified jobs which the Spanish population was unwilling to take[13] was one of the main reasons that led immigrants from non-industrialised countries to settle in those geographical areas. These immigrants represent almost 75% of the total foreign labour force and most are employed in the ser-

---

[10] Ecuadorians already showed a 56% net increase and Brazil 30% from 1996 to 1997 (see *Indicadores de la Inmigración y el Asilo en España*, n. 2, August 1998, published by the Permanent Observatory of Immigration (OPI) of the IMSERSO – Ministry of Labour and Social Affairs). The increase of Ecuadorians has gone on since then in geometrical progression having become in 2001 the second largest group of immigrants in Spain after the Moroccans, with Colombians in third place.

[11] The so called economic immigrants are nationals from Eastern European countries and Turkey, Latin America, Africa, Asia except nationals from Israel and Japan, plus the stateless.

[12] This percentage is rapidly increasing as the Canary Islands have recently become one of the main targets for irregular immigrants from Africa because of the strong measures which have been taken to block their entry in many parts of the coastline on the Spanish mainland.

[13] This points to the segmented character of the Spanish labour market and partly explains why there should be a demand for foreign labour in a country where the rate of unemployment is still very high (15.6% in 1999) according to the Survey of the Active Population for the 2nd Term of 1999, in spite of its continued decrease during the past 3 years.

vice, agricultural or construction sectors. Employment in these sectors is further reinforced by the government through the yearly quota system which determines the types of jobs for which it will grant work permits. By continents, Europeans (except those belonging to the EU) as well as Latin-Americans and Asians are more likely to work in the service sector and Africans in agriculture and construction. Table 3 shows the percentage distribution by continent and sector of occupation of the foreign population (except EU citizens) holding a work permit.

Table 3: Distribution of Work Permits by Continent and Sector of Activity (Year 1999, Horizontal Percentages)

Continents	Services	Agriculture	Construction	Industry	Other
Europe	62.7	11.2	15.4	9.2	1.5
North America	80.0	0.2	1.3	16.2	2.2
Central and South America	85.2	3.5	4.9	4.8	1.5
Africa	30.8	43.0	13.0	8.6	4.6
Asia	87.4	3.1	2.0	6.0	1.5
Oceania	73.0	1.2	2.4	19.8	3.6
Sateless or Unknown Origin	51.0	14.7	18.6	13.7	2.0
TOTAL	58.5	21.2	9.4	7.4	3.6

Source: *Anuario Estadístico de Extranjería 2000*, Ministry of the Interior

Madrid and Catalonia absorb each more than 25% of the foreign labour force, not counting EU citizens (these do not appear in the statistics as they no longer have need of a permit to work in Spain).

The distribution by gender shows a prevalence of men in the foreign population with legal working permits. In 1999, these represented 65.3% as against 34.7% of women in the active population. Nevertheless there are large differences by continent of origin. Men are dominant amongst Africans (82.6%) and to a lesser degree amongst Asians (62.1%) as well as amongst Europeans from non EU countries (61.5%). On the contrary, amongst those originating from the Americas it is the women who prevail, representing 63.7% of the working population from that continent. The balance in favour of women is even greater in this case if we examine the distribution of the working force by gender and by countries: thus, for instance, one finds that 83.4% of the workers from the Dominican Republic and 64.7% of those from Peru are female. Thus there is an evident feminisation of the active foreign population in particular that which proceeds from Latin-American countries. This feminisation nevertheless seems to be slightly decreasing. The data on work permits for 1999 showed an increase of 2.6% for this sector of the population, while the number of work permits for men increased 3.6%.

The unbalance in favour of men in the distribution of the active foreign population with valid work permits tends to disappear when the figures are viewed from the perspective of the total population. The gap between the sexes becomes then more reduced, men representing 53.3% and women 45.8% of all foreigners, which is approximately the same distribution of the Spanish population. Some of the differences between continents and by countries of origin which were pointed out before nonetheless remain. Thus although amongst Europeans and Asians the proportion of women and men is similar, there is a predominance of males (68.5%) amongst Africans and of females (61.5%) amongst Latin-Americans.

The unbalance between the genders within the foreign population from the non industrialised countries witnesses to the still recent character of the phenomenon of immigration in Spain, showing that as far as many of the nationalities are concerned it is still mainly a population of workers, in which family reunification is only beginning to take place[14].

This is also made apparent when looking at the composition by age groups of the foreign population as shown in table 4.

---

[14] This is not true for the foreign population taken as a whole. Figures show that the general proportion of workers to the rest of the foreign population has evolved in a short span of time. Thus while workers represented 75% of the foreign population in 1992, in 2000 they have decreased to 52.2%. This means an important increase of the dependent population (ascendants and descendants) which no doubt will have important consequences on the integration of immigrants and subsequently on policies.

Table 4: Foreign Residents by Age and Continent of Origin in 1997

Continent	Under 16 yrs	16-18 yrs	19-24 yrs	25-44 yrs	45-64 yrs	65 yrs Over
EU	20,361	5,425	18,987	127,207	86,650	49,073
Rest of Europe	6,068	1,078	4,703	27,373	8,344	3,171
Africa	48,605	10,585	31,283	144,845	23,645	2,422
Asia	10,168	2,380	8,574	37,789	10,670	1,953
North America	1,583	260	1,410	6,023	3,725	2,797
Central and South America	19,995	5,697	20,209	108,535	25,969	6,239
Oceania	59	7	34	430	257	115
Other	126	23	114	465	124	165
TOTAL	106,965	25,455	85,314	452,667	159,384	65,935

Source: Own elaboration from *Anuario Estadístico de Extranjería 2000*, Ministry of the Interior

Thus we find that almost 81% of all the foreign population is of working age, 82.7% in the case of immigrants from countries outside the EU. Immigrants in the 25 to 44 years bracket make up the bulk representing 50.7% of all immigrants in active age and 55.4% if EU citizens are left out, showing the youth of this section of the foreign population. In contrast, the aged foreign population, that is the population 65 years and over, only represents 3.0% if we again leave out EU citizens who hold a very large share in this age group. If we look at the figures for the Spanish population in 1996, although the data are not strictly comparable, we find considerable differences: 64% are in active age, with only 35% in the age bracket from 25 to 49 years, and 17.7% are 65 years and over.

The presence of an already significant number of foreigners who are under 16 years of age is a sign that immigrants are settling in the country and plan to stay and that the immigration process is beginning to become "normalised". Figures show that 11.4% of the total immigrant population finds itself in this category; this percentage rises to 15.9% amongst the foreign population from non-industrialised countries. In the latter case, the proportion is only slightly lower than for the Spanish population under 16 years of age which according to the estimates made by the INE (National Institute of Statistics) for 1998 amounts to 16.9%. What this may be showing is that the birth rate for this section of the population, although figures are not available to confirm it, is comparatively higher than the one for the Spanish population which in any case is very low by any standard[15].

Although in absolute numbers the amount of immigrant children under 16 is small compared to the Spanish population of the same age, their presence already makes itself felt particularly in the school system as well as in the social and health services. This presence is bound to grow in the near future considering that the children of immigrants from countries who have been established for a longer period of time in Spain far outnumber those of the immigrants proceeding from countries which have only more recently appeared on the scene (such a Peruvians, Ecuadorians, etc.). These are already adding their children to the present numbers.

The concentration of the foreign population in certain geographical areas as well as in certain areas of the cities and towns is one of the causes of the pressure put on the school system by the presence of immigrant children. Another is the great difference in their cultural backgrounds. This is apparent when we look at the distribution by country of origin of the foreign population under 16 years of age and see, for instance, that Moroccans alone represent more than one third of the children in that category.

From another angle, figures show that the age group from 6 to 15 years is the largest, representing 66.5% of the under 16's in the immigrant population. Then come the groups from 3 to 5 years with 18.4% and with 0 to 2 years which represents 15%. Thus one observes that the upper age segment of the population of under 16's prevails over two the lower ones. This distribution is similar to that of the Spanish population, although the reasons for it may not be the same, as a close examination of the distribution by nationalities reveals. In this sense we find that the higher percentages of children in the upper age brackets – with percentages which are far above the average – belong, on one side, to some of the nationalities who have been longer in the country, and, on the other, to some of the more recent ones. Argentineans with 63.2% of the children in the age group from 11 to 15 years are an example of the first case and the Dominican Republic with 51.1% or Peru with 47.8% are of the second one. What the latter is suggesting is that a marked family reunification process is going on within these nationalities.

---

[15] The birth rate, i.e. the number of births in Spain per every thousand inhabitants, has decreased from 21.8 in 1960 to 9.2 in 1995 and has become one of the lowest in the EU.

Table 5: Foreign Population under 16 Years of Age: Main Nationalities

Nationality	Number	Percent
Morocco	40,246	39.3
Dominican Republic	4,219	4.1
China	4,100	4.0
Germany	3,824	3.7
U.K.	3,658	3.6
Portugal	3,210	3.1
France	3,045	3.0
Gambia	2,911	2.8
Colombia	2,718	2.6
Peru	2,462	2.4
Ecuador	2,097	2.1
Italy	2,027	2.0
Argentina	1,923	1.9
Cuba	1,782	1.7
Philippines	1,506	1.5
India	1,347	1.3
U.S.	912	0.9
Rest of Nationalities	20,282	19.8
Total	102,269	100.0

Source: Own elaboration from data obtained by the OPI from the Ministry of the Interior, 2000

Once they have begun to settle, immigrants from these nationalities are bringing over the children which had been left in their country when either the mother – in both these cases probably the mother – or the father emigrated to Spain. Thus most of these children will have been born in their parent's country of origin. On the other hand we find that it is the nationalities with a relatively longer presence in Spain than that of the citizens from the Dominican Republic or the Peruvians but shorter than that of others like the Argentineans, who have the highest proportion of children in the lower age brackets, therefore children in many cases probably born in the country. This would be the situation of the Moroccans with 43.3% in the age group from 0 to 5 years, or of the Gambians with 60.5% in the same age group, or again of the Senegalese with 52.3%[16]. The process of family reunification which seems to be going on as well as the existence of relatively significant numbers of children born in Spain from immigrant parents are once again signs of a progressive normalisation in the composition of the immigrant population, as well as of a certain degree of integration in the country of choice.

To sum up, foreign immigration to Spain is a recent phenomenon whose main feature has been that of the fairly rapid growth of the population coming from non industrialised countries. This fact as well as the concentration of this population in a limited number of geographical areas has contributed to its visibility and hence, to the alarm caused by its presence and the fear of "invasion by foreign hordes".

Together with an increase in the rate of flows to Spain in the past two or more years there have also been shifts in their composition as well as in the patterns of settlement. Although still concentrated for the most part in a few autonomous communities and in large urban areas, immigrants now tend to be found in significant numbers in more and more parts of the country. All this speaks of a still continuously changing scenario as far as some aspects of immigration are concerned.

On the other hand, there are also clear indications that immigrants of longer standing are beginning to settle. A clear signal in this direction is the evolution in the relative proportion of the foreign workers to the rest of the foreign population. The proportion of the active population has been constantly decreasing, reaching the point where it now only represents little more than half of the total foreign population, while in 1992 it was 75%. The explanation for this is that family reunification is underway and that the number of children of immigrants born in Spain and brought over from their country of origin is acquiring significant proportions. This is a clear step in the integration of the immigrant population.

1.2. Political and Societal Definition of the Situation of Immigration in a Historical Perspective

Until the 1980's Spain was regarded as a country of emigration rather than of immigration. Thus the entry of immigrants in Spanish territory is still a very recent occurrence and perceptions of this influx of people tend to be shaped by two sets of experiences. First, the experiences of those Spaniards who only a few

---

[16] In contrast, we find much smaller numbers in the age group from 0 to 5 years amongst the nationalities recently arrived to Spain. Thus amongst the Ecuadorians, children in that age group represent 21.1% – less than half the Moroccans in the same age group – of the under 16's; and amongst the Colombians this percentage is still lower: 14.8%.

years back had immigrated to Central Europe and Latin America. Second, media coverage of events in other countries in the European Union and the United States.

This would serve to explain the ambivalent attitude in Spanish society towards immigrants: on the one hand, they view the situation of immigrants with a sense of collective benevolence as they equate their predicament with that of other immigrants, that is, their fellow Spaniards; on the other, they approach the situation not without certain reservations and a sense of prejudice, springing from the disturbing images of the problems posed by immigrants portrayed in the media in the US, Germany and France.

A conceptual issue underlies this ambivalence, which explains why the question of whether Spain should consider itself to be a country of immigration or not has not become a subject of debate in Spain. Thus the expression "country of immigration" is understood in a purely descriptive sense and not in a normative sense, as simply referring to the question of whether countries are or are not receiving immigrants. In this sense, as it is obvious immigrants are coming to Spain, we can obviously call it a *country of immigration* and there seems to be no need for discussion on this matter. If we were to pose the question of whether Spain *ought* to take the immigrants that come to this country, most Spaniards would certainly reply that it *must* take them as there is simply no alternative.

It is worth noting that social perceptions of the prevailing situation of migration are noticeably different from those of political circles. This difference can be explained very easily. On the one hand, as immigration is still a new phenomenon Spaniards have not had much time to develop a common social discourse on this matter. Coherent opinions have not emerged in favour or against immigration. On the other, a view of events has developed much more quickly in political circles, where it is formed by small, tight-knit groups which are better-informed about the Spanish case and other foreign cases.

The following characterise the stance adopted by political agents: The perception of immigration as a rather negative phenomenon, but an inevitable one all the same[17]. The perception of the need to offset in the middle term the shortage in the workforce caused by the low demographic evolution among the

---

[17] The National Plan for the Integration of Immigrants in force since January 1995, starts with the following words: "Immigration is for the present an unstoppable fact for which Europe must be prepared". In this way it is suggesting that the plan would not be necessary if immigration were not unstoppable, because otherwise entry could simply be denied to all.

Spanish population[18]. The perception of the integration of immigrants as a necessary task, which, if unsuccessful, might threaten social peace and safety in towns and cities in Spain[19]. The perception that the task of integrating immigrants must be carried out very carefully in order to avoid nationalist and xenophobic reactions[20].

Apart from these ideas, shared by politicians of all persuasions, the approach to immigration differs. Left-wing parties strive to give the impression to the general public that they are the advocates of rights of immigrants, in contrast to the passive attitude adopted by the right. As the left is currently in opposition, it can project this image by homing in on certain details, without placing them within the context of the economic situation or that of safety in towns and cities. Right-wing parties in contrast aim to maintain the economic situation and that of safety in towns and cities, whilst stressing their affirmation and respect for human rights. No party or legally-constituted institution in Spain dares to oppose immigration openly, as this stance tends to be equated with neo-fascist ideologies.

As mentioned above, the prevailing view of immigration in political circles coexists with the highly fragmentary and dispersed stance taken by Spanish society. The data available show that less-educated people from the lowest socio-economic sectors are more openly hostile to the idea. But in some of the middle-class sectors in closer contact with immigrants, such as civil servants or school teachers, there are many indications that these tend to discriminate

---

[18] Successive reports on the subject published since 1998 by the Bank of Spain, the Banco Bilbao-Vizcaya and the Banco de Santander have put emphasis on this point and politicians have taken note of them. But in Spain it was unpopular to recognise it because of the connection public opinion establishes between competition in the labour market and risk of unemployment. The strong echo which the United Nations' report published in the year 2000 has had in Spain seems to have given politicians an excuse to speak more openly on the subject.

[19] In her presentation of the National Plan for the Integration of Immigrants, the then Minister of Social Affairs, Cristina Alberdi, wrote: "Migratory movements constitute one of the great challenges before us. On our capacity to direct, to channel and to achieve their integration will depend, in the final balance, an outcome in which the positive contributions are able to overcome the difficulties that may appear in the way" (see official edition of the Plan, published in 1995 by the Ministry of Social Affairs). A concern for the possible problems arising from a failure in the integration of immigrants is patent, even when these are named only euphemistically.

[20] In Spain it is politically incorrect to name the existing racism, except when its hideousness can be discharged on parafascist groups. But politicians do not deceive themselves on the fact that xenophobia is very extended outside these groups. This conviction is not made public, but it has often been evidenced in the contacts the IEM, to which I belong, has had with high officials from the Ministry of Labour and Social Affairs, the Home Office and the Ministry of Foreign Relations.

against immigrants who have not integrated fully in Spanish society. The statistics systematically elaborated since 1991 on this topic show that up to 47% of the Spaniards with a low educational level are somewhat or very racist (ASEP 1998, 15) and politicians are for this reason very careful when they talk about these themes. The presence amongst civil servants of a latent xenophobia appears in numerous life stories collected from immigrants in researches carried out by the IEM. Nevertheless, such views seldom receive media coverage, as the media, the general public and even those who espouse them, regard them as politically incorrect.

1.3. Emergence of an Integration Policy

The following factors mark the beginnings and evolution of Spanish immigration and integration policy since immigrants started to arrive in the country in the 1980's:

▸ The geographical location of Spain as a country of transit for the Maghreb/ Europe and Latin America/Europe routes.

▸ The ongoing debate in public opinion on migration matters, frequently imported from other EU countries, but different from that of other European countries.

▸ The fact that the first influx of immigrants coincided in Spain with the redistribution of the population within the different areas of the labour market, due to the economic changes associated with Spain's entry in the European Community, as well as a significant rise in the educational level. The jobless rate was high, the black economy thrived and a large number of women entered the labour force for the first time.

As regards the first point, it is worth noting that the first measures adopted in Spain were taken at the time of the Schengen agreements and mainly because a significant proportion of the migrants who arrived from the North of Africa and from Latin America wanted to use Spain as a point of entry to other European countries with a better standard of living. Given the fact that this happened when the European Union wished to co-ordinate the control of inflows, and thus the control of frontiers, Spain was obliged to establish severe control policies for immigrants when hardly any other policies or problems existed.

The above accounts for the lack of integration policies for immigrants in Spain during the 1970's and 1980's, and for the fact that, up to 1994, the government dealt with this issue mainly in accordance with the Law 7/1985 *"On the Rights and Liberties of Foreigners in Spain"*, which was later called the "Ley de Extranjería". That is to say, the Foreign Office handled entry visas, the Home Office (i.e. through the police) controlled the entry of migrants and work permits, and the Ministry of Labour (now Ministry of Labour and Social Affairs) granted these permits.

As for the processes of integration, the aforementioned law controlling immigration had two unwanted consequences. The first of which was that they only took into account those aspects related to work and the economy, considering immigrants implicitly as only workers and neglecting other personal aspects.

The second consequence was that police control procedures took precedence over other elements of migratory policy for some years, thus distorting the perception of the problems encountered. But this situation ceased to exist after political debates at a national level and contact with other European countries with more experience in this field called it into question and in turn led to the creation of a *"General Office for Migration"* dependent on the Ministry for Labour and Social Affairs in 1993. The aim was to transfer the management of migratory policies from the hands of the police to another body, which could deal more effectively with the complex demands which immigration presented in Spanish society.

Thereafter, and on the initiative of the aforementioned General Office for Migration, an official conception of integration policies began to be made explicit; the first version of which would be included in the so-called *"National Plan for the Integration of Immigrants"*, approved in 1994[21].

The main thrust of this plan was that the integration of immigrants must be achieved by facilitating their gradual access, as in the case of other Spanish citizens, to basic civil and social rights, not to political rights[22]. To put the integration policies into practice, criteria and measures were devised concerning the ways in which immigrants qualify for these rights. The first of these criteria was to introduce a control of the migratory flows so that Spanish society could offer all those who arrive in the country the same social rights enjoyed by the Spanish population. Again the emphasis was placed firmly on control in migratory policies.

---

[21] "Interministerial Plan for the Integration of Immigrants" approved by the Council of Ministers on 2 December 1994. Its purpose is to serve as "a frame of reference for the administration, a proposal of action for the autonomous regions and the local governments and a channel for the active participation of civilian societies in the integration of the immigrant population".

[22] This plan did not contemplate granting political rights to foreigners from non EU countries holding residence permits, albeit it opens up the way by which they can acquire Spanish nationality and hence full citizenship. These ways are made particularly easy in the case of certain nationalities.

This control of inflows is realised through a system of entry quotas which are granted in accordance with the situation of the labour market, so that priority is given once more to migrants' availability for work in policies on integration, relegating their social and personal condition to second place.

Nevertheless, the most important element of this concept of integration was probably not either of these two explicit traits, but an implicit one in it. As the aim of integration was to facilitate immigrants' access to the same civil and social rights and to assume the same duties as Spanish citizens, the plan assumes that the only adjustments to be made in Spanish society are those by immigrants and it fails to consider the effect the arrival of immigrants might have on Spanish society. The entire burden of immigration falls firmly on their shoulders and it is taken for granted that Spanish society remains as it is.

Thus, on an explicit level, the measures implemented are legally directed by the emphasis they place on the access of immigrants to the exercise of civil and social rights and duties which Spanish society grants to its citizens. However, at an implicit level, aspects related to work and the economy take precedence because of the convergent influence of three factors: the pressure exerted by native social sectors who consider the immigrants' arrival to be a threat for labour markets; government concern to reduce the volume of the underground economy; and the influence of political decisions in which relations between workers and employers are considered the key to justice and social peace. And this attitude is also adopted by the Catholic Church, whose organisation of centres, volunteers and publications, in practice, are highly influential in immigration matters.

Apart from the general orientation towards access to the rights and duties of citizenship and access to the labour market, a third concept is emerging in Spanish immigration policies. It stems from the work of numerous NGOs which collaborate with immigrants in Spain and which are beginning to influence the immigration policies drawn up by the administration. This concept is based on the criticism of a controlling *economism*, stressing the fact that an immigrant is not just a worker whose labour situation has to be controlled, insofar as it is possible, by external agents. A common expression in the language of the NGOS is to say "we asked for workers and persons arrived". Or also, on a more abstract and political level: "It is necessary to move from considering immigrants as a workforce in precarious conditions to count them as citizens"[23]. An immigrant is a subject of social interaction, regardless of whether he/she is employed or not, does or does not have a residence permit, simply by virtue of the fact that he/she is in Spanish territory and this has a number of

---

[23] Both expressions and their subsequent explanation can be found, for instance, in page 6 of the booklet *"A dignified Status for Immigrant Workers"*, prepared by the Catholic Church in Madrid for the celebration of the Day on Migrations (edited by the Servicio de Formación de la Delegación Diocesana de Migraciones, Madrid, 1999)

consequences. Integration should not depend on work alone nor should it only be viewed from the outside; the initiatives and strategies promoted by the immigrants themselves (which tend to differ depending on their ethnic and cultural origin) should not be overlooked.

These points of view greatly influenced the elaboration of the new law on the rights and liberties of foreigners and their social integration promulgated by Parliament in January of the year 2000, which guaranteed the regularisation of all immigrants with two years' residence in Spain regardless of whether they had entered the country illegally; it also extended the right to receive free health care to irregular migrants and stipulated that illegal residence or work could not be considered causes of expulsion. And for the first time it gave legal status to the possibility of obtaining permanent residence, it regulated the right to family reunification and stipulated sanctions for those promoting illegal human traffic.

But this law was approved, on the eve of the elections which took place in the year 2000, with the opposition of the governing political party who then announced that they would change this law if, as a result of the elections, the composition of Parliament permitted it. As this was the case, the law was modified mainly on three points: lengthening to five years the time of permanence in Spain required for the regularisation of irregular migrants on the basis of being settled in the country; hardening the conditions required for family reunification and, once again considering irregular residence and irregular work as conditions of expulsion.

Although still restrictive, the new legislation undoubtedly changes and betters the conditions under which the integration of immigrants was taking place, but the span of time elapsed since it has come into force is too short for an evaluation of its practical effects.

2. Types and Instruments of Integration Policies

2.1. General Societal Integration Policies which include Immigrants

If we mean by *general societal integration policies* those procedures by which every country tries to maintain a sense of union and to bridge the principal divisions which tend to occur among its members, and if we accept that social class, religion and the diversity of regions produce most of those divisions, then we could say that in Spain the integration policies are officially based on the equality of all citizens before the law (Constitution, Article 14), the separation between state and church (ibid., Article 16) and the decentralisation of the administration of the different regions tempered by principles of interregional solidarity (ibid., Article 138,1) and the exclusion of those social and economic privileges which would favour some citizens over others (Article 138,2 and 139).

Other divisions arise in Spain because of the plurality of languages, which also places the cohesion of society in jeopardy. The Constitution tries to overcome this obstacle by granting every language official status in its territory (Article 3.2), but establishing Spanish as the official state language that all citizens must learn and that may be used throughout the nation (Article 3.1).

According to the framework proposed for this research, we need to go beyond these structural features in our definition of the Spanish mode of integration. It is necessary to take into consideration the different kinds of political and institutional entities which Spain has promoted in order to harmonise the existing social strains.

These policies and agencies are very similar to those existing in other democratic European states and an analysis of them would therefore fall short of defining the specific mode of integration prevalent in Spain. The lack of institutional procedures aimed at reducing the indirect cultural discrimination which may arise among Spaniards is likewise not enough to define this specific mode of integration. It could therefore be said that the Spanish integration mode could be called *liberal*, that is, one based on the full participation of the political citizenship and of the cultural elements belonging to it, but considering other cultural questions and their influence in everyday life to be private and, therefore, free.

It is obvious that an official classification of the general mode of integration in Spain does not go very far towards specifying its distinguishing characteristics and cannot be used to explain to what degree the general mode of integration affects the way in which immigrants can be integrated in the country. For that purpose, it would be necessary to take stock of the recent historical events determining this integration mode and the *identificational* dimension of integration which Spaniards share.

Three factors therefore should be taken into consideration, on which the identification of an individual with a community usually depends: the satisfaction of an individual with the role played in his group, opposition to external opponents or difficulties and sustaining accepted identity narratives in the group that validate self-esteem. This is arguably the distinguishing characteristic in the Spanish mode of integration. It could be characterised by what has happened with the validation of Spaniards' identity narratives, and with the way citizenship and the cohesive principle that all are equal in the eyes of the law have been interpreted in Spain.

As regards identity narratives, the most important aspect is the fragmentation that occurred following Franco's death. During Franco's regime these narratives were sustained by the teaching imparted in schools and the media, which portrayed a highly traditional view of the history of Spain and of the Spanish condition (supposed nobility and the heroism of the medieval victory against Islam or "Reconquista", the discovery and conquest of America, the high level of the artistic and literary genius of Spaniards...). But these narratives, lionising the role of Spain on the world stage, were also embedded in the ideology represented by Franco. And by the mid-1960's they were already considered absurd, as Spain opened up to the rest of Europe through tourism. Thus when Franco died these narratives disappeared completely from the mass media and schools.

As there were no identity narratives of a general scope to replace them, specific narratives of diverse ideological strains, different regions and opposed social sectors were validated. Thus the Spanish condition became overloaded with individual and local meanings which could hardly serve to integrate Spaniards. And it even acquired a negative overtone: to be Spanish means not to be from anywhere else and to be fated to struggle against all those born in the same country[24].

In short, we can argue that the collective identity of the nation formed by the Spanish people is hardly conducive to integrating them together in a positive way. This is because the said identity lacks positive meanings and is overloaded with individual and local signifiers, interconnected by a fatal link to a specific territory. But it does integrate them in a negative way, insofar as it brings them together in a struggle against the aspects of social life which in their opinion hinder them from achieving their individual goals.

---

[24] Many Spanish thinkers from the late nineteenth century have examined this point. It is one of the main strand running through the writings of the so-called "Generación del 98" (Unamuno, Antonio Machado, Azorín, Baroja...), which criticise the individualism, envious nature and fragmentation of the Spanish nation of their time. Ortega y Gasset raised the history of Spain to a philosophical level in his work "España Invertebrada", in which Castile, once the central nervous system of the global historical project uniting Spain, from the seventeenth century onwards, shifts away from this central role towards individualism, in such a way that "Castile would have made and unmade the unity of Spain". P. Laín Entralgo analyses this problem in a historical context in *"España como Problema"* (Seminario de Problemas Hispanoamericanos, Madrid, 1948) republished many times (see p. 24, 42 s., 61-64 of the first edition). In 1986 Laín returned to this subject in *"En Este País"*, and his study *"La España de Ortega"* (Tecnos, Madrid, 1986). In 1988, to mark the tenth anniversary of the Spanish Constitution, M Sagrera wrote in the newspaper *"El País"* that thanks to the Constitution Spaniards could stop being Spaniards by force, by virtue of being born in Spain (see Sagrera's collection of articles published with the title *"Las Mil Españas"*, Editorial H-F, Madrid, 1989, p. 83).

It is in this context that the citizen's role and the political aim of all being equal in the eyes of the law gains special significance in Spain. The citizen's role is understood as an exercise in monitoring the rights that prevent a return to the authoritarianisms, restrictions on freedom and inequalities which are now regarded as arguably the main cause of Spain's lack of prosperity. The proclamation of all being equal in the eyes of the law is understood as described in article 10.1 of the 1978 Constitution: 'the dignity of the person, the inviolable rights inherent to him, the free development of his personality, the respect of the law and of other people's rights, are the basis of the political order and of social peace'.

All this is linked in practice, on the one hand, with the hypersensitivity of Spaniards today towards anything that could be interpreted as a flagrant attempt to go back to former inequalities and authoritarianisms; and on the other, to what could be interpreted as a belittling of local, ideological and class identities.

A Spaniard therefore feels nowadays that he has been discriminated against and not integrated if he believes that the development of his personality is curtailed in any way, or if he feels he receives less favours compared to others. This is likely to lead to various situations of unease in many segments of the population due to a sense of *comparative grievance* ("agravio comparativo", an expression in common usage in Spain today), that is, due to the opinion that a sector of people, to which one belongs, has been discriminated against by the administration in comparison to other sectors. The unease stemming from comparative grievances may result in the loss of swathes of voters or even become explosive. Many of the problems besetting Basque or Catalan nationalism illustrate this very clearly.

In sum, the general policies aimed at integrating Spaniards are based on equality for all in the eyes of the law and equal access to state assistance in the areas of education, health care and public expenditure. Such policies are characterised by a concern to lighten the burden of recent history, which has made Spaniards hypersensitive to anything that could be perceived as being to the detriment of the group to which they belong, in comparison to the favours enjoyed by others.

It is evident that the approach adopted in these general policies aimed at integrating Spaniards has conditioned the approach to the integration of immigrants laid down officially for the first time in the "Plan Nacional para la Integración de los Inmigrantes" (National Plan for the Integration of Immigrants) of 1994. In it the integration of immigrants in Spain is emphatically understood in terms of (legalised) immigrants being granted full citizenship, sharing the same civil and social rights and responsibilities as Spanish citizens (with the exception of political rights). The GRECO Programme (Global Programme to Regulate and coordinate Foreign Resident's Affairs and Immigration in Spain) of the Government Delegation for Foreigners and Immigration which was approved in 2001 and was meant to substitute the former Plan has not altered in any way this standpoint.

However both these plans fail to address openly the underlying feeling of comparative grievance. But it is conveyed in the way in which anything that could appear to be positive discrimination toward immigrants in those policies stimulating their access to labour, housing and social services is presented in the aforementioned plans for the integration of immigrants. Those who have access to political circles know too well how that fear of comparative grievance is expressed by them off the record much more plainly and explicitly[25]. Likewise, in decision-making environments we find a strong ambivalence between what is required by an awareness of the need for integration or by anti-racist ideological postulates – common to every Spanish political party – and what is advised by the fear of losing votes and people's good will.

All this finally has an effect on the members of the administration more directly connected with immigration matters (consulates, police, social services...), above all on those at the lower levels. On the one hand, they are aware of their superiors' ambivalent attitude, on the other hand, they are close to the opinions and ways of life of those who would like better jobs, more housing aid and better opportunities for their children.

In short, the degree of integration of Spanish society is weak and in the lower strata it is exposed constantly to cracks, due to the strength with which comparative grievances are felt. The not unfounded fear of the manifestation of the latter checks politicians when drawing up integration policies and can also mean that these policies are not executed properly by state officials in the lower ranks. It is evident that in order to enhance the promotion of the integration of immigrants a more effective integration of the Spanish population as a whole would be required.

2.2. Special Integration Policies for Migrants

As shown in section 1.3., the specific policies for the integration of immigrants that have been developed in Spain have taken the legal criteria of full citizenship as a starting point, while they are in practice centred on the controlled placing of immigrants in the labour market, including some measures to train immigrants for employment. Implicitly therefore, this places the burden of integration on the immigrants' shoulders.

---

[25] During 1996, in the capacity of advisor to the autonomous government of Madrid, Rosa Aparicio took part in a regional project for the integration of immigrants, which, by the way, has not yet been enacted. She therefore had the opportunity to follow the way in which such projects are carried out.

The first policies immigrants have to deal with are those associated with entry controls. These controls, usually carried out by immigration officers, are in line with a system of entry quotas which are granted each year according to the needs of the labour market. And this approach to the influx of immigrants according to their future placement in the labour market acts as the corner-stone for other integration policies.

Other specific policies are built on this foundation and together they aim to reach so-called *"normalisation"*, that is, channelling civic participation and en-joyment of immigrants' rights through the same bureaucratic and legal means, and financial resources which normally regulate Spanish citizens' participation in society. Regarding this aspect, the legal framework is opposed to setting up, for example, specific ways of gaining access to social services reserved for immigrants and in which they would benefit from positive discrimination. Nonetheless, it admits that immigrants are disadvantaged in their access to social services, and thus accepts and recommends that measures of "affirmative action" be taken in order to facilitate this access, thus compensating for any *"indirect discrimination"*. The language of the Spanish administration sets a clear difference between what it calls *actions of positive discrimination* and *affirmative actions*. The first, which would follow from norms directed exclusively to favour immigrants in some kind of social benefit, are reprobated, no doubt to avoid possible complaints from Spaniards who could feel that they are being treated less favourably in comparison with immigrants. Affirmative actions on the other hand would be directed at making accessible to immigrants the same social benefits to which the Spanish population is entitled, helping them to avoid the difficulties which they might encounter because of their cultural differences or because of latent xenophobia.

The lack of political measures specifically directed at immigrants in Spain is in consonance with the approach to the integration of immigrants mentioned above. In practice, these measures only embrace the following: setting up special channels to inform immigrants about the regulations affecting them, regulating the regrouping of families and providing, for those immigrants from countries who have signed agreements with the Spanish state and those professing other religious creeds, complementary schooling in the language and culture of their country of origin[26] or in their religious beliefs[27].

---

[26] This is the case, for example, of immigrants from Morocco. Moroccan children are able to study Arabic with native teachers thanks to the agreements signed between Spain and their country of origin.

[27] The Federación Española de Asociaciones Islámicas (Spanish Federation of Islamic Asso-ciations) signed an agreement (see TEIM 1999) with the Spanish government in which the religious content to be covered by the teachings of Islam are described in great detail, for those children whose parents ask for this instruction within the Spanish state school system.

2.3. New Special Integration Policies

It can be argued that few things are carried out through specific policies, and this also extends to indirect or special policies. Three of these policies are outlined here; two focusing on discrimination, albeit in different ways, and the third of a more basic and general nature.

First, sustained official support and considerable financial assistance is given to anti-racist associations such as *"S.O.S. Racismo" (Racism SOS)* or *"Jóvenes contra la Intolerancia" (Young People against Intolerance)*. These associations, which have good media access and organise events in schools regularly, run several ongoing programmes, especially information and complaints services, linked with cases of direct or indirect discrimination of immigrants. Regrettably it appears that the views these associations espouse on racism and xenophobia, which echo those of political correctness and those held by most of the population, do not reach the discriminators. Indeed the latter tend to believe that the way in which they deal with immigrants is not the product of racism or xenophobia at all, they feel that their treatment of immigrants simply reflects the behaviour of the latter and that anybody would treat them in the same way.

Counsels in which Immigrants' Associations, NGOs and the administration are represented are a much more effective tool against discrimination, albeit via a less direct route. The first of these forums was set up in Catalonia, inspired by advisory bodies created by several local governments in other European countries. But they were soon to be organised at regional and central government levels. Administrations running these forums must inform its members about the regulations in force or the major programmes it plans to put in place and representatives from the immigrant community are able to state their demands.

The main problem these forums have posed up to now is how to select the participants. On the one hand, immigrants' associations are not very developed in Spain, moreover most of the existing ones are unaware of the existence of other groups and have a low membership. This situation means that the representatives chosen are not always very representative of that community as a whole and most immigrants do not feel that they represent them. The same dilemma arises with representatives from NGOs. It follows that interest in the debates held at these meetings often falls away, even on the part of the administration organising them.

The body created by central government in order to follow migratory processes called the OPI (Observatorio Permanente de la Inmigración – Permanent Immigration Observatory) also exerts an influence on the integration of immigrants at the basic and general level. This body's mission, as its name suggests, is purely information-based. But it has begun to collaborate fairly closely with research centres, NGOs and immigrants associations in Spain. This enables all of the above to update continually the facts and figures used in their immigration projects.

In addition, it is worth noting that the Spanish Ministry of Labour and Social Affairs, and the main trade unions in Spain have signed agreements with Morocco in order to carry out a joint monitoring process of the legal status of Moroccan workers. These agreements aim to ensure that these workers are neither discriminated against in comparison to Spanish workers nor absorbed by the black economy[28]. And although it appears that the effects of these agreements are likely to be more symbolic than real (as apart from these agreements Spanish legislation sets heavy penalties for employers who fail to abide by the regulations on equality in work contracts), the fact that Moroccan immigrants know that their own government can intervene in their work situation still promotes integration.

3. Areas of Integration Policies: Aims, Measures, Resources

As part of our study it is important to distinguish between *structural* integration policies, concerning the integration of immigrants in the framework of the organisation of the state and its basic welfare services; and *cultural* policies embracing education, language and religious aspects associated with their outlook on the world and coexistence. In other countries two further areas are usually covered: *social integration* policies, relating to the ethnic differences in everyday life, and *"identificational"* policies, referring to the types of group membership created amongst immigrants and for them. But in Spain we can not talk about these last two kinds of policies as they have yet to be developed. We illustrate below the first two policy types, starting with *structural integration policies*.

3.1. Structural Integration Policies

This section includes policies related to acquiring nationality, education and *welfare state* benefits, as well as access to the labour market and housing.

3.1.1. Nationality Law and Citizenship

As full citizenship is the cornerstone of Spanish ideas on integration, it is not surprising that emphasis is placed on opening up the ways an immigrant can obtain citizenship.

---

[28] The text from one of these agreements has been published recently in the journal *Migraciones*, no 6 (1999), p. 153 - 158.

For this reason although Spanish citizenship is basically governed by the concept of *ius soli*, it may be acquired by origin, by option, by naturalisation or by residence[29].

1. *By origin*, by all those adopted by a Spanish citizen before the age of 18 and also by all those born in Spain when one of the parents is a Spanish citizen, or when both parents are foreign but one was born in Spain, with the exception of those in the diplomatic or consular services. Acquisition by origin is also possible when the parents are stateless or the legislation of their country of origin does not attribute their nationality to the offspring, or when the parents are unknown.

2. *By option*, by all foreigners, born in Spain, when one of the parents is a Spanish citizen and by the foreigners who are subject to the paternal authority or the protection of a Spanish citizen.

3. *By naturalisation patent,* by all foreigners over 18 years old, or over 14 if assisted by his legal representative, when exceptional circumstances may be considered.

4. *By residence,* by all foreigners over 18 years or emancipated, who can document legal and continued residence in Spain during the time required by the law (1 year for applicants born in Spain, 2 years for nationals from Latin America, Andorra, Equatorial Guinea, Philippines, Portugal, Sephardic Jews; 5 years for refugees; 10 years for all others).

From this review of the main aspects of the naturalisation law, it can be seen that the norms are on the whole very generous or liberal and favour the naturalisation of the children of immigrants. For migrants coming from countries historically attached to Spain the norms are also liberal but not free from bureaucracy and delays (up to 3 or 4 years).

---

[29] The following legal texts can be used by immigrants and their children to acquire Spanish citizenship:

1. The Spanish Constitution of 1978, articles 11 and 149.

2. The Civil Code: articles 17 to 26, drawn up in accordance with the Law 18/1990 of December 17 on the reform of the Civil Code in matters related to the acquisition of nationality, then modified by the Law 29/1995, of December 2nd 1995. Articles 17: d, 21, 22, 23 and 26 refer to questions pertaining to foreigners wanting to acquire Spanish nationality on the basis of residence. The others articles apply to Spanish emigrants.

3. Law of June 8, 1957 on the Civil Register: in particular articles 63 to 68 and 96. Decree of November 14, 1958 by which the Regulations of the Law on the Civil Register is approved.

3.1.2. Education

Spanish legislation establishes that all children of compulsory school age (i.e. 6 to 16 years) have the right to receive schooling, including children of immigrants in a situation of irregularity. Before the recent changes in legislation, the first was in accordance with the "Law 7/1985 on the Rights of Foreigners in Spain"[30] which stated that all foreigners – and their children – having legal resident status in the country, enjoyed the same rights as Spanish nationals, amongst which is the right to education. On the other hand, the schooling of children of irregular immigrants was recognised in the resolution on Office for School Centres[31], which is based on the UN's International Convention on Child Rights ratified by Spain. This resolution establishes the principle that, at the level of compulsory education, the rights of the minor take precedence, regardless of the legal status of the family. Thus an immigrant child was not required to present any official documents when he applies to enrol in a school run or funded by the state.

This right is now also recognised by "Law 8/2000 on the Rights and Liberties of Foreigners in Spain and their Social Integration". The recent changes in legislation have also extended to regular migrants and their children the possibity of receiving education at the non-compulsory (i.e. access to free education after 16 years, grants for university studies, etc.), rights which were previously barred to them.

Insofar as the general mode of integration in Spain tends to reflect the integration of immigrants through the channels that prevail for the native population, this is also the general rule for the schooling of children of migrants. Thus, generally speaking, there are no special policies – with the exceptions which we will later mention in section 3.2. dealing with language and cultural gaps – concerning their education. They will then normally be enrolled in a school within the general education system and will be asked to follow the same curriculum as Spanish children, helped where appropriate through the general measures that are established for all children (Spanish or not) with special educational needs.

However policies relating to the number and distribution of children of migrants or other minorities in schools do vary. In Spain, only Catalonia has a ruling on this matter, which states that no school may have more than 15%

---

[30] This is also established in the L.O.D.E. (Ley Orgánica 8/1985 reguladora del Derecho a la Educación).

[31] Resolution of May 3rd 1995, Office for School Centres, Ministry of Education and Culture.

of its pupils belonging to minority groups[32]. This includes not only immigrant children, but also gypsies and other minority groups. In the other autonomous regions, the place of residence determines which school the child must attend as a general rule for all. An unwanted consequence of this general regulation is that in certain suburbs or residential areas, with a high density of immigrants, ghettos may arise, particularly in state-run schools[33]. This happens as a result of several factors: the small proportion of Spanish children because of the declining birth rate or because the neighbourhood population tends to be old; native parents taking their children to other schools because they do not want them to mix with migrants' children or other minority groups.

Apart from the regular school system described above, some foreign schools exist, but no information is forthcoming on the number of these schools or the number of children who enrol in them. Limited information is available on Koranic schools for Muslim immigrants, but these, like Chinese schools mostly operate on Saturdays or Sundays and are compatible with attendance to regular schools. Some full-time schools have also been opened by Moroccans, but these are nevertheless an exception.

3.1.3. Access to Welfare State Benefits, especially Health Care

Up till recently the right to receive full health care on the same level as Spanish citizens as guaranteed to all immigrants with legal residence in the country by article 1, point 2 of the General Health Law 14/1986, 25 April. Illegal immigrants therefore were not covered by this law, although some autonomous regions – Catalonia and the Basque Country in particular – had made provisions through the mediation of NGOs so that these immigrants could be attended by regional health services.

As regards illegal minors until recently, different interpretations prevailed relating to their right to receive health care. The conflict existed between which law or regulation should be given priority: the regulation for the enforcement

---

[32] The purpose of this measure is to avoid the concentration of immigrant the concentration of immigrant children in schools and its negative consequences. The main negative consequences it seeks to prevent are generating xenophobic feelings and conducts amongst the parents of Spanish school children and the drop in school levels. The Autonomous Community of Madrid has adopted a similar measure for schools financed with public funds although it has put the limit in 25%.

[33] An example of this in the Madrid area is the Antonio Morales School with almost 80% foreign children, and this number in some classes rises to 95%.

of the "Ley de Extranjería"[34], approved on 2 February 1996, ruled that all foreign minors resident in the Spanish territory – whether legally or illegally – should be treated in accordance with the 1989 UN Convention on Child Rights, which Spain signed in 1990, giving minors the right to health care; the Organic Law for the Protection of Minors[35] approved on 5 January of the same year restricted this right to minors at risk or under the guardianship of the state or competent public administration (article 10.3). The problem was that the latter was a higher ranking law.

The coming into force of Law 8/2000 recently put an end to the need for such special measures by granting all immigrants registered in the municipal census – no matter if they are illegal – the right to receive full health care[36]. It also made the same provision for minors and for pregnant women before and after the birth of their child. Irregular migrants not registered in the municipal census are also eligible for public health care but only in cases of emergency.

Immigrants with legal residence in Spain also have by law all the other social rights enjoyed by Spanish citizens. It remains to be seen whether they are effectively put into practice in the same way. Thus children of migrants may receive grants for school fees and books, as well as financial aid to attend crèches or nurseries or for food and clothing, in this case regardless of their legal status.

3.1.4. Access to the Labour Market

The granting of initial work permits in Spain – and in consequence of residence permits – depends on the situation of the labour market, which means that immigrants only have access to those jobs for which there is little or no demand by Spanish nationals. The types of jobs offered in the quotas of new permits established each year by the Spanish Government, the majority of which are in areas of domestic service, hotel and catering business, construction, agriculture and others which are not highly regarded, show where the openings lie.

On the other hand, as immigrants are employed for the most part in jobs which are by their very nature highly precarious and unstable, and as for many years a residence permit is dependent on obtaining a contract and having a

---

[34] Reglamento de Ejecución de la Ley Orgánica 7/1985 sobre Derechos y Libertades de los Extranjeros en España approved on 2 February by Royal Decree 155/96.

[35] Ley Orgánica 1/96 de Protección Jurídica del Menor.

[36] Proving that one's permanent place of residence is within the municipality is the only prerequisite for registering in the census.

work permit, immigrants tend to be at constant risk of falling into irregularity or illegality, a situation which can hardly be said to be conducive to integration.

No special measures exist to help immigrants obtain employment or to help them get training. Nevertheless, legal foreign residents have access to all the measures for the promotion of employment open to Spanish citizens. This means that, although there are no specific measures for young immigrants, these also have access to the measures for youth employment offered to Spanish young people. It remains to be seen whether more specific measures will be taken when the state and the different autonomous regions become aware that an important number of youth of immigrant origin will soon be seeking to enter the labour market and may encounter specific problems to do so.

Few studies[37] have as yet been conducted in Spain into discrimination in the labour market, although there are many indications that point towards differences in salaries and opportunities relating to access to jobs and promotion based on ethnic origin[38].

3.1.5. Housing

There are no specific policies for immigrants in the area of housing. Once again, following the general mode of integration, immigrants with legal residence have access to the different housing opportunities available to all those on low incomes. Occasionally, some ad hoc measures have been taken at regional (autonomous) or municipal levels to eliminate shanty towns by assisting immigrants to acquire housing in other areas with better living conditions; state help is also provided to rent lodgings, particularly by acting as intermediary between the owners and the migrants, when they are felt to be subject to discrimination on the part of the latter. But no policies exist in this area to help young immigrants and migrants' children in particular. Few exist in any case – and all at the autonomous level – for Spanish youth.

---

[37] One such study has been carried out by the Colectivo IOE (1995): *La discriminación laboral a los trabajadores inmigrantes*, Ginebra, Oficina Internacional del Trabajo; another by Lorenzo Cachón (1995): *Prevenir el racismo en el trabajo : informe sobre España*, Dublín, Fundación Europea para la Mejora de las Condiciones de Vida y de Trabajo.

[38] Colectivo IOE 1998, 228.

3.2. Cultural Integration Policies

The 1994 *"Plan Nacional de Integración de los Inmigrantes"* provided for "actions to raise awareness and appreciation of the culture and history of the countries of origin of immigrants"[39], but this aim has not lead to the development of specific cultural policies for the adult population.

As regards the cultural integration needs of children of immigrants, as mentioned above, general measures are applied in an attempt to solve the linguistic difficulties encountered as well as to bridge other cultural gaps which apply to all children with special educational needs (including children from minority groups such as gypsies, as well as children suffering from any type of disability.). In Spain this is known as "Compensatory Education" and it is governed by the L.O.G.S.E. in its Vth Title[40], as well as by the L.O.P.E.G.[41], which in its second additional provision defines the school population with special needs as that with needs derived from physical disabilities or behavioural disorders as well as from needs related to social or cultural situations of disadvantage[42].

Although "Compensatory Education" is made obligatory whenever such needs arise in a school, the way it is put into practice may differ depending on the autonomous regions. Thus in schools which were until recently under the jurisdiction of what in Spain is called the "MEC territory"[43], generally children attend special classes during part of their school hours (classes which are most often perceived by the other children as "the class for thick children")[44]. In

---

[39] Nr. 3.0, p. 67.

[40] L.O.G.S.E. (Ley Orgánica 1/1990 de Ordenación General del Sistema Educativo), this is the Law which now regulates the whole of the Spanish educational system and which was first put into practice in 1990.

[41] L.O.P.E.G. (Ley Orgánica 9/1995 de la Participación y Evaluación y el Gobierno de los Centros Docentes).

[42] In addition to the former, there is the Royal Decree 299/96, which regulates all matters concerning the education of children with special needs associated to social or cultural disadvantages.

[43] This refers to those centres which were under state control through the Ministry of Education and Culture and have recently been transferred to their respective autonomous regions. MEC territory until then covered all autonomous regions except Catalonia, Madrid, Andalusia, the Basque Country, Valencia, the Canary Islands, Navarre, and Galicia.

[44] Quoted by Adela Franze and Celia Ruiz in an unpublished report from their research on "The Cultural and Linguistic Integration of Immigrants in the Autonomous Region of Madrid", carried out in 1996.

contrast to this, in Catalonia it is the teachers and not the pupils in need of compensatory education who receive the necessary support to help their disadvantaged pupils. Andalusia, on the other hand, has recently established a system for immigrant children that could be regarded as a more specific measure, although it is designed in connection with the general norms of "Compensatory Education"[45]. Thus in this community immigrant children are placed for a certain length of time (4 or 5 months) in a separate class, while they acquire the necessary linguistic skills and competence in other subjects to be able to follow the normal classes.

The allowance made for programmes to preserve and extend the immigrants' language and culture of origin could be considered a specific measure. The "National Plan for the Integration of Immigrants" of 1994 introduced as one of its action proposals that the teaching of the language and culture of origin should be co-ordinated with the normal classes. But there is no general rule as to how this should be carried out. These programmes are specifically regulated through bilateral agreements between the Spanish Ministry and the Ministries or Embassies of the respective states. A number of agreements exist at present: one with Morocco called the "Hispanic-Moroccan Experimental Programme" by which that country provides native teachers to teach Arabic (classes are also open to the Spanish children as well as to children from other nations) and other aspects of Arab culture to all children who wish to attend these classes outside school hours; another with Portugal, which embraces all students from Portuguese-speaking countries (Brazil, Cape Verde..., etc.). There is little information available on the former but the latter functions particularly in 5 autonomous regions[46] with 74 native Portuguese teachers. In 1997, 2,000 Portuguese-speaking children and 5,000 Spanish children attended these classes. These classes are given during school hours and the teachers are integrated with the rest of the school staff, working alongside them as a team.

NGOs and immigrant associations also play a role in giving additional educational support, and in preserving the children's mother tongue and culture. Programmes implemented by these organisations are localised, but they are usually funded by the administration, either at state, regional or municipal level. An example of a state-funded programme run by an NGO is the one called "Bienvenidos Amigos" (Welcome friends)[47] by which children of immigrants are helped after school hours to do their homework and are offered sports and other recreational activities together with Spanish children. Further-

---

[45] Decreto 1/2002 *Plan Integral para la Inmigración en Andalucía.*

[46] These are Galicia, Asturias, Leon, the Basque Country, Navarre.

[47] This programme is carried out by the NGO "Madrid Puerta Abierta".

more, there is a programme for the teaching of the Chinese language and culture carried out by the Chinese associations and funded by the Hispanic-Chinese Fund. These associations have agreements with several schools to use their facilities on Saturdays. Chinese children whose parents wish it attend "Chinese Schools" for the whole of that day, where they are usually taught Mandarin Chinese and the traditional way of writing, which can create conflicts because for many the language of origin may be a dialect or their parents may know and use modern characters.

4. Political Actors on National, Regional and Local Levels

The relative decentralisation, albeit not uniform, of the administration in Spain today, underlies many of the differences found in the form integration takes and the social roles played by immigrants.

As regards this decentralisation, we must first observe that in Spain, as well as in other countries, we need to distinguish between state and local levels in decision-making processes for specific integration policies. But we must also emphasise the fact that co-ordination between these two levels is made more complex due to the existence of seventeen regional governments – the autonomous regions –, which have their own parliaments and exercise different powers in matters of social welfare, education etc. Thus the lack of co-ordination which might be expected of the disorganised Spanish bureaucratic tradition becomes even more entangled.

In this context it is worth mentioning the official aid that the government encourages citizens to provide, principally through the NGOs involved with immigrants. In fact, the latter play an important role in drawing up and executing migratory policies. This is the result of the political trend towards shifting as much responsibility as possible regarding the administration and immediate implementation of social services to civilian society, whilst maintaining control over them through the allocation and distribution of the financial resources required for the day-to-day running of these services. NGOs hence come to represent another level of the conception and implementation of migratory policies.

Therefore if we draw a distinction between the areas of conception, decision and execution of the immigration policies, we must take into account the following levels:

Figure 1: Levels of Conception, Decision and Execution of Immigration Policies in Spain

Social Agents	Conception	Decision	Execution
Central Government[48]	X	X	███████
17 Autonomous Governments	X	X	███████
Local Agencies / Municipal Government	X	X	X
NGOs	X	███████	X
Social Workers, Civil Servants, Police	███████	███████	X
Immigrant Associations	X	███████	X

The differences found between the levels of decision-making and implementation of integration policies vary the said policies significantly. Some regional governments, for example those of Catalonia, Andalusia and Madrid where most immigrants settle, naturally place greater emphasis on the integration of immigrants than others. Moreover, NGOs are more numerous and powerful in those regions and social workers are better trained in immigration matters.

There is evidence to suggest that immigrants feel that the treatment they receive from social workers is, generally speaking, very good, unlike that of civil servants and still less so of the police. But it is nevertheless true that the government is making a serious attempt to improve the treatment immigrants receive.

---

[48] Particularly through the Ministry of Foreign Affairs, the Home Office and the Ministry of Labour and Social Affairs. As regards the functions they fulfil, Carrillo and Delgado have noted that the importance of each ministry has altered over time (see Carrillo/Delgado 1998, 31). And they add: "In 1994 the link between the Home Office and the Ministry of Labour was tightened in an attempt to stamp out illegal workers, through co-operation between the Labour and Social Security Inspectorate and police forces and bodies. The work groups mentioned [as they aim to stamp out illegal work] are headed by the Government's representative or Civil Governor [in their respective territory] and are composed by: the Provincial Director of Labour, Social Security and Social Affairs; the Head of the Provincial Labour and Social Security Inspectorate; the Legal Representative of the State, Head of the respective Government Office or Civilian Government; the Provincial Police Commissioner and the Head of the Civil Guard. When measures against illegal foreign workers are taken this also includes the Head of the Provincial Documentation Division and the Head of the Office for Foreigners where it exists". This demonstrates very clearly the labyrinthine responsibilities and duties that exist in Spain to deal with migration issues.

As outlined above, immigrant associations do not wield much power in Spain. However, mosques do play a more significant and positive role in the integration of the Muslims in Madrid and Andalusia, in a certain way acting as a substitute for immigrant associations.

Agencies dealing with economic and labour relations, those promoting training and education of migrants, health care services and those dedicated to territorial coexistence and housing are key to the integration of immigrants. Of the above, the state exerts more influence over labour issues. Additionally, the policies monitoring the contractual situation of immigrants are determined by the dominant practices of employers with regard to said control in civilian society.

The implementation of immigration and integration policies is very uneven in the area of labour. On the one hand, Spanish morals are very permissive with small enterprises employing ten or less than ten workers, and, on the other, the vast majority of the jobs available to immigrants are precisely those offered by those small firms. And this permissiveness allows employers very often, although not always, to discriminate against immigrants thus hindering their integration in the labour market. The state and employers, as well as the immigrants themselves and social agents, dictate the level and mode of integration that can be achieved.

The decisive social agents for integration are completely different in the field of education and training. In this case power is decentralised; the regional authorities in many instances decide and manage the respective policies. It falls to said authorities and the teachers dependent on them to carry the heavy burden of responsibility for the integration of migrant children.

Nonetheless there are other entities involved in this process. In accordance with Spanish legislation, every educational institution must have a Parents' and Students' Association, acting as a consultative and monitoring body. Thus they can become, and in fact sometimes do so, social agents of integration or discrimination in schools (for instance, by blocking the entry of certain pupils, as has occurred in a number of cases with gypsy children). In other cases it is the government that is responsible for promoting integration, given the fact that it has established agreements with the countries of origin of immigrants (for example, Morocco), in order to provide teaching in their native language in Spanish schools.

There are strong indications that currently teachers in general genuinely favour integration, although they have not always received suitable training to help those pupils whose parents are immigrants. Parents' and Students' Association, as well as the pupils themselves, do not always look favourably on integration, and occasionally display discriminatory and xenophobic tendencies.

Local authorities carry even more weight in actions related to territorial coexistence and housing. In this area, the promotion of the integration of immigrants is supposedly drawn up and put into practice by local authorities rather than the central government. There is little data available on the above; information is limited to a number of difficult situations or pioneering initiatives.

In short, major differences emerge among the areas promoting the integration of immigrants, owing to the various levels of decision-making and the varying degree of public interest shown in these different matters. As they are under state jurisdiction, areas concerning entry controls and placing immigrants in the labour market receive greater political attention, have a stronger impact on public opinion and the implementation of policies in this field tends to be more uniform. Family and territorial coexistence issues, which are largely entrusted to local authorities, are dealt with in diverse and non-standard ways and only come to light in isolated and extreme cases. Finally, education and training issues occupy the middle ground: they have less impact on public opinion and the policies implemented are not so controversial (at the moment they are the least controversial) and do not give rise to serious conflicts.

5. Conclusion

The pages above describe the scenario for migrants entering Spain, as well as the legal and political measures that underpin this scenario. It is clear that the presence of immigration in Spain is still a recent phenomenon, and the Spanish population has not had time to form definite opinions on specific questions of integration.

The integration process of immigrants is mainly made up of general practices and policies that aim to promote integration within Spanish society. And this society, born with the will to overcome the lack of freedom and social divisions and discord that characterised the end of Franco's regime, is still very keen to defend equal rights, freedom and opportunities for all those living in Spain.

As regards social coexistence migrants in general and children of migrants in particular will be principally referred to the same bodies and laws protecting the human rights and freedoms in Spain, as well as the equal opportunities, of the different social groups that exist in society. Albeit, of course, with the restrictions generally imposed upon citizens who are not Spanish nationals, as occurs in other countries.

In fact we find that immigration policies in Spain, up to 1994, seldom refer to anything other than legal entry (border controls), and they take for granted that once immigrants have entered the country their civil and social rights will be amply covered by existing laws. And it is precisely the failure of border controls, with the subsequent presence in Spain of a high number of undocumented migrants, that has sparked many of the legal and political debates. For example, concerning the rights of undocumented children to schooling or to health care. Or, on a more general level, regarding the discrimination suffered by immigrants in the housing and labour markets. The process is nearly always roughly the same: specific problems suffered in particular by undocumented migrants become conspicuous, this raises awareness of the fact that regularised migrants are also affected by these problems and this leads to changes in legislation and the introduction of new political measures. But these changes and new measures almost always have a common objective: to ensure that the social rights and freedoms of immigrants are protected more effectively by the same bodies and channels as Spaniards.

Some regional governments, especially in Catalonia and the Basque Country, have made more headway than the central government in this respect. This points very clearly to the need to take into account in immigration policy-making the administrative decentralisation of health care, schooling and social protection services in Spain at the present. Although the differences in the end are not very considerable and tend to follow the very uneven distribution of immigrants across the country. From this uneven distribution it follows that the presence of migrants is noticed earlier and more intensely in regions where immigration is greater, and these areas are quicker to take action and to implement more specific measures to solve the problems they face.

Nonetheless this decentralisation and the lack of co-ordination that often accompanies it must be taken into account, especially as in Spain the Ministry of Labour and Social Affairs handles some immigration matters (work permits, on which residence permits depend; as well as social services and other matters related to integration) the Home Office deals with other matters (residence permits, family regrouping, regularisation) and the Ministry for Foreign Affairs with a number of others (border controls, entry visas and visa exemptions). Immigration and integration policy-making in Spain depends on all these authorities and the implementation of such policies involves many official bodies and subcontracted NGOs, the co-ordination of which is not very well defined at an institutional level. This does not help to provide coherence and uniformity in the attempts to take action in this field.

References

ASEP - Juan Díez Nicolás 1998:

Actitudes hacia los inmigrantes, Madrid: Ministerio de Trabajo y Asuntos Sociales, Colección Observatorio Permanente de la Inmigración

Cachón, L. 1995:

Prevenir el racismo en el trabajo: informe sobre España, Dublín: Fundación Europea para la Mejora de las condiciones de vida y del trabajo

Carrillo, E. / Delgado, L. 1998:

El entorno, los instrumentos y la evolución de la política de inmigración en España (1985-1996), Madrid: Instituto Universitario Ortega y Gasset

Colectivo IOÉ 1998:

Inmigración y trabajo. Trabajadores inmigrantes en el sector de la construcción, Madrid: Ministerio de Trabajo y Asuntos Sociales, Colección Observatorio Permanente de la Inmigración

Constitución Española de 1978

Delegación del Gobierno para la Extranjería y la Inmigración, Ministerio del Interior:

Programa Global de Regulación y Coordinación de la Extranjería y la Inmigración (G.R.E.C.O.)

Dirección General de Ordenación de las Migraciones 1995:

Plan de Integración Social de los Inmigrantes, Madrid: Ministerio de Asuntos Sociales

Franzé, A. / Ruiz Alonso, C. 1996:

La integración cultural y lingüística de los inmigrantes: un proyecto de innovación/investigación coordinada, Memoria Final de Investigación, Madrid: Instituto Ortega y Gasset (inédito)

Izquierdo, A. 1992:

La Inmigración en España 1980-1990, Madrid: Ministerio de Trabajo y Seguridad Social

Ley Orgánica 7/1985, de 1 de julio, de derechos y libertades de los extranjeros en España

Ley Orgánica 8/1985 reguladora del Derecho a la Educación (LODE)

Ley Orgánica 1/1990 reguladora de Ordenación General del Sistema Educativo (LOGSE)

Ley Orgánica 9/1995 de la Participación y Evaluación y Gobierno de los Centros Docentes (LOPEG)

Ley Orgánica 1/1996 de Protección Jurídica del Menor

Ley Orgánica 4/2000, de 11 de enero de 2000, sobre derechos y libertades de los extranjeros en España y su integración social

Ley Orgánica 8/2000, de 22 de diciembre, de reforma de la Ley Orgánica 4/2000, de 11 de enero, sobre derechos y libertades de los extranjeros en España y su integración social

López García, B. (ed.) 1996:

Atlas de la inmigración magrebí en España, Madrid: Universidad Autónoma de Madrid Ediciones

Ministerio de Trabajo y Asuntos Sociales de España y Ministerio de Desarrollo Social, de la Solidaridad, del Empleo y de la Formación Profesional de Marruecos 1999:

'Acuerdo administrativo entre España y Marruecos relativo a los trabajadores de temporada, de fecha 30 de Septiembre de 1990', *Migraciones*, 6, pp. 153-158

Ministerio de Trabajo y Asuntos Sociales:

Anuario de Migraciones (several years)

Ministerio del Interior:

Anuario Estadístico de Extranjería (several years)

Ministerio de Trabajo y Asuntos Sociales, OPI:

Indicadores de la Inmigración y el Asilo en España, nos. 1 to 10

Reglamento de ejecución de la Ley Orgánica de Extranjería 7/1985 promulgado mediante R.D. 155/1996, de 2 de febrero que sustituía al anterior Reglamento (RD 1119/86)

TEIM 1999:

Lengua y cultura de origen: niños marroquíes en la escuela español, Madrid: Ediciones del Oriente y del Mediterráneo

Friedrich Heckmann / Dominique Schnapper

Conclusion

This volume has presented analyses of national modes of immigrant integration for eight different European countries. In a concluding remark we shall make some summarising comparisons. The main motive for comparing these national modes of integration comes from an interest to learn something about the kinds, degrees and relevance of *national differences* vs. the kinds, degrees and relevance of *convergences in integration policies* between European countries. Is there a trend for a Europeanisation of integration policies? Is there, as we have asked in the introduction, one national mode of integration that could serve as a European model?

There is no single and simple answer to this question: *There are, undoubtedly, strong tendencies of convergence, but relevant national differences do remain.* There is both convergence and national difference. We shall first look at national differences and then at trends of convergence.

The migration process has been roughly parallel in the main countries of immigration, UK, France, The Netherlands, Germany, Sweden and Switzerland. Large waves of migrants arrived between 1955 and 1973, when the Western European countries' economies developed quickly and needed extra manpower. For France, UK and The Netherlands, it was also the end of colonial empires and the return or arrival of former colonialists and colonised populations. Except for the colonial population, in all countries, but particularly in Germany and Switzerland, both the migrants and the local authorities and population thought that immigration was provisory. The migrants would go back to their country, when they would become useless for the economy. In all countries, the authorities tried to send the migrants back to their country of origin when the oil crisis seemed to make them useless between 1973 and 1975. But this did not happen. The former migrants were somehow acculturated to the country they had been living in. Because of democratic values, they had acquired some social and economic, but also some political rights, the right to stay and to be protected by law. A policy of temporary labour migration with limited and temporary integration could not be upheld anywhere. The former migrants settled in the European countries with their families. What was first considered as a labour migration became a settlement migration. For the last twenty five years, the migration towards Western European countries was mainly due to family reunification and to asylum rights. Spain or Finland that changed only recently into immigration countries repeated the experience of the other European countries: "Workers were needed, but human beings arrived". Therefore an integration policy had to be adopted.

253

None of the European countries has started with a detailed concept of an integration policy when migrants arrived and stayed. Such a concept, instead, seems to be an end or in-between-product of a longer development. The different countries have rather approached upcoming necessities and problems resulting from immigration in the way they were traditionally used to when solving social problems and approaching questions of social cohesion and conflict avoidance. In none of the European countries, the policy of immigration and integration has been publicly and democratically debated and organised. For years, many countries have not admitted that they were "immigration countries". The very notion of "integration policy" has to be understood as a retrospective construction by the politician or the sociologist.

Political actors – like other actors – work with a particular "definition of the situation" which effects their perceptions, reflections and decisions. In the introduction to this book we have therefore developed the concept of the "societal definition of the immigration situation" which can be regarded as a paradigm for action in immigration and integration policies. The *societal definition of the immigration situation* and the relations between migrants and the native populations in the preceding chapters have clearly been shown to be nationally specific. The differences in the definition of the situation manifest themselves in different linguistic terms: speaking about the incoming population as foreigners, immigrants, ethnic return migrants or ethnic minorities, for example.

Thus integration policies towards migrants in different countries have been determined by the *particular national history* of institutions engaged in this process: by the national history and traditions of welfare state institutions; by the national history and traditions of political systems as to their concepts of democracy, their understanding of nation and their degree of centralisation or federalism; by the national history and practices of the economic and educational institutions.

Thus, the structure, the similar patterns of institutional practices on a national level allow one to speak of a national mode of immigrant integration. French universalism, British and Dutch multiculturalism, or German, Swedish and Finnish welfare state concepts for migrants' integration are not the result of a consciously devised national plan for an "integration strategy" for migrants, but result from the history and common characteristics of national institutions engaged in integration work. The states represented in our book are modern democratic welfare states, but they are not the same as welfare states: There are very different "worlds of welfare capitalism" (Esping-Andersen 1990). Germany and France have organised their education and qualification systems in very different ways, many core institutions in The Netherlands are related to the ideological, political and religious "pillars" in the country, the Finnish welfare system is different from the Swiss or the Spanish, labour markets in

Britain and Germany have very specific national features, to give only a few examples. Since migrants generally have access to the core institutions of the settlement society they are much affected by the particular characteristics of national institutions in each country. The particular strengths or weaknesses of the general institutions in the country thus affect the integration process. Therefore the inclusion of immigrants in general societal integration institutions and policies is much more important for immigrant integration than any targeted special policies. The results of the EFFNATIS field studies in France, Germany and Great Britain have shown that the *national context* explains most of the variance compared to other variables. This means that it is still *very relevant*.

At the same time, the analyses of the national policies of integration in this volume reveal *processes of convergence and Europeanisation* as well. This is not a new phenomenon for the scientific public, as Hammar (1985), Schnapper (1992) and Freeman (1995) have written about such processes before. What is relevant is that it is a continuing phenomenon.

All countries adhere to basic democratic values and human rights, they are also submitted to the same European Courts of justice. By their very logic these values and rights cannot be restricted to citizens, but must generally be granted to non-citizen inhabitants as well. The migrants have the same rights as the autochthonous, except political rights in the narrow sense (suffrage and right to be elected to political appointments). Since the middle of the 1950's, they are entitled to the same civil, economic and social (i.e. the welfare state) rights as the autochthonous. This has been done first at the national level. For instance, the 1955 treaty between Germany and Italy gave the Italian workers the same conditions of pay, health insurance, unemployment and pension benefits as natives. But the equality of civil, economic and social rights between the foreigners and the national population is now part of the European legislation, and therefore obligatory to all countries of the EU. There are now practically no legal barriers to the labour market for the foreigners in the country. All countries give the right for family reunion to migrants. All countries have opened the core institutions of their societies to the migrants: labour market, self-employment, education, housing, training and qualification, health services, social security and even citizenship. Convergence and Europeanisation of migration and integration policies are presently accelerated by direct interventions of the EU. Directives against discrimination in the labour market and against racist and xenophobic discrimination are examples of this trend as well as the Amsterdam Treaty that aims at a common immigration and asylum policy.

No democratic country can escape the necessity of granting political rights to the children of international migrants. This is the reason why most countries have changed their nationality law during the 1980's or 1990's, making it easier for them to acquire nationality and citizenship. Old immigration countries like UK and France have always made some place to the *jus soli* (since 1889 in France). It is now the case for Germany that is usually considered as the most "ethnic" of the European nations. The new citizenship law that has come into effect on January 1st 2000 introduced some elements of *jus soli*, has eased naturalisation and, in special cases, tolerates double citizenship. Even the conservative opposition, which was opposed to the *jus soli*, raised the possibility of giving the newly born foreign children a paper guaranteeing them citizenship at their maturity and giving them an unconditional right to live in the country until then. It means that the main political forces agreed on giving political rights to the children of international migrants. This example shows the strength of the "civic" values on all European countries: they cannot escape the fundamental fact that citizenship is potentially universalistic and cannot be restricted on the basis of "ethnicity". In Switzerland as well, which is not an EU country, a lively public discourse on the reform of the nationality law has developed.

Not only has the juridical access to citizenship been eased, but the very concepts of citizenship and underlying concepts of nation have approached one another. The so-called opposition of "ethnic" vs. "political" nation or of *jus soli* vs. *jus sanguinis,* which was always more ideological and historical than analytical (Schnapper 1998), is getting increasingly obsolete. The convergence of citizenship laws includes a convergence in the "philosophy of naturalisation" within the integration process: naturalisation increasingly is regarded everywhere as an instrument of integration, not as something finishing the integration process.

As to *policies in relation to ethnic difference,* European countries generally do not aim at forming new ethnic minorities out of their immigrant populations, but follow policies of acculturation. Great Britain has been an exception to this trend, although a formal recognition of "ethnic communities" never existed, but in 2001 seems to have started changing its views under the impression of "race riots" and September 11th. More and more, discourses on multiculturalism and the so-called multicultural policies are not meant to form and reproduce cultural or ethnic minorities, but intend to understand and recognise the meaning and values of the migrants' former cultures. Multiculturalism is not a policy, but a general tolerant intellectual attitude.

Thus one can observe that the schooling policies are more and more alike. Some countries develop a political discourse in favour of universalistic values, but they have still taken some special measures (France), in other countries, the discourse is more sensitive to cultural pecularities, but the policies also refer to the universalistic values of knowledge and citizenship (Germany, Britain or Sweden). All countries have realised that the school is the main instrument for integrating the children of international migrants. Even in countries like

Sweden that adopted a "multicultural policy", or in The Netherlands traditionally tolerant towards cultural diversities, all efforts tend to provide the migrants' children the main tools to participate to the country they live in: mastery of the local language and of the scientific and technical knowledge necessary to access the labour market on an equal basis with the autochthonous. The debates on whether the aim of the schools is to integrate foreign children into the main culture or to reinforce their ethnic identity are getting more and more obsolete. Integration is now seen as the only possible policy.

Convergence does consist not only of what one does in a common or similar way, but may also consist of what one does not and evades. To increase the social and economic opportunities of migrants European states so far have stuck to "conventional" welfare state policies and have not embarked on policies of positive discrimination like affirmative action. Affirmative action would be a complete change of political philosophy as it implies the idea of the equality of groups, not of individuals.

Islam is the religion with most followers among Europe' s new immigrants. All countries make an effort to give Islam a place in their societies' religious lives. Although all governments favour the religious organisation of Moslem populations that are settled in the European countries, it is more or less difficult according to the national tradition of the relations between the state and the churches and according to the characteristics of the different national traditions of the Moslem populations. In the UK and in the Netherlands, there is a tolerant political tradition and an established form of relations of the state with religious organisations. In Britain, the Moslems are less divided (most of them come from the Indian peninsula) than they are in France or Germany, their leaders are accepted by the local authorities to negotiate the special needs of the Moslem population. The French and German governments try to organise – or in the German case to stimulate – the formation of a common body of representatives of the Moslem populations, but these are divided by their national origin (Turks and Moroccans, for instance) or by their history (Algerians and Moroccans and among the former Algerians for instance, former FLN militants and former *harkis* refuse to collaborate). Until now, it has been impossible to organise the Moslem population on the same pattern as, for instance, the Christian churches and the Jewish communities in Germany or to apply the laws of secularism ("laïcité") to them in France. The "Moslem scarf" issue is symbolic of this issue. One should add that the national populations are still more or less reluctant to accept that Islam would be recognised and organised as one of the official churches. European countries have a Christian and secularist tradition. Any project to build a mosque encounters the opposition of the local population with the danger of developing strong reactions from the extreme-right movements.

Trends of convergence make it more and more obsolete, as has been done in so many cases, to look at one particular country as a "model country" for integration or to believe that "it's always better in the other country". It also destroys stereotypical images of integration policies that have been upheld for a long time. For example, the refusal to recognise an immigration situation has often been portrayed as a particular German attitude, but nowhere has there been a recognition of the immigration situation by governments or societies when the settlement process came under way in the 1970's. In none of the European countries the policy of immigration and integration has been publicly and democratically debated. France expected that the workers who were recruited in the 1960's and early 1970's would return to their native country after the oil crisis. In 1998, the Dutch minister responsible for migration still found it necessary to declare The Netherlands an immigration country. Germany has only been slower in recognising the immigration situation than other European countries. Switzerland still refuses to see herself as an immigration country.

In a recent statement during a visit to Germany[1], Doris Meissner, the former Commissioner for the US Immigration and Naturalisation Service, remarked: *"Integration is difficult, everywhere"*. This may sound like a banal statement, but it is not. Labour market integration of often little qualified immigrants is difficult in all highly developed knowledge based European economies. All countries struggle with the problems of racism, xenophobia and other forms of discrimination and prejudice. This does not mean that some things are not done better in some countries than in others, but it implies that the integration of immigrants is not an easy, straightforward process and that there is no easy way of copying a particular national "model of integration".

---

[1] May 15, 2001, at the American consulate in Munich.

References

Esping-Anderson, G. 1990:

The Three Worlds of Welfare Capitalism, Cambridge: Polity Press

Freeman, G. 1995:

'Models of Immigration Politics in Liberal Democratic States', *International Migration Review*, 4, pp. 881-902

Hammar, T. (ed.) 1985:

European Immigration Policy. A Comparative Study, Cambridge: Cambridge University Press

Schnapper, D. 1992:

L'Europe des Immigrés. Essai sur les politiques d'immigration, Paris: François Bourin

Schnapper, D. 1998:

Community of Citizens. On the Modern Idea of Nationality, New Brunswick and London: Transaction Publishers

Authors' Affiliations

Aparicio, Rosa, Prof. Dr.; Director of Instituto Universitario de Estudios sobre Migraciones, Universidad Pontificia Comillas Madrid

Dingu-Kyrklund, Elena, M.A., LL.M.; Senior researcher at the Centre for Research in International Migration and Ethnic Relations (CEIFO), Stockholm University

Doomernik, Jeroen, Dr.; Senior researcher at the Institute for Migration and Ethnic Studies (IMES), University of Amsterdam

Heckmann, Friedrich, Prof. Dr.; Professor of sociology, Director of the european forum for migration studies (efms), University of Bamberg

Krief, Pascale, Dr.; Researcher at Ecole des Hautes Etudes en Sciences Sociales Paris, Centre de Recherches Historiques

Kyntäjä, Eve, Dr.; Senior researcher at the Finnish Centre for Russian and East European Studies, University of Helsinki

Mahnig, Hans († May 20, 2001); Senior researcher at the Swiss Forum for Migration Studies (SFM), University of Neuchâtel

Peignard, Emmanuel, Dr.; Researcher at the Department of Educational Sciences, Université de Dijon, Teacher

Rex, John, Prof. Emeritus; formerly Director of the Centre for Research in Ethnic Relations, University of Warwick, and President of the International Sociological Associations' Research Committee on Racial and Ethnic Minorities

Schnapper, Dominique, Prof. Dr.; Director at Ecole des Hautes Etudes en Sciences Sociales Paris, Member of the French Conseil Constitutionnel

Tornos, Andrés, Dr.; Senior researcher at Instituto Universitario de Estudios sobre Migraciones, Universidad Pontificia Comillas Madrid

Westin, Charles, Prof. Dr.; Director of the Centre for Research in International Migration and Ethnic Relations (CEIFO), Stockholm University

Wimmer, Andreas, Prof. Dr.; Director of the Center for the Comparative Study of Ethnicity, University of California at Los Angeles

Europäisierung nationaler Migrationspolitik
Eine Studie zur Veränderung von Regieren in Europa

von Verónica Tomei

2001. 228 S. kt. € 24,90 / sFr 43,60. ISBN 3-8282-0156-3
(Forum Migration Band 6)

Am Beginn des 21. Jahrhunderts bildet die Frage, wie der Nationalstaat mit den Herausforderungen umgeht, die sich aus der Zunahme transnationaler wirtschaftlicher, politischer, sozialer und kultureller Interdependenzbeziehungen ergeben, eines der Leitthemen. Zu diesen Herausforderungen gehören auch die internationalen Wanderungsbewegungen. Die Staaten der Europäischen Union sind zu einer der größten Einwanderungsregionen der Welt geworden, wobei die Bundesrepublik Deutschland als das bedeutendste Aufnahmeland hervorsticht.

Die Studie untersucht die Strategien, die diese Staaten im Umgang mit internationalen Wanderungsbewegungen entwickeln. Es wird der Frage nachgegangen, wie sich die Bedingungen nationaler Politik durch eine multilaterale Kooperation im Politikfeld Migration verändern. Zielsetzung der Arbeit ist dabei, einen Beitrag zur Erforschung der Veränderung von Regieren in Europa zu leisten.

Deutschland - ein Einwanderungsland?
Rückblick, Bilanz und neue Fragen

herausgegeben von Edda Currle und Tanja Wunderlich
(europäisches forum für migrationsstudien (efms))

2001. 538 S., kt. € 39,- / sFr 69,-. ISBN 3-8282-0196-2

Der Band knüpft an die von Friedrich Heckmann 1981 gestellte Frage "Die Bundesrepublik: Ein Einwanderungsland?" an und führt in einem aktuellen Überblick Erkenntnisse aus dem politischen wie wissenschaftlichen Diskurs zum Thema Migration und Integration zusammen.

Autoren aus Wissenschaft, Verwaltung, Politik und Medien diskutieren aus ihrer jeweiligen Perspektive die ausländer- und migrationspolitischen Entwicklungen der letzten Jahre und stellen einschlägige theoretische Erkenntnisse und empirische Untersuchungsergebnisse bezüglich der Konsequenzen von Zuwanderung für die Bundesrepublik Deutschland vor.

Die Darstellung behandelt die folgenden Themenbereiche: Migration im politischen und wissenschaftlichen Diskurs • Migrations- und Integrationspolitik in Deutschland • Migration und Sozialstruktur • Migration und Integration in Städten • Migration in internationaler Perspektive • Interkulturalität und das Fremde.

 *Stuttgart*

Soziologie der Migration

Erklärungsmodelle · Fakten · Politische Konsequenzen · Perspektiven

von Prof. Dr. Petrus Han, Paderborn

2000. XI, 374 S., 13 Tabellen, 7 Übers., kt. UTB 2118. € 19,90 /sFr 37,-.
ISBN 3-8282-0117-2 (L&L), 3-8252-2118-0 (UTB)

Seit Jahrzehnten nehmen die Migrationsbewegungen weltweit stetig zu. Die einstige Einteilung zwischen den sog. Aus- und Einwanderungsländern relativiert sich. Viele Länder sind gleichzeitig Aus- und Einwanderungsländer. Vor diesem Hintergrund beschreibt das Buch die komplexen Themenbereiche der Migrationssoziologie. Es hat zum Ziel, Studierenden, sozialen Fachkräften in den Migrationsdiensten und interessierten Lesern einen strukturierten Überblick über migrationssoziologische Zusammenhänge zu vermitteln.

Asylgewährung

Eine ethnographische Verfahrensanalyse

von Thomas Scheffer

2001. 249 S. kt. € 23,- / sFr 41,20. (ISBN 3-8282-0165-2)

Qualitative Soziologie Band 1
(hrsg. von K. Amann, J. R. Bergmann und S. Hirschauer)

Asyl wird nicht anerkannt, sondern in überschaubarer Zahl gewährt. Die praktizierte Asylgewährung fungiert als Filter zwischen globalen Wanderungs- und Fluchtbewegungen auf der einen und dem nationalen Wohlfahrtsstaat auf der anderen Seite. Das Asyl fußt auf einem höchst eigensinnigen und eigenmächtigen Prüfverfahren, das mit "unsichtbarer Hand" und abgekoppelt von den je aktuellen Flüchtlingskrisen immer wieder neu stabile Anerkennungsquoten fabriziert.

Die Frage, wie diese Regulation praktisch ermöglicht und vollzogen wird, steht im Zentrum der detailreichen Feldstudie von Thomas Scheffer. Seine Beobachtungen zum Asylverfahren führten ihn zu den Kontrollgängen an der "grünen Grenze" Ostdeutschlands, zu den Prozeduren einer Erstaufnahmeeinrichtung, zu den "aufenthaltsbeendenden Massnahmen" einer Zentralen Ausländerbehörde und zur Endstation Abschiebehaft. Die Fülle an Material wird wie in einem Brennglas auf die entscheidende Asylanhörung und deren Nachspiel gerichtet. Scheffer zeigt lebensnah, wie die bürokratische Mühle mahlt - und auch zuweilen ins Stottern gerät.

 *Stuttgart*

Ethnische Minderheiten, Volk und Nation

Soziologie inter-ethnischer Beziehungen

Von Prof. Dr. F. Heckmann, Hamburg.

1992. XII, 279 S., kt.
sFr 31,- /€ 17,-
(ISBN 3-8282-4532-3)

Beziehungen zwischen ethischen Gruppen rücken in das Zentrum öffentlichen und wissenschaftlichen Interesses. Die Integration ausländischer Zuwanderer, ein neuer Nationalismus in Osteuropa, ethnische Konflikte, die den bisherigen Systemkonflikt abgelöst haben, sind zentrale Aspekte des Themas.

Systematische Überblicke vom soziologischen Wissensstand und Weiterführrungen kennzeichnen die vorliegende Arbeit, die auch als Lehrbuch gut geeignet ist.

Migration Policies: a Comparative Perspective

Herausgegeben von Prof. Dr. F. Heckmann und
Dipl. Sozialwirt W. Bosswick, Bamberg.

Forword by Richard von Weizsäcker.

1995. 373 S., 2 Tab., 4 Übersichten, kt.
'sFr 46,30 /€ 26,-
(ISBN 3-8282-4531-5)

Migration policies have become a major issue of internal and international politics. This volume examines the migration policies of major European countries (France, Germany, Great Britain und Italy), and informs about such policies in classical immigration countries like the United States and Australia. In addition, topics such as East-West migration, economic development and migration push, and migration policies of European institutions are discussed. The authors from eight countries are leading experts in their respective fields.

  *Stuttgart*

Zeitfracht Medien GmbH
Ferdinand-Jühlke-Straße 7
99095 Erfurt, Deutschland
produktsicherheit@kolibri360.de